Can We Know Anything?

I0327384

In this book, Michael Huemer and Bryan Frances debate whether – and how – we can gain knowledge of the world outside of our own minds. Starting with opening statements, the debate moves through two rounds of replies.

Frances argues that we lack knowledge because, for example, we cannot rule out the possibility that we are brains in vats being artificially stimulated in such a way as to create an illusion of living in the real world. Huemer disagrees that we need evidence against such possibilities in order to gain knowledge of the external world, maintaining instead that we are entitled to presume that things are as they appear unless and until we acquire specific grounds for thinking otherwise. The authors go on to discuss how one should think about controversial issues wherein the experts persistently disagree. Frances argues that we should generally withhold judgment about such issues or at least greatly reduce our confidence. Huemer agrees that people are often overconfident about controversial issues but tries to carve out exceptions wherein one can rationally hold on to controversial views.

Accessible while also detailed and substantial, this thoughtful debate is suitable for readers at all levels, from those encountering the topic for the first time through those who are deeply familiar with the issues.

Key Features

- Showcases arguments from two leading philosophers in standard form and in clear language
- Presents definitions in an easily accessible form
- Summary boxes recap key arguments
- Includes an annotated bibliography and glossary of all specialized vocabulary

Michael Huemer is Professor of Philosophy at the University of Colorado. He is the author of numerous academic articles in epistemology, ethics, political philosophy, and metaphysics, as well as several books, including *Skepticism and the Veil of Perception*, *The Problem of Political Authority*, and *Understanding Knowledge*.

Bryan Frances has taught and conducted research in universities in several countries. He has published books and articles in epistemology, metaphysics, the philosophy of language, the philosophy of mind, and the philosophy of religion. His books include *The Epistemic Consequences of Paradox*, *An Agnostic Defends God*, *Scepticism Comes Alive*, and *Disagreement*.

Little Debates About Big Questions

About the series

Philosophy asks questions about the fundamental nature of reality, our place in the world, and what we should do. Some of these questions are perennial: for example, *Do we have free will? What is morality?* Some are much newer: for example, *How far should free speech on campus extend? Are race, sex and gender social constructs?* But all of these are among the big questions in philosophy and they remain controversial.

Each book in the *Little Debates About Big Questions* series features two professors on opposite sides of a big question. Each author presents their own side, and the authors then exchange objections and replies. Short, lively, and accessible, these debates showcase diverse and deep answers. Pedagogical features include standard form arguments, section summaries, bolded key terms and principles, glossaries, and annotated reading lists.

The debate format is an ideal way to learn about controversial topics. Whereas the usual essay or book risks overlooking objections against its own proposition or misrepresenting the opposite side, in a debate each side can make their case at equal length, and then present objections the other side must consider. Debates have a more conversational and fun style too, and we selected particularly talented philosophers – in substance and style – for these kinds of encounters.

Debates can be combative, sometimes even descending into anger and animosity. But debates can also be cooperative. While our authors disagree strongly, they work together to help each other and the reader get clearer on the ideas, arguments, and objections. This is intellectual progress, and a much-needed model for civil and constructive disagreement.

The substance and style of the debates will captivate interested readers new to the questions. But there's enough to interest experts too. The debates will be especially useful for courses in philosophy and related subjects – whether as primary or secondary readings – and a few debates can be combined to make up the reading for an entire course.

We thank the authors for their help in constructing this series. We are honored to showcase their work. They are all preeminent scholars or rising stars in their fields, and through these debates they share what's been discovered with a wider audience. This is a paradigm for public philosophy, and will impress upon students, scholars, and other interested readers the enduring importance of debating the big questions.

Tyron Goldschmidt, Fellow of the Rutgers Center for Philosophy of Religion, USA
Dustin Crummett, Ludwig Maximilian University of Munich, Germany

Published Titles

Do We Have Free Will?: A Debate
By Robert Kane and Carolina Sartorio

Is There a God?: A Debate
by Kenneth L. Pearce and Graham Oppy

Is Political Authority an Illusion?: A Debate
By Michael Huemer and Daniel Layman

Selected Forthcoming Titles

Should We Want to Live Forever?: A Debate
by Stephen Cave and John Martin Fischer

What Do We Owe Other Animals?: A Debate
by Bob Fischer and Anja Jauernig

Consequentialism or Virtue Ethics?: A Debate
By Jorge L.A. Garcia and Alastair Norcross

For more information about this series, please visit:
www.routledge.com/Little-Debates-about-Big-Questions/book-series/LDABQ

Can We Know Anything?

A Debate

Michael Huemer and
Bryan Frances

Routledge
Taylor & Francis Group
NEW YORK AND LONDON

Designed cover image: JamesBrey / Getty Images

First published 2024
by Routledge
605 Third Avenue, New York, NY 10158

and by Routledge
4 Park Square, Milton Park, Abingdon, Oxon, OX14 4RN

Routledge is an imprint of the Taylor & Francis Group, an informa business

© 2024 Taylor & Francis

The right of Michael Huemer and Bryan Frances to be identified as authors of this work has been asserted in accordance with sections 77 and 78 of the Copyright, Designs and Patents Act 1988.

All rights reserved. No part of this book may be reprinted or reproduced or utilised in any form or by any electronic, mechanical, or other means, now known or hereafter invented, including photocopying and recording, or in any information storage or retrieval system, without permission in writing from the publishers.

Trademark notice: Product or corporate names may be trademarks or registered trademarks, and are used only for identification and explanation without intent to infringe.

ISBN: 978-0-367-20886-8 (hbk)
ISBN: 978-0-367-20887-5 (pbk)
ISBN: 978-1-003-43493-1 (ebk)

DOI: 10.4324/9781003434931

Typeset in Sabon
by Apex CoVantage, LLC

Contents

Foreword — ix
DUNCAN PRITCHARD

Opening Statements — 1

1 The Illusion of Knowledge — 3
   BRYAN FRANCES

2 The Reality of Knowledge — 53
   MICHAEL HUEMER

First Round of Replies — 105

3 The Skeptic's Response to the Realist — 107
   BRYAN FRANCES

4 The Realist's Response to the Skeptic — 137
   MICHAEL HUEMER

Second Round of Replies — 159

5 When Will It Ever End?: Response to Huemer's Reply — 161
   BRYAN FRANCES

6   It Ends Here: Response to Frances' Reply   178
    MICHAEL HUEMER

Further Readings   194
Glossary   198
Bibliography   202
Index   206

Foreword

Skepticism is a familiar part of the contemporary social media world. Many of the most pressing public debates that face us involve skepticism in some form, such as skepticism about vaccines, skepticism about gender identity, skepticism about cryptocurrency, and so on. And then of course there are the forms of skepticism in the public realm that are perennial, such as skepticism about politicians or skepticism about weather forecasts. It can often be rational to take a skeptical stance towards a topic. If a technology is new and untested, for example, then it's reasonable to be skeptical about its effectiveness until it proves itself. In general, the rough-and-ready principle in play here is that if there are insufficient reasons to regard something as reliable, then it is rational to be skeptical about its reliability (even if one must rely upon it).

While that general principle might work as an everyday rule of thumb, it is not without its problems. For example, it's often important to trust people rather than being circumspect about them. Someone who is always seeking good reasons to rely on someone before they do so will likely miss out on developing significant relationships. Reasonable people will thus depart from this rule of thumb when circumstances are appropriate. Another concern about this skeptical principle is that embracing the reasonable, localized skepticism that is entailed by this principle can easily lead one into drifting into a more disturbing and generalized form of skepticism. Indeed, we find this happens quite often in contemporary life. People who get used to being skeptical about the familiar things like politicians and weather forecasts can slide into more substantive forms of skepticism, such as regarding vaccines or about science itself, and soon just about everything is being called into question. Moreover, such a transition isn't obviously unreasonable. If it's sensible to be skeptical about politicians, then why not the vaccines that the politicians are advocating? And if one is skeptical about vaccines, then why not be skeptical about science too, given that vaccine effectiveness is underwritten by science? One can see how conspiracy theories can quickly become attractive once one starts down this skeptical path. If one is skeptical about political and scientific authority, then why believe that there was a moon landing, or that the earth is round? In short, how does one contain one's skepticism and prevent it from becoming wholesale?

Of course, one option here is to embrace the drift towards a radical skepticism and be skeptical about everything, or at least as much as one feasibly can at any rate. Perhaps it simply isn't psychologically possible to doubt everything, after all. Try seriously doubting what you clearly see right in front of you of right now, for example. It's not easy, is it? Still, that leaves an awful lot that one can seriously doubt. So why not? Interestingly enough, one finds a wide-ranging skeptical doubt of this kind right back in antiquity, in the very earliest philosophical discussions. In ancient Greece, for example, one can find schools of thought, like Pyrrhonism, which were serious attempts to consistently live a form of skepticism whereby everything that could be realistically doubted was held up to critical scrutiny. Indeed, the Pyrrhonians treated such skepticism as an ethical position, in that the good life was thought to be a life of perpetual skepticism.[1]

But isn't there a cost to such radical doubt? We don't normally regard the reasonable person as being someone who is skeptical to this extent, but rather think of them as someone who moderates their skepticism in response to legitimate reasons to doubt. Moreover, it seems that to get on in life one needs to know a great deal, as knowledge guides one's reasoning about what to do and what to believe. How is one to do that, if one doubts (almost) everything? Doubt undermines belief, after all, and without belief one doesn't have knowledge.

---

1. Note that skepticism of this kind is not confined to ancient Greece, as we find similar forms of skepticism in other world philosophical traditions. Indeed, we find similar ideas in the Madhyamaka Buddhist tradition. The ancient Greek philosopher, Pyrrho of Elis (360-270 BCE), after whom Pyrrhonism is named, famously travelled with Alexander the Great on his campaigns, ending up in ancient India, where he interacted with the early Buddhist scholars of the day. For further discussion of the overlaps between Pyrrhonism and Madhyamaka Buddhism, see Kuzminski 2008; Beckwith 2015; Brons 2019.

Thus far we have considered skepticism as a *stance*, which is usually how it features in contemporary public debate. But philosophers are also interested in skepticism as the product of arguments, whether anyone endorses the conclusion of these arguments or not. The distinction might seem too subtle to be significant. If there are good arguments for skepticism, then surely that would legitimate skepticism as a stance? In order to see point of the distinction, however, we need to consider the very radical forms of skepticism that appeared in the early modern period, starting with René Descartes (1596–1650) and his famous *Meditations on First Philosophy* (first published 1641). In this work Descartes puts forward a form of skepticism so extreme that almost everything that one might believe is exposed to skeptical doubt. Part of the reason why Descartes can be so radical in this regard is that, unlike the Pyrrhonians, he was not advocating skepticism as an ethical position, but rather using it as a methodology to help him forge a new theory of knowledge (and much else besides). Consequently, it isn't important to Descartes that it might be psychologically impossible for anyone to ever actually endorse the conclusions of his radical skeptical arguments. Rather the purpose of these arguments is to help clarify how we should think about knowledge so that it can be resistant to such skepticism. A distinction thus opens up between radical skepticism as a philosophical puzzle and radical skepticism as a philosophical stance or position.

Descartes thought that these radical skeptical arguments could be successfully resisted, but as so often happens in philosophy, the presentation of the problem is held to be more persuasive than the solution that is offered to that difficulty. As a result, Descartes is now more widely known for his skepticism than for his anti-skepticism, even though the whole point of him offering his radical skepticism was to motivate his *response* to that skepticism. In any case, it is skepticism of this kind that has generated the most interest among philosophers ever since. For if these radical skeptical arguments are successful, then they threaten nearly all, if not all, of our knowledge, and that seems like an unacceptable situation to be in. It is thus imperative that we find a way to diagnose where they go awry. Relatedly, if radical skepticism of this kind is granted, then it follows that the prospects for a moderate skepticism as a position are bound to be poor. If one doesn't really know very much, then why shouldn't one adopt a skeptical attitude to just about everything?

This volume brings together two leading philosophers to offer their own unique perspectives on the skeptical debate. Each author is known for making an important contribution to the discussion of skepticism, and this is reflected here. Bryan Frances has made an influential case for thinking that disagreements of a certain kind can motivate skeptical conclusions, and you will find this skeptical line nicely set out here. In contrast, Michael Huemer is known for his defense of an important anti-skeptical position, called phenomenal conservatism, which can in principle explain how our everyday knowledge might be able to resist the radical skeptical challenge. Again, you will find this stance well represented in this volume. The result is that the authors can weave a compelling narrative about both what might motivate skeptical doubts and also what might be put into service to answer such doubts. Naturally, the volume doesn't cover all the main issues regarding skepticism, or even concerning contemporary discussion of this topic, as that simply wouldn't be possible in such a concise book.[2] Nonetheless, reading this volume will give you a good sense of some of the interesting philosophical terrain that's covered by this topic, and hence will provide an excellent foundation for thinking more about the philosophical puzzles raised by skepticism. With that in mind, I urge you to set any skepticism you may have about this book to one side and dive straight into chapter 1!

Duncan Pritchard
University of California, Irvine
January, 2023

---

[2]. For my own take on radical skepticism, see Pritchard 2015. See also Pritchard 2019, which is aimed at a more general audience. If you're interested in learning more about skepticism, you might also find the following MOOC (= Massive Open Online Course) useful: https://www.coursera.org/learn/skepticism.

Opening Statements

Chapter 1

The Illusion of Knowledge

Bryan Frances

Contents

1 Introduction	4
2 Traditional Skepticism	7
2.1 Introduction: What Skepticism Is, and Isn't	7
2.2 Premise 1: The Consequences of Knowing One's Hands Are Frostbitten	15
2.3 Premise 2: The Consequences of Being Able to Know You're Not a Mere Brain in a Vat	18
2.4 Premise 3: Ruling Out the Mere Brain-in-a-Vat Hypothesis	22
2.5 "But Thinking of Brains in Vats Is Silly"	25
2.6 Challenging the Skeptic: Sensory Experiences	26
2.7 Challenging the Skeptic: The Fact That There Are No Brains in Vats	28
2.8 Challenging the Skeptic: The Practicality of Knowledge	30
2.9 Challenging the Skeptic: Incomplete Meanings	31
2.10 Challenging the Skeptic: Reliable Belief-Forming Mechanisms	32
2.11 Living Life as a Skeptic	34
2.12 Can We Really Take Skepticism Seriously?	36
3 Subtle Skepticism: Consistency with Knowledge	37
4 Controversy Skepticism	41
4.1 When Disagreement Does *Not* Ruin Knowledge	42

DOI: 10.4324/9781003434931-2

4.2 When Disagreement May Ruin Knowledge 47
4.3 Two Objections to the Arguments for Controversy
     Skepticism 50

I Introduction

People have all sorts of opinions that don't amount to knowledge. For instance, a person on a jury might have excellent overall reason to believe that the defendant is guilty, but if the defendant is perfectly innocent and has been cleverly framed, then the jury member doesn't *know* he's guilty even if the prosecutor's presentation was quite convincing and the juror did an excellent job assessing the evidence that was presented in court. You can't know what isn't so, even when you've got excellent reason backing you up. For another example, imagine a man who despite loads of contrary evidence convinces himself that his partner is sexually faithful to him. In reality, his partner is cheating on him, and the only reason he believes otherwise is that he has been engaged in wishful thinking. He believes his partner is faithful, but this belief doesn't amount to knowledge.

It should be uncontroversial that there are plenty of perfectly ordinary, sober reasons for thinking that we know *a lot* less than we think we know – even when we are not guilty of any irrational thinking. There are many cases from ordinary life in which a little reflection should make one be more cautious with one's opinions: we should *suspend judgment*, neither thinking the main claim at issue is true nor thinking that it's not true. We all suspend judgment on many issues. For instance, most of us suspend judgment on "The planet Venus once had living bacteria on it", since we realize that we have no good evidence either way (we aren't astronomers who specialize on the billions of years of history of Venus). We also suspend judgment on claims such as "It will rain on 21 May next year in Chicago" or "The New York Yankees will win the World Series in the next couple years". Here are few types of cases in which we usually (with exceptions) should, if we're being reasonable, suspend judgment.

Problem 1: *group disagreements*. Suppose I know that my group disagrees with another group, and I have no good reason to think that my group has any key advantage over the other group – an advantage that means that we were in a better position to figure out whether the contested claim is really true. For instance, suppose the two groups disagree over whether capital punishment is a good crime deterrent. If I am sufficiently reflective, then I will wonder whether my group knows something their group doesn't – something that makes it reasonable for me to stick with my belief about capital punishment even though I'm perfectly aware that there are loads of intelligent people out there who disagree with me. I will also wonder if they know something we've missed – or maybe we've made an error that they've avoided. If I have no reason whatsoever to think that my group knows something the other group has missed, then it often, but not always, means I should withhold judgment on my original belief, even if that's psychologically hard to do in practice.

Problem 2: disagreements with people I recognize to be my *epistemic superiors*. If I think Jupiter has about ten moons because that's what my vague memory tells me from my childhood science education, and then I encounter an astronomer who assures me the number is in the dozens, I will defer to her and drop my belief that Jupiter has about ten moons. But if I encounter a renegade scientist who says global warming isn't happening, I won't defer to him even though I know he's an expert and I'm not: for I know that virtually all experts think he's wrong. These are easy cases! For many interesting cases from real life, it's not clear what one should do in response to disagreement with people you recognize to be your epistemic superiors on the topic at hand.

Problem 3: cases of *disagreement among experts* taken as a collective body. Suppose I start out confident that claim C is true. But then I discover that the experts on C are more or less split on its truth. After my discovery of this expert disagreement, what should I, the amateur, think about C? For instance, suppose I discover that 40% of the experts say C is true, 30% say C is false, and 30% say they don't know. In this case, 33% more experts agree than disagree with me (since 40 is 33% more than 30), but this hardly seems very comforting, right? After all, the percentages on each side are still pretty close. Or suppose 20% agree with me, only 5% disagree with me, but a whopping 75% withhold judgment on the matter. The fact that four times as many experts agree with me compared with those who disagree with me may be initially reassuring, but the fact that the vast majority of experts have suspended judgment suggests I should be like them in having no opinion. Finally, imagine that current expert opinion is solidly in my favor: 80% agree, 10% disagree, and 10% withhold judgment. Although this looks promising – it looks as though I will be reasonable in sticking with my belief in C – what if I learn that expert opinion on C has undergone wild swings over the recent years, from endorsing to rejecting C and then back again, multiple times? That is good reason to distrust the significance of the *currently* favorable view toward C since there is good historical reason to think the consensus is merely temporary.

Problem 4: the real possibility that our *evidence is unrepresentative* in lots of important cases. Even when I've done an excellent job assessing my evidence, if my evidence is unbeknownst to me skewed, then my conclusion may be off. A few minutes of research on the internet shows that for a huge percentage of the topics we typically have disagreements about, there is a large body of relevant evidence out there just waiting to be discovered by you. And if you aren't a fool, you'll know full well that your opinion is based on just a tiny fraction of the available evidence (e.g., think of how much you really know about the economics of or laws regarding various high-profile political issues). If a person is reflective and aware of the staggering amount of information out there, then she will know that for many interesting beliefs she has, she has based those beliefs on very partial, incomplete, and potentially one-sided bodies of evidence. Even if she has been a diligent thinker and done her best to judge fairly the evidence she knows about, she will know she has excellent reason to think there is an enormous body of relevant evidence out there that she knows nothing about even though it's directly relevant to her belief. The scary part is that she will also know that there is a real chance that the evidence she is unfamiliar with will, taken collectively, go against her settled views.

Problem 5: *historical variability*. Suppose you are a fan of the New York Yankees or some other sports team. You realize, of course, that if you had grown up outside of New York – say, somewhere in Estonia or Turkey – you would most likely not be a Yankees fan. Acknowledging this fact hardly shows that there is anything foolish about your current attachment to the Yankees. In fact, it's totally irrelevant. But now consider a couple beliefs of yours: your belief that Jesus rose from the dead and your belief that global warming will be catastrophic. If you had grown up in a scientifically warped environment, then you would not currently think that global warming will be catastrophic. But that doesn't give you even the slightest reason to think there is anything wrong with your current global warming belief. But if you had grown up in some other cultural environment, perhaps in the United Arab Emirates, you would probably not believe that Jesus rose from the dead, and this time it does seem to some experts as though there is something amiss here. You could have lived your life pretty much the same when it comes to religion – following your culture, reading the accepted holy books, engaging in certain prayers, etc. – and end up with the opposite religious beliefs. Does this show that our religious – and political, and moral – beliefs are somehow not based on real evidence?

2 Traditional Skepticism

2.1 Introduction: What Skepticism Is, and Isn't

The five issues just introduced are incredibly valuable to think about, since they suggest the important truth that most of us know a lot less than we typically think we know. For my own part, when I had these realizations, many years ago, it made a large positive effect on my life. The issues having to do with disagreement specifically will be explored in section 3.

Over the centuries, philosophers who study knowledge have spent much of their time on a *much* more radical idea, one that suggests that we know virtually nothing. Do you think you know that Spain is a country in Europe? Or that there are other people in the world? Or that you sometimes eat food? Or that you have hands? Just look at your hands for a moment: don't you *know* that they exist? For many centuries, a significant portion of philosophers have answered: "Nope: you know no such things, even if they are straightforwardly true and there is nothing whatsoever atypical about your mind or powers of perception and reason: *no one* knows these things!"

In this section, I go over the basic line of reasoning that leads to **traditional skepticism** ("skepticism" for short). I present the good reasons – rooted in our everyday lives – behind the premises that collectively lead to this wildly counterintuitive philosophical view.

Skepticism says we know virtually nothing. I will define it more carefully in the rest of this section, but keep in mind that skepticism doesn't merely say that you don't know your best friend's motives or know what your favorite color was five years ago. Rather, it says that you don't know that you eat food or have skin: it's a radically counterintuitive thesis. In order to see if it's true, we need to know in detail what it means. And in order to know what it means, we need to get a handle on what knowledge is supposed to be, since skepticism has to do with the alleged virtual nonexistence of knowledge. It would be asking too much to ask for a precise definition of "knowledge" – there are precious few words that we have precise definitions of – but we need to make at least some progress in narrowing down its meaning.

Before we get to that task regarding what knowledge is, we need to get straight on how we are going to use "belief".

A belief is an opinion about things, a view of how things are, a claim about what's true. But what does it mean to believe something is true? What does it mean to believe that God exists or that bees make honey? Here is a pretty good answer, even if it is vague:

- You *accept* those ideas as being true.
- You would bet on them as being very likely true.
- You have enough evidence so that additional evidence is unnecessary as far as you are concerned.
- You have made up your mind and consider the case closed.

Beliefs can be *positive* or *negative*: the belief that I have a laptop is positive, while the belief that God doesn't exist is negative. Beliefs can be utterly *trivial*: we all believe that 2 + 2 = 4 and that red is a color. Others can be *controversial*: the belief that abortion is morally wrong in most cases. They can be *serious*: some of us think the capital punishment system in the USA has caused great moral harm. Some are *silly*: we all believe that Winston Churchill was not a church on a hill and that Earth is more than five minutes old. Some beliefs are held for just a few seconds and then discarded: while walking down a hallway at work, you come to think that someone moved the trash can in the hallway at work since yesterday; this belief leaves your mind pretty quickly provided you don't have occasion to think about it again. Other beliefs you have almost your entire life: we believe that cats have four legs. Beliefs come from religion (the belief that heaven exists), sports (the belief that the New York Yankees were the best team in baseball in the 1950s), ethics (the belief that euthanasia is wrong), politics (the belief that prostitution is illegal in most parts of the USA), entertainment (the belief that Lady Gaga plays the trumpet), philosophy (the belief that we don't have free will), science (the belief that Venus is about the same size as Earth), art (the belief that Michelangelo's statue *David* is much better than almost all other statues), and just about every other walk of life. Each of us has countless beliefs, many true and many false.

A belief, in the strict sense used in this book, is something whose meaning is expressed by a *complete declarative sentence*: it's a *claim*, something that's true or false, that someone thinks is true. If Kia says that one of her beliefs is abortion, well she hasn't really told you much of anything. Maybe she believes abortion should be legal. Maybe she believes it is morally acceptable. Maybe she believes both claims. In any case, we need a *full* claim before we have a genuine belief, and saying, "One of my beliefs is abortion" only tells us a *topic* one might have beliefs about. Throughout this book, whenever I talk of a belief, I mean a claim that someone can believe and that is expressed by a complete declarative sentence.

On some occasions, you hear someone contrast knowledge with "mere opinion". When we say that a belief is a "mere opinion" or "just someone's opinion", usually we mean that the belief doesn't amount to knowledge and doesn't have much evidence backing it up. In this book, we use "belief" in such a way that we leave open whether the belief amounts to knowledge. Some beliefs have so much backing evidence that according to common sense, they count as knowledge (e.g., we believe, and know, that Jane Austen wrote *Emma*), others have no supporting evidence (e.g., the belief that Albert Einstein was an alien), and the rest lie in between.

Often I will use the letter "C" to indicate a belief in some claim. So when Jack believes bees make honey, and I say, "Jack believes 'C'", "C" stands for the claim expressed by the declarative sentence "Bees make honey". If Jill believes that bees don't make honey, then I would say, "Jill believes not-C", where in this context "not-C" means the same as "Bees don't make honey".

Usually, it's easy to determine if someone has a belief. Often all you have to do is find the right opportunity to ask them. But other times it's quite difficult. If Caucasian Chris is racist against African people, does that mean he *believes* African people are inferior to Caucasians? He certainly *acts* that way, virtually all the time, but if you ask him, he may well vehemently deny that he is racist against Africans or that he thinks they are inferior to Caucasians. Not all racists are aware of their own racism. When it comes to human behavior, we may want to say that he believes that African people are inferior to Caucasians, but when it comes to ideas that he will explicitly agree with, we want to say he doesn't *believe* it although he *acts* it, so to speak. In this book, we will ignore this issue since even though it's an important one in other contexts, it doesn't affect our arguments regarding skepticism.

Let's get back to getting a preliminary handle on what knowledge is. Suppose you're playing poker with a fool. He thinks he can predict what the next card from the deck will be, even though only a few cards have already been dealt. He's drunk, which is temporary, but he's also arrogant, which in his case is not temporary. He announces that the next card will be the queen of clubs. He's guessing! He can't "count cards" any more than you can. He's just being stupid.

Even so, this time around he got incredibly lucky and guessed correctly: the next card really was the queen of clubs. As you might guess, when the card was revealed, he shouted, "See?! I knew it! I'm a genius!" But this is nonsense. He made a dozen other predictions about cards that evening while playing poker and was wrong every time, as is to be expected when one is guessing. Clearly, he didn't *know* that the card was the queen of clubs even though his belief about it was perfectly true. So, true belief is not always knowledge: knowledge ≠ true belief.

Neither is knowledge the same thing as belief that is based on excellent overall evidence. The jury case that opened this chapter illustrates this. You are a member of the jury at a murder trial. The prosecutor has been extremely impressive, revealing all sorts of key pieces of evidence that collectively make it overwhelmingly likely that the defendant is guilty. Moreover, the defense attorney has been unable to poke any significant holes in the prosecutor's case. Neither was she able to reveal any alibi or other evidence that suggests her client's innocence. So, you believe *the defendant is in fact guilty* based on the excellent overall evidence you have.

Despite all this, the defendant is in fact innocent: he did not even touch the murder victim. He has been very cleverly framed by multiple people working together. So, your belief in his guilt is false. More to the point, you do not know that *the defendant is in fact guilty*. You can't know that X is a fact if X is not a fact. Hence, knowledge ≠ belief based on excellent overall evidence.

The same stories show that knowledge isn't *confidently held belief*, as both believers in the stories might have been highly confident in their respective beliefs and still not have either belief amount to knowledge. So what is knowledge?

Here's an intriguing idea: knowledge = *true belief based on excellent overall evidence*. Here we combine the first two guesses as to what knowledge is. Even though this proposal is definitely closer to the truth, it has serious flaws. One problem with the proposal involves the notion of evidence. For instance, you know that 0 + 0 = 0. But what is your evidence for this? It's hard to see what it might be. A person could know that 0 + 0 = 0 but be unable to produce anything remotely like a proof of it (especially if she is a child). And it's not like she could point to some physical evidence for it either. This suggests that you can know certain facts without any *standard* kind of evidence.

Another problem is that on occasion even when someone has a true belief that is definitely based on excellent overall evidence, there is good (but not to say conclusive) reason to think it may, if circumstances are odd enough, fail to count as knowledge. Suppose you arrive at a waiting room for your doctor's appointment. There is a digital clock on the wall that reads 11:23. So, naturally, since you know it's morning, you come to believe that it's 11:23 am. But it turns out that the clock has been broken since the previous evening. It just happened to stop at 11:23 pm last night. The next morning, no one bothered to fix it or cover it up. It is still lit up as though it's working fine.

Your belief that it's 11:23 am is straightforwardly true, since it in fact is 11:23 am. And you have excellent reason to think you're right: after all, you can see the clock clearly, it has no visible signs of being broken, the doctor's office is completely normal, etc. You have every reason to accept what the clock says. And yet, do you *know* that it's 11:23 am?

Many people who think about odd cases like this one answer negatively. They say that your belief is true and based on excellent overall evidence but does not have what it takes to count as knowledge. In order for it to qualify as knowledge, there can't be any "funny business", like the belief being true by weird chance, as in the broken clock case. Most people who investigate knowledge think that the following is roughly accurate: you know C just in case C is true, your basis for believing it is solid, and there's no funny business going on. The main challenges in improving this idea involve fiddling with the "no funny business" clause and elaborating on what it means for a belief to have a solid basis. Let's leave the precise characterization of knowledge behind and return to figuring out what skepticism is all about.

If you've ever talked to a philosopher for more than a few hours, then you know how inclined they are to think of outrageous situations that are purely hypothetical. For instance, right now you're reading a book. It's either a book made of paper, glue, and other physical materials, or it's on an electronic screen of some kind. But is that really true – are you really reading a book right now? How do you *know* that earlier today you didn't have horrible accident, you are currently in a coma, and right now all your experiences are illusory – including the ones you're having of reading a book? Maybe you're lying in a hospital bed *right now*, and all your visual, auditory, tactile, gustatory, and olfactory experiences are illusions had while in a deep coma: your brain is going crazy with stimulation, but this neuronal activity is producing mere illusions of sight, smell, sound, etc. You are not reading a book at all right now! It's just an amazing illusion created by your brain.

The *skeptic* says that you don't know that you are reading a book. Roughly put, she says this because she thinks you don't have evidence that rules out scenarios like the coma one I just described.

It's easy to misunderstand the skeptic. She doesn't think you are in a coma. She doesn't think we are seeing illusions. She doesn't think that ordinary perception is completely unreliable. She does not think there is excellent evidence that you're in a coma. She is not a nutcase. She just thinks that in order for a true belief, such as the one you have that's expressed with "I am reading a book", to amount to knowledge, a particular hurdle must be cleared: we need evidence of some kind or other that rules out the coma scenario. She isn't saying that your belief that you're reading a book is *false*. Rather, she's saying that even though it's perfectly true, it's not good enough for knowledge. *When she says, "You don't know C", she IS NOT saying that she thinks C is false.*

This point gets confused a lot, so let me make it perfectly clear. The skeptic does not have to prove that you are in a coma. Instead, she thinks that as far as your evidence goes, you have insufficient evidence for knowing you aren't in a coma right now, yet you need such evidence in order to know that you are reading a book. Your evidence regarding your ordinary beliefs might be sufficient for getting on with your day and assuring other people that you are normal, but it's not sufficient for knowledge. There's more on what it's like to live life as a skeptic later in this chapter.

But *why* does the skeptic believe these weird things? Well, she is a philosopher, which means she has an *argument* for her thesis, and in centuries of exceedingly careful investigation, no one has ever been able to convince the philosophical community what's wrong with her argument, if anything. For the most part, it is a distraction to imagine what life is like as a skeptic; it is better to focus on her argument.

Skeptics like a little drama. The coma story is nice, but a more exciting story involves brains in vats (BIVs). Although it certainly *seems* as though you are reading a book right now, maybe when you were ten years old, some mad scientists captured you, cut off your head, took your brain out of your skull, destroyed the rest of your body, put your brain in a vat of nutrients, plugged a bunch of electric cables into your brain, and have been sending electronic signals into your brain via the cables so as to trigger sensory experiences that make it seem as though you are living a normal life, with hands and feet and philosophy books. But in reality, since the age of ten, you've been nothing more than a brain immersed a vat of nutrients. You have all the visual, tactile, auditory, olfactory, and gustatory sensory experiences that a full-bodied person has, but it's just an awe-inspiring artificial illusion produced by scientific manipulation of your brain.

That's science fiction, of course. But is there anything you can do to show that it's not actually true? It seems not, or so the skeptic suggests. Anything you could point to in order to try to prove that it's false could easily be the deceptive product of the grand manipulation. You could respond to the skeptic by insisting that scientists don't have the technology to pull off such an illusion. But of course you can't rule out the hypothesis that everything you've read about science was part of the manipulation: the scientists made sure you were deceived about what technology can do. You might object that no sequence of artificial sensory experiences could be as rich, consistent, and detailed as yours are. But of course you can't rule out the hypothesis that your opinions about the limitations of artificial sensory experiences are the product of manipulation as well. You might object that scientists would have no good motive to bother doing this. But who are you to say why they might want to do this? Your opinions on science, technology, and human nature could be the product of manipulation. You might retreat from the goal of refuting the BIV idea in order to object that it doesn't matter if it's all an illusion as long as it continues for the rest of your life. That's fine, but now are you admitting that the skeptic is right but you don't care?

You aren't supposed to be convinced of skepticism based on the earlier paragraph! That's just a warmup for the real skeptical argument, which I present and partially evaluate in the rest of this section. In my evaluation, I will articulate and comment on a few strategies people have offered to try to poke holes in the skeptic's argument.

I have said that according to skepticism, we have *virtually* no knowledge. The reason for that use of "virtually" is that most skeptics grant that we can know purely abstract and simple truths, such as "$0 = 0$", as well as definitions, such as "A square has four sides". But even setting aside the bit about "virtually", we need to say more about what the skeptic is saying.

Based on our discussion so far, it is no surprise that most philosophers think that knowledge requires four things: in order for you to know that bees make honey, (1) you have to *believe* that bees make honey, (2) it has to be *true* that bees make honey, (3) your belief that bees make honey has to be *backed up appropriately* (for instance, it has to be based on good reasons, or excellent overall evidence, or something similar), and (4) there can't be any "funny business", like in the broken clock scenario in which the true belief was backed up appropriately (with excellent evidence) but didn't seem to amount to knowledge because the connection between the believer's evidence and the truth of the matter was so weird. The "backed up" condition (3) is tricky to characterize. Most philosophers would label it "justification": so if you know that bees make honey, then your belief is "justified". The notion of justification is not that of *moral* justification. For instance, we might say that although Jill hit Jack, she was morally justified in doing so. When we use "justified" to talk about condition (3) on knowledge, we don't mean moral justification. Instead, we mean to indicate something along the lines of evidence, or reasons, or something similar.

Skepticism is the idea that we know almost nothing *due to* the fact that *our beliefs almost always have inadequate justification.* So, skepticism is the idea that even if we have loads of objectively true, reliably formed, fully reasonable beliefs that were not tainted by faults such as wishful thinking or motivated reasoning (or any "funny business"), they *still* don't have what it takes to qualify as knowledge because they aren't sufficiently justified despite the fact that many of them are rational according to ordinary standards of rationality. Hence, skeptics focus on condition (3) for knowledge, arguing that it is rarely met. Let's define **realism** as the view that we know a great deal about the world around us. Hence, realism goes beyond the mere denial of skepticism to include the idea that we know *an enormous number of truths* about the world around us. For instance, according to realism, doctors and medical scientists could (and have) fill a book 3,000 pages long with detailed knowledge of human blood and bones.

2.2   Premise 1: The Consequences of Knowing One's Hands Are Frostbitten

The skeptic's argument targets a typical putative piece of ordinary knowledge and attempts to show that it doesn't really qualify as knowledge. For instance, Jo, an ordinary person like you or me, seems to know quite well that her hands are frostbitten, as it's winter, she's been hiking in the wilderness for many hours, her hands are in fact definitely frostbitten, she has examined her own hands, and she has lots of prior experience with this type of situation (we can suppose she is a doctor who has treated people with frostbite before). The skeptic's first premise:

> *Premise 1*: if Jo knows that her hands are frostbitten, then she can know that she isn't a mere BIV being fed electrical signals to give her the illusion of having a full body and a normal life.

Thus, premise 1 says that if Jo has *one* particular piece of knowledge (that her hands are frostbitten) then she can have *another* piece of knowledge (that she is not a mere BIV). So it's a claim connecting two *pieces of knowledge*: Jo can't have the first piece without also having the ability to have the second piece. It doesn't say anything about whether skepticism is true or not! Premise 1 is an "if-then" claim: if X, then Y. So in order for it to be false, X would have to be true while Y is false. That is, in order for premise 1 to be false, this has to happen:

> Jo *knows* her hands are frostbitten, but she *can't know* she isn't a mere BIV, *even if* she tries to reason from "My hands are frostbitten" to "So, I'm not a handless BIV."

Thus, if you think 1 is false, then in order to convince your audience that you're right about 1 you need to show us how (i) Jo knows that her hands are frostbitten, even though (ii) she can't know that she isn't a mere BIV. Premise 1 does not say, "If Jo's hands are frostbitten, then Jo is not a BIV". Instead, it says if Jo KNOWS her hands are frostbitten, then she can KNOW she is not a mere BIV. The latter "if-then" sentence is about knowledge; the former one has nothing to do with knowledge.

The main reason premise 1 is so likely to be true is this: *one can come to know things by inferring them from other things one knows*. If Jo knows her hands are frostbitten, then it should be the easiest thing in the world for her to know that she is not a *mere* BIV, as a mere BIV has no hands by stipulation (that is, we are using "BIV" to mean a *mere* brain, one without hands, feet, nose, etc.). All Jo has to do is think to herself, "My hands are frostbitten. But if my hands are frostbitten, then of course I'm more than just a brain. Thus, I'm more than just a brain. So, I'm not a mere BIV". This line of reasoning looks about as simple and reliable as any could be, so it should be extremely easy to go from knowledge of "My hands are frostbitten" to knowledge of "I am not a mere BIV". And that's just what premise 1 is saying! So that's why premise 1 seems obviously true.

Here are some more thoughts on the matter, just to drive the point home:

Suppose you know that a guy in Oklahoma owns a snake that has two heads. You've seen the videos and read a brief article about it on some popular science website. So you know S1: a guy in Oklahoma has a snake with two heads ("S" is for "snake"). From piece of knowledge S1, you can *very easily* make some elementary inferences. For instance, from S1, you can infer that some snakes have more than one head. That's belief S2. S2 follows from S1 without the aid of any other beliefs. On other occasions, we can use S1 plus some background beliefs to infer new beliefs. For instance, with S1 plus S3, "Snakes are reptiles", you can infer that some reptiles have more than one head. That's S4: "Some reptiles have more than one head". So you start out with S1, can infer S2 immediately, and can use S1 together with previous knowledge S3 to infer S4. This kind of inferring happens to each one of us every single day in a great many little ways. It's basic reasoning, and it's very easy to do.

The point is that it's easy to start with one bit of knowledge (e.g., S1 qualified as knowledge) and use it to come to other, closely related, bits of knowledge (e.g., S2 and S4). That is, we can come to know some things via inference from other things.

Here's another example, one closer to what's going on with premise 1. Suppose you know that your brothers are silly. So, you know B1, "My brothers are silly" ("B" is for "brothers"). From B1 you can easily infer that anyone who thinks you have parents but no brothers is mistaken. You do have parents, so she is right about *that* matter, but you know she's wrong when she says you don't have brothers and hence don't have silly brothers. That is, from B1 you can easily infer B2, "It's not true that I am an only child, with no brothers". You start out knowing B1, and since you easily and competently deduced B2 from B1, you know B2.

Premise 1 is saying the same thing. It starts out with the provisional assumption that you know F1, in which F1 is "My hands are frostbitten". ("My hands are frostbitten" is like "My brothers are silly".) From F1 you can easily infer that anyone who thinks you have a brain but no hands is mistaken. You do have a brain, so she is right about *that* matter, but you know she's wrong when she says you don't have hands and hence don't have frostbitten hands. That is, from F1 you can easily infer F2, "It's not true that I am a mere BIV, with no hands". (F2, "It's not true that I am a mere BIV, with no hands" is like B2, "It's not true that I am an only child, with no brothers".) You start out knowing F1, and since you easily and competently deduced F2 from F1, you know F2. See the comparison:

Brothers Story
B1: My brothers are silly.
B2: It's not true that I am an only child, with no brothers.

Hands Story
F1: My hands are frostbitten.
F2: It's not true that I am a mere BIV, with no hands.

Since it's true that *if you know B1, you can know B2*, it should also be true that *if you know F1, then you can know F2*. Hence, if you know F1, then you can know F2. That's exactly what premise 1 is saying, applied to Jo.

Premise 1 doesn't say Jo knows F1! All premise 1 says is that *if* Jo knows F1, *then* she can know F2. When the skeptic says that premise 1 is true, she isn't saying that anyone knows either F1 or F2. Instead, all she's saying is that if Jo knew F1, then she could easily come to know F2.

Furthermore, premise 1 doesn't suggest that Jo ever actually thinks to herself, "Well, my hands are frostbitten. So, it's not true that I'm a mere brain with no hands". No one outside of a philosophical conversation would have such thoughts go through her head! All premise 1 is saying is this: if Jo knows F1, then she *can*, if she likes (even if she never ends up thinking about it), know F2. Maybe a person doesn't *consciously* or *explicitly* know F2 unless it explicitly comes into her consciousness. Okay, but all premise 1 is saying is that if Jo starts out knowing F1, then she *could* come to know F2: that knowledge of F2 is "open" to her, so to speak. In order to know F2, Jo wouldn't have to do anything special like acquire new evidence. That's just like the situation with B2: if you know B1, then in order to know B2, you hardly need anything other than a super-easy inference.

What would things be like if premise 1 were false? Here's what it would be like: Jo knows F1 but *can't* come to know F2, even though F2 obviously follows from F1 via a very simple line of reasoning. If you want to argue that premise 1 is false, then you've got to argue that Jo knows F1 but she can't know F2 even if she tries.

So, there are some decent reasons to think premise 1 is true. But if you have the right people in mind, then you might think it's obvious that 1 is false. A five-year-old child, you say, knows that the blanket is warm, the ice is cold, the dog is outside, and mommy is laughing. But it's obvious, you continue, that the child cannot know that she isn't a BIV who has been fed electrical signals that make it only seem as though there is a blanket, ice, dog, and mommy. After all, she hasn't the foggiest idea what brains, vats, electrical signals, or illusions are. Hence, even if an individual has ordinary empirical knowledge, it's often the case that she cannot come to know that any of various BIV scenarios aren't really true.

In response to this comment on premise 1, we have to better understand the use of "can" in "If Jo knows her hands are frostbitten, then she can know she is not a mere BIV". It has to mean something like this:

If Jo knows her hands are frostbitten, then she can, if she takes the time to understand the whole BIV story, know that she is not a BIV.

In this chapter, I will ignore issues about the age and cognitive limitations of potential knowers.

2.3 Premise 2: The Consequences of Being Able to Know You're Not a Mere Brain in a Vat

So, premise 1 says, when applied to Jo, that if she knows that her hands are frostbitten, then she can know she isn't a mere BIV. The obvious question to ask next is: "Well, can Jo know that she isn't a mere BIV?" The combination of the next two premises give a negative answer to this question.

The skeptic presents her second premise:

> *Premise 2*: if Jo can know that she is not a mere BIV, then there is something that rules out for her the scenario in which she is a mere BIV.

Premise 2 is similar to premise 1 in the sense that it's a claim connecting two things, in this case, a certain piece of knowledge (Jo's alleged knowledge of "I am not a mere BIV") and a certain thing (something that rules out the BIV scenario for Jo; more on that issue later). It says that IF Jo can know she is not a BIV, THEN there is a certain thing. It doesn't say that she is a BIV; it doesn't say that she knows she is not a BIV. It doesn't say anything like that! All it says is this: if Jo can know that she isn't a mere BIV, there is something that rules out the BIV scenario for her. The skeptic says this because she thinks that *in order for someone to be able to know that some situation hasn't occurred, there has to be something that rules that situation out for her*. Well, no kidding: you can't know that X hasn't occurred unless there is something that shows X hasn't occurred. In order for me to be able to know that there is no cat of mine in the kitchen, there has got to be something – such as my knowledge that I have just one cat and she is sleeping on my lap in the living room – that rules out for me the scenario in which there's a cat of mine in the kitchen. That sounds right. So, premise 2 sounds right, too.

In sum, then, premises 1 and 2 say the following:

> If Jo knows her hands are frostbitten, then she can know she is not a mere BIV.
>
> If Jo can know she is not a mere BIV, then there is something that rules out the mere BIV scenario for her.

It doesn't take a genius to see that when you put those two premises together, you get this result:

> If Jo knows her hands are frostbitten, then there is something that rules out the mere BIV scenario for her.

Of course, virtually any level-headed person thinks that Jo does indeed know that her hands are frostbitten! If you are an intelligent and modest person who has reflected on the five "problems" from the introductory section, then you already accept that we know significantly less than we think we know. But you probably do not go so far as to think that Jo fails to know that her hands are frostbitten, as this piece of knowledge seems awfully easy for her to obtain. Skeptics are pretty rare nowadays despite having a fascinating argument for their positions (it takes a certain amount of intellectual courage to openly defy nearly universal common sense). So if we do have ordinary knowledge, then according to the combination of the first two premises, for each of us, there is something that rules out the BIV scenario. Here's the argument that proves it for Jo:

a. Suppose Jo knows her hands are frostbitten.
b. The combination of premises 1 and 2: if Jo knows her hands are frostbitten, then there is something that rules out the mere BIV scenario for her.
c. Therefore, from (a) and (b), there is something that rules out the mere BIV scenario for Jo.

But is (c) true? This is the focus of the next section.

As hinted at earlier, premise 2 is an instance of a general principle, something along the following lines:

> *Generalized 2*: if you can know that C is false (e.g., let C be the situation in which your hands aren't frostbitten), then there is something that rules out for you the scenario in which C.

However, what does it even mean to "rule out" some scenario? This issue is addressed in multiple places in this chapter.

For my part, when I hear the phrase "rule out", one image that comes to mind is that of a detective such as Sherlock Holmes slowly pacing back and forth in a large, beautiful living room while he patiently and conclusively argues to the enthralled audience that we have evidence that rules out the possibility that the butler is the murderer. This seems like a paradigmatic case of someone "ruling out" some possibility. But even the skeptic admits that that's an implausible model to use in evaluating Generalized 2. There is little reason to think that in order to know that the butler wasn't the murderer, you must be able to give an argument – a *piece of reasoning*, with premises and a conclusion – that proves your case. After all, it's reasonable to think the butler himself knows he didn't murder anyone even if he is awful at giving arguments in public – or private for that matter. He hardly needs an argument to pass through his mind.

Or consider another, more illuminating, case. For a week, Jasmine has had a splitting headache. She has been to multiple doctors, who have examined her extremely thoroughly. She even went to the best doctors in the world – and they found nothing wrong with her. They have come to think she is lying about her pain; they think she is a fraud. But she can quite easily know that she's not faking it. According to Generalized 2, if Jasmine can know "I am not faking it", then she must have something that rules out the faking-it hypothesis. And Jasmine does in fact have such an item: her *awareness of the pain*. She hardly needs an *argument* (a piece of reasoning) to be the thing doing the ruling-out job. Jasmine's simple and overwhelming awareness of her pain is sufficient for the task of ruling out the doctors' "She is just faking her pain" hypothesis. The skeptic need not object to any of this.

If you like, you can substitute an alternative, less loaded, term for "ruling out", such as "eliminate" or "neutralize". That may help avoid the connotation that the only thing that can rule out a hypothesis is an argument that passes through one's mind.

Finally, it's tempting to think that anything that rules out a scenario must count as a piece of *evidence*. However, I am going to use the neutral "there is *something* that rules out the mere BIV scenario" instead of "there is *evidence* that rules out the mere BIV scenario" language because I suspect that the meaning of "evidence" is pretty open-ended or incomplete (or however one wants to put it). Due to that semantic problem, disputes over theses that are expressed with sentences using "evidence" can involve parties using "evidence" differently, talking past one another. For instance, a detective will insist that some pieces of "evidence" are literally ordinary physical objects, such as a bloody knife. Someone else might say that strictly speaking, it's not the knife itself that is evidence but the *fact* that the knife was bloody and found at the crime scene. A third person insists that it's our *knowledge* of this fact and not the fact or the knife itself. I'm happy to bypass that dispute entirely, thank you very much.

2.4 Premise 3: Ruling Out the Mere Brain-in-a-Vat Hypothesis

Premise 3 completes the skeptic's argument:

> *Premise 3*: there isn't anything that rules out that BIV scenario for Jo.

When we add 3 to 1 and 2, we end up with the result that Jo doesn't know that her hands are frostbitten.

Premise 3 is not an "if-then" like 1 and 2 are. It just says that there isn't anything that rules out the BIV scenario for Jo, end of story. Obviously, the only way to cast doubt on 3 is to give good reason to think that there is something that rules out the BIV scenario for her. The only way to show that 3 is false is by completing the sentence "There is something that rules out the BIV scenario for Jo, and that thing is just this: . . ." Note that 3 is not saying that Jo doesn't know that she is not a BIV; neither does it say that she doesn't know that her hands are frostbitten. *It says nothing at all about knowledge.* It just says something about a *specific absence*. All it says is this: there is nothing that rules out the BIV scenario for Jo.

You might think that it's easy to rule out the BIV scenario by appealing to scientific facts about the brain. However, for two reasons, many philosophers don't think this will work.

First, for what it's worth, I have yet to see any solid scientific reason why the BIV scenario is impossible. If you like, you can include, along with the brain, the brain stem and the rest of the nervous system (you can go on the internet and see awesome pictures of what the nervous system looks like when carved out of a body). Thus, I don't think one can rule out the BIV scenario by appealing to fancy scientific knowledge.

Second and more important, all the skeptic is saying is that it's *imaginable* for a person to live a normal mental life – including sensory experiences such as visual and tactile ones – with nothing but a brain. The skeptic need not insist that it's medically or scientifically possible to take a brain (or nervous system) and make it have a normal mental life without a body. Perhaps certain biological facts would have to change in order to make this happen. That's fine. Her point is that it's imaginable for a mere brain to have a normal mental life, and the vast majority of us don't possess anything that rules this out. We already know that an extraordinary amount of our mental lives can be artificially produced (e.g., a pain that seems to be in the thumb can be produced by careful brain manipulation without ever touching the hand at all). The skeptic is just extending this idea and adding that her scenario is imaginable.

In sections to follow, I will look at better possibilities for defeating the skeptic, although my examination will be brief. For now, we need to keep in mind a few points about what the skeptic is claiming.

The skeptic is concluding that we, like Jo, don't know perfectly ordinary things, like the fact that we eat food. But the skeptic is not concluding that we merely lack *perfectly certain* knowledge. Nope, she's saying we lack *ordinary* knowledge. Her position is that when in an ordinary conversation your mom says, "I know you rode on that awful motorcycle last night", what she says is really false, even though the skeptic will be happy to grant that your mom saw perfectly well you riding on the awful motorcycle last night. That's exactly what premises 1–3 entail: your mom doesn't know that fact about you and the motorcycle even though she saw you on it, as clearly as one sees just about anything. Under one interpretation of his work, the great scientist, mathematician, and philosopher René Descartes probed the question of whether we have *perfectly certain* knowledge. That's an interesting question, but the skeptic says we not only lack perfect knowledge of the fact that we eat food but we have no ordinary knowledge of that fact as well. When you assess the skeptic's argument – her three premises – keep in mind that what's at issue is the existence of everyday, ordinary knowledge.

Relatedly, as a professor, I occasionally encounter students who complain that the skeptic is implausibly assuming that ordinary empirical knowledge has to be based on *absolutely conclusive evidence*. I don't think that is accurate. Instead, the skeptic is saying . . . well, *she's saying 1–3* – no more and no less. She's saying, first, that if Jo really knows that her hands are frostbitten, then she has the ability to know, perhaps through easy and immediate inference, that she isn't a handless BIV. This hardly seems objectionable or even hints that knowledge requires conclusive evidence. She's saying, second, that if Jo can know she isn't a mere BIV, then there must be something that rules out the mere-BIV scenario for Jo. There's no requirement that the ruling-out item has to be absolutely conclusive evidence, whatever this might mean. (The notion of "partial" ruling out will be discussed later.) And of course she's saying, third, that there isn't anything that rules out the BIV scenario for Jo. I don't think there's anything about super-high standards of evidence here. The skeptic has offered a logically valid argument – "logically valid" being used in the sense that *if* the argument's three premises are true, *then* the argument's conclusion simply must be true as well. The anti-skeptic has to find a flaw *in the premises* and not just offer vague talk that fails to target one or more premises. The vague talk is perfectly okay *at the beginning*, when one is first thinking through the issues, just brainstorming, but eventually one has to get serious and say which premise is false and why it's false.

Finally, remember that the skeptic doesn't think we can't know *anything*. At least, the person who endorses the skeptical 1–3 argument need not hold such a radical view. Her argument only denies us *some* knowledge, albeit an incredibly enormous chunk of knowledge: most of our knowledge of the physical world. Usually skeptics think we can know that 2 + 2 = 4, that squares have four sides and facts about our own internal mental states (e.g., what your current thoughts and feelings are).

Summary

It might be tempting to think that we can ignore skepticism, since the arguments for the three premises are less than airtight. It's up to the skeptic to prove her point. Since her arguments for her premises aren't totally convincing, why not just ignore her?

I think this thought is mistaken. At the minimum, we have learned that at least one of the following simply must be true:

- Premise 1 is false. That means Jo knows that her hands are frostbitten, but she can't know that she isn't a mere BIV – even though the inference from "My hands are frostbitten" to "I am not a mere BIV" is about as simple as can be and certainly looks sufficient for Jo to know that she isn't a BIV provided she knows that her hands are frostbitten.
- Premise 2 is false. That means Jo can know that she is not a mere BIV, but there is nothing that rules out for her the BIV scenario. This means one can know that a situation doesn't obtain even though there is nothing that rules out its obtaining.

- Premise 3 is false. This means there is something, call it *X*, that rules out the BIV scenario for Jo. This is true even though it seems that anything in Jo's sensory experience could also be had by a BIV, so it doesn't seem like *X* is in her sensory experiences. If *X* is thought to be some fact about Jo or BIVs, it means that *X* is doing the ruling out job even though it appears that Jo need not have the slightest idea what *X* is.
- Skepticism is true. That means we don't know many perfectly ordinary things, such as the fact that we sometimes eat food.

Speaking just for myself, part of the interest in the argument for skepticism is the fact that it shows that at least one of the foregoing is true, which I find fascinating. I may not know which is true, but it's a real advance to know that at least one of them is.

2.5 "But Thinking of Brains in Vats Is Silly"

Yes of course it is! Well, it's silly in some ways.

Any philosopher who teaches epistemology – which is the study of notions including knowledge, evidence, rationality, certainty, and wisdom – is familiar with the response just quoted. A course in epistemology starts out serious and deep: "Let us proceed to investigate the notion of *knowledge*". But then we end up thinking about silly science fiction scenarios involving brains in vats. Surely, it might be said, the BIV scenario is silly enough that it shouldn't matter to whether we know things.

Well, that seems to be saying that it should be *awfully easy* to rule out the BIV scenario. After all, if the BIV scenario is so absurd or non-serious or silly or irrelevant or whatever, then it should be a piece of cake to show that it isn't true. But that's to say, by implication, that it should be easy to refute premise 3, which said there isn't anything that rules out the BIV scenario for us.

You may think the BIV scenario is just wild science fiction. But the idea that we are all part of a vast computer simulation is not at all fanciful: some scientists and philosophers think that there is an excellent chance it's really, objectively true.

In philosophy, you have to deliver the goods. If you think the skeptic is mistaken, then you're saying that her thesis is false. But her thesis is definitely 100% true *provided 1–3 are true*. Hence, if you think she's wrong, then your position is that there is a mistake in 1–3: at least one of them is false. You think there is a mistake there? Fine: prove it.

In the next five sections, I'm going to investigate five ways one might initially challenge the skeptic's argument.

2.6 Challenging the Skeptic: Sensory Experiences

Let's focus on premise 3. If you think it's false, then you simply must complete this sentence: "Here is the thing that rules out the BIV hypothesis [BIVH] for Jo. . . ." Otherwise you're fooling yourself if you think you have a good objection to premise 3.

Here is a plausible candidate for ruling out (neutralizing) the BIV scenario: *Jo's awareness of her sensory experiences of her body parts other than her brain.* (Or perhaps the ruling-out work is done by the sensory experiences themselves and not our awareness of them; I won't try to figure which is more plausible as a ruling-out candidate.) This anti-skeptic makes three key claims. (a) It's a fact that Jo has sensory experiences of her hands and legs (she sees them and feels them), (b) her awareness of these experiences can do ruling out work, (c) her awareness of them suffices to rule out the BIV scenario for her. So, premise 3 is false according to this anti-skeptic.

The skeptic need not object to the anti-skeptic's claim (a): she objects to claims that Jo *knows* certain facts, but she need not object to facts about Jo, such as the fact that she has hands and legs and has sensory experiences of the hands and legs. The skeptic says that Jo lacks knowledge of her hands, not that she lacks hands. More interestingly, the skeptic can accept the anti-skeptic's claim (b). Consider again the hypothesis from before that medical patient Jasmine is merely faking her headache pain. The skeptic is happy to acknowledge that Jasmine's awareness of her pain sensations is enough to neutralize, eliminate, or rule out the Jasmine-is-just-faking-her-pain hypothesis.

Therefore, the skeptic has no quarrel with the idea that Jo's sensory experiences, or her awareness of them, can rule out *some* hypotheses. The big question when it comes to the argument for skepticism is whether Jo's sensory experiences have what it takes to rule out the BIVH in particular – that's claim (c). With her use of premise 3, the skeptic is denying the anti-skeptic's (c) even though she accepts (a) and (b).

Well, what should we think about (c): is it true, or is it false?

It is irrelevant what would happen if Jo *tried* to rule out the BIV scenario. After all, we tend to think that Jo knows her hands are frostbitten even if she hasn't done anything to *try* to rule out the BIV scenario. The Realist position is that Jo, who has never done any philosophizing and knows virtually nothing about skepticism, *already* knows that her hands are frostbitten.

Again, claim (c) says that the brute physical fact that Jo has seen and felt her body parts is enough for the BIV scenario to be ruled out for her. Unfortunately, the skeptic can respond that that seeing and feeling doesn't do the ruling out job because *all Jo's sensory experience could be happening even if she were a handless BIV*, as the mad scientists could create these illusory experiences in her. The skeptic says this:

So *what* if Jo is having sensory experiences that seem to come from hands? That doesn't favor the commonsensical hypothesis "Jo has hands" over the skeptical hypothesis "Jo is a BIV who has *illusory* experiences of hands". Pointing out that she has certain sensory experiences doesn't favor the commonsense hypothesis over the skeptical hypothesis.

In order to see what is going on here, the skeptic asks us to consider an analogous case. You and a friend are debating whether some celebrity is rich. Your friend says the celebrity used to be rich but last week sued her accountant for embezzlement and filed for bankruptcy, so she's no longer rich. In response, you say that the celebrity still owns three houses, so she's still rich. Your friend points out that the fact that the celebrity owns three houses hardly suggests she is still rich, as her debt – indicated by the bankruptcy and lawsuit – may be much greater than the value of the homes. Here is the key point about your debate with your friend: *you appealed to a thing X in defense of your position, but your opponent pointed out that X in no way favors your position over hers*, where in this story X is the fact that the celebrity still owns three homes, your position is "The celebrity is still rich", and your friend's position is "The celebrity is no longer rich".

Similarly, you and the skeptic are debating whether there is something that rules out the BIV scenario for Jo. You say her sensory experiences can do the job. Your friend points out that the fact that she has certain sensory experiences hardly does the ruling out job, as these experiences can be had by a BIV. The key point is analogous to the one made in the celebrity case: *you appealed to a thing X in defense of your position, but your opponent points out that X in no way favors your position over hers*, where X is Jo's relevant sense experiences. That is, although Jo did indeed have sensory experiences that seem to require her having hands and legs, these experiences aren't a reliable sign of real hands and legs because she could have the same experiences without these body parts at all – just like how the three homes aren't a reliable sign of being rich. Or so the skeptic says! The rest of this book explores the issue further.

2.7 Challenging the Skeptic: The Fact That There Are No Brains in Vats

The anti-skeptic may have a better option for maneuvering around this objection. Here is her general idea:

I agree that having certain sense experiences doesn't *100%* rule out the BIV scenario. But maybe having these sense experiences rules it out *enough* so that she can know she's not a BIV. After all, the cold hard fact is that there are no BIVs who have sensory experiences that seem to be perceptions of hands and legs! That fact has to count for something! So, sure: the skeptic is right that it's *possible* that Jo has the sense experiences without having hands. I'll admit that. But the BIV possibility is extremely unlikely given the sensory experiences that seem to call out for hands, and this fact is all it takes to *sufficiently* rule out the BIVH for her – even if it doesn't rule it out completely.

Here is one way of converting the anti-skeptic's idea into a relatively precise argument:

- Here is truth T: there aren't any BIVs with sense experiences like the ones Jo has when she sees and feels her hands.
- Jo can know that T is true.
- If Jo can know that T is true, then this ability rules out or neutralizes, for her, BIVH enough so that she is able to know she's not a BIV.
- Hence, BIVH is ruled out enough for Jo to be able to know she's not a BIV. So, premise 3 is false.

This argument is poor. According to its second premise, a five-year-old child is in a position to know the exceedingly complicated truth T. But surely that's wrong: five-year-olds aren't like that. For one thing, they are a million miles from even understanding it. For another thing, even if they do come to understand it, they may well not endorse it, for any of a variety of confused reasons. For yet another thing, it's question-begging against the skeptic to assert that we are in a position to *know a plainly external world claim*, which is what T is. It's worth keeping these criticisms in mind when substituting some other, perhaps better, truth for T.

Here is an improved version of the anti-skeptic's argument against the skeptic's premise 3:

- Here is truth T: there aren't any BIVs with sense experiences like the ones Jo has when she sees and feels the gloves on her hands.
- If T is true, then all by itself – without its being known or even knowable – it neutralizes, for Jo, BIVH enough for her to be able to know that she's not a BIV.
- Hence, BIVH is ruled out enough for Jo to be able to know she's not a BIV. So, premise 3 is false.

This argument is an improvement over the first one because it requires the mere truth of T and not the idea that Jo is in a position to know it. The anti-skeptic admits that she would be begging the question against the skeptic to claim, in an argument against the skeptic, that Jo has *knowledge* of an external world claim. That would be similar to concluding that a particular religious text is infallible based on an argument that used nothing but claims from the text. But all the anti-skeptic is doing with T is saying it is true, not known.

I see four problems with the second premise (the second bullet point) of this anti-skeptical argument against premise 3.

i) It's not clear that a truth (such as T) can rule out an alternative scenario for a person without the person being in a position to know the truth. In most cases, in order for a truth or group of truths to rule out a scenario for someone, she has to be in a position to *know* these truths.

ii) Even if a truth can rule things out for a person who isn't in a position to know that truth (so problem (i) is dodged), it's not clear that there are degrees of ruling out. There are degrees of *evidential support* – e.g., although you and I both believe C, your evidential support for it might be better than mine – but that doesn't mean there are degrees of *ruling out*.

iii) Even if an unknown truth can rule things out and there are degrees of ruling out (so both (i) and (ii) are dodged), it's hardly clear that knowledge requires something less than 100% ruling out.

iv) Even an unknown truth can rule things out, there are degrees of ruling out, and knowledge need not require 100% ruling out (so we get around all of (i)–(iii)), it seems that Jo's knowledge that her hands are frostbitten is about as strong as knowledge ever gets; remember, she is a doctor familiar with frostbite, she has examined her own hands, etc.). So, one would think that we must have ruled out alternatives to "My hands are frostbitten" to the maximum extent – 100%.

These four problems do not, in my opinion, *obviously* destroy the anti-skeptic's attack on premise 3. However, the anti-skeptic would need a convincing response to them. Can you think of one?

2.8 Challenging the Skeptic: The Practicality of Knowledge

We navigate our lives by relying on the word of others. My fiancée says she'll be home at 7 pm, so I plan to have dinner ready by then. Doctors tell us that the sugar in highly processed food is bad for us, so we try to avoid this sugar. We trust some but not all the assertions we hear. If the U.S. military makes a significant claim, in a great many cases, wise people are hesitant to believe them, since the U.S. military has a track record of significant lying. In contrast, when my doctor says I cracked a rib, I trust her, since doctors have an excellent track record in cases similar to this one. In general, the following formula is very roughly true: if someone tells us that C is true, we trust her just in case we take her to *know* C is true. So, trust, knowledge, and communication appear to be closely linked. The links aren't perfectly tight, but they are pretty good.

Some philosophers emphasize the practical usefulness of knowledge to such an extent that they will reject any principles about knowledge that severely restrict its usefulness. And, of course, knowledge can't be useful if it almost never exists. For them, even though 1–3 look true, at least one of them has to be rejected because it simply *must* turn out that we have lots of ordinary knowledge of the world around us. The true principles of knowledge don't have so much to do with matters like evidence as they do with truth, trust, communication, and related issues. Or so some people think.

All by itself, this doesn't help us with the skeptic's argument, as it gives us no clue as to where there is a mistake in it. It's fine to argue for a conception of knowledge that has it intimately connected to trust and communication. But the skeptic's argument is denying just that: she is saying that trust and communication aren't linked to knowledge (because there is so little of it) but are linked to true belief that satisfies certain social standards for assertion but fails to satisfy the standards for knowledge. If we are to reject skepticism by finding a flaw in the skeptic's argument, well, then we have to find a flaw in the argument – and not merely protest that skepticism isn't true because it violates our conception of the extent of knowledge.

2.9 Challenging the Skeptic: Incomplete Meanings

Imagine a perfectly ordinary table that one occasionally uses as a chair. When no one is sitting on it, is it a chair? Or imagine what looks to be a perfectly standard chair – but one that magically vanishes whenever no one is sitting on it but reappears whenever someone comes within ten centimeters of where it last was, so he or she can sit on it. Is it a chair when it has vanished? In each case, we might be tempted by the thought that the meaning of "chair" is *incomplete enough* that when it comes to applying "chair" to certain bizarre circumstances, neither "It is a chair" nor "It isn't a chair" is true.

Analogously, many of my students over the years have suspected that there is something deeply wrong with "Jo can/cannot know that she isn't a BIV". They suspect that neither claim is true because each is just too damn weird. In particular, they think that perhaps the meaning of "knows" is incomplete enough that when it comes to applying "knows" to certain bizarre circumstances, neither "She can know it" nor "She can't know it" is true. In particular, one might think that this holds for the admittedly bizarre BIV circumstance: the meaning of "knowledge" is incomplete enough that neither "Jo can know she isn't a BIV" nor "Jo can't know she isn't a BIV" is true. This would probably mean that premise 1 is neither true nor false, as its "if" part is true but its "then" part is neither true nor false. The "if" part of 2 will be neither true nor false as well. If we say that "rule out" is akin to "knowledge" in having an incomplete meaning, then both the "then" part of 2 and all of 3 may fail to be true or false too.

There are two problems with this "incomplete meanings" proposal. First, there are reasons from the philosophy of logic and language to think that in virtually all cases "She can know it" or "She can't know it" has got to be true. I won't go into that here. Second, it isn't difficult to imagine realistic situations in which "She can't know she isn't a BIV" and "There isn't anything that rules out the BIV scenario for her" are clearly true:

Suppose BIVs become technologically and fiscally possible; a team of mad scientists ends up ruling the world; certain top secret documents detailing plans for massive kidnapping and BIVing are stolen and leaked to the public; impenetrable 100,000-square-mile complexes of laboratories are set up in the wilds of Canada, Brazil, and elsewhere; over a period of years, hundreds of thousands of people mysteriously disappear in the middle of the night to become BIVed. You can see how at least one BIVH – "I have become a BIV as the result of these crazy mad scientists" – could become something close to a real, live possibility for almost any person. Even if you are never BIVed in that world, it seems pretty straightforward that if you happen to keep insisting that you are not a BIV, the assertion "She knows she isn't a BIV" is just plain false.

That proves that "She can/cannot know she isn't a BIV" can have a definite truth status (true or false) when BIVs are realistic. It is hard to see how "She can/cannot know she isn't a BIV" could fail to have a truth-evaluable meaning depending on how realistic the possibility of BIVs is.

2.10 Challenging the Skeptic: Reliable Belief-Forming Mechanisms

The clock on my phone is reliable: it's virtually always accurate. Google Maps is pretty accurate too, although it is not as accurate as my phone's clock. Here's another thing that's pretty accurate: the biological mechanisms in my central nervous system and peripheral nervous system that lead to my perceptual beliefs.

When Jo is looking at her hands upon taking off her inadequate gloves, she sees them and forms the belief "My hands are frostbitten". For the most part, we can't help but form the beliefs we adopt: for instance, if you look in the refrigerator and see an apple in there, you're going to come to believe that there's an apple in the fridge. When you looked in the fridge, the light from inside it went in your eyes and initiated a sequence of events in your nervous system that eventually ended up with your forming the belief that there's an apple in the fridge. And this biological process is *reliable*: it almost always produces beliefs that are true if the "inputs" are true, too. For instance, if the thing in the fridge wasn't a real apple but an extremely realistic-looking plastic apple, your perceptual system would still give the "output" belief that there's a real apple in the fridge.

Some philosophers have thought that the mere fact that many of our belief-forming physical mechanisms are highly reliable is enough to make a good portion of our true beliefs count as knowledge. It's an attractive idea: a true belief is knowledge formed in a highly reliable fashion. This principle might not be exactly correct (remember our discussion of "funny business" from before), but it has seemed to many people to be on the right track.

Perhaps this means that premise 3 is false: the fact R of the reliability of our cognitive systems is enough to rule out the BIV scenario enough for Jo to be able to know she isn't a BIV. Of course, Jo might not have any conception of R. And if we told her about it, she may well misunderstand it and as a consequence not believe it. R is a pretty advanced and complicated fact. So perhaps R does its ruling out work without Jo being aware of it or even disposed to believe it once she is made aware of it.

So, one might think that R shows that premise 3 is false. But one might have another idea on how R relates to the skeptic's argument.

Perhaps the real lesson of reliability is this: on occasion, in order to be able to know that scenario C hasn't occurred, there doesn't need to be *anything at all* that rules out C. So, we don't need R to do any ruling out work. That is, maybe the way to understand the reliability idea is to say that premise 2 is false, since it says that in order for Jo to be able to know that she's not a BIV, there has to be something that rules out the BIV scenario.

Then again, maybe the whole notion of "ruling out" or "eliminating" or "neutralizing" is vague enough that there's no fact of the matter as to whether it's premise 2 or premise 3 that is false – although we can be sure that at least one of them is false.

What do you think R's effect on 1–3 is? Does it show that 3 is false, that 2 is false, or that one of them is false but we don't know which, or does it fail to make a significant dent in any of 1–3?

Summary

Over the past five subsections, we have seen that the "obvious" or most straightforward ways of objecting to the skeptic's premises have serious weaknesses. However, this doesn't mean the skeptic wins! Just because it's not going to be a piece of cake to defeat her doesn't mean she is actually right.

You probably knew that before we started: why would anyone write a book evaluating a position that could be defeated pretty easily?

We will be returning to the core ideas of 2.6–2.9 in subsequent chapters to see if they can be developed in ways that make them stronger and reveal fatal weaknesses in the skeptic's argument. Much of philosophy involves digging deeper and deeper into certain ideas, with a great deal of patience, care, and creativity.

2.11 Living Life as a Skeptic

Someone is a skeptic just in case she thinks the conclusion of 1–3 is true. So, she thinks she herself doesn't have knowledge of the world around her. For instance, she will hold that she doesn't even know that she has hands. But does she *believe* she has hands?

Before I answer this question, it is important to see that *it doesn't matter*. I mean: it doesn't matter to the truth of 1–3. Whether these claims are true is independent of both (i) whether there are any skeptics and (ii) whether there is anything peculiar about being a skeptic.

To answer the question about what skeptics believe, first consider a couple stories.

You're hiking through the mountains on a trail. You come to a fork in the trail and need to decide which fork will send you on the correct way to your destination. But there are no markings to indicate the right way. You choose the left fork arbitrarily and proceed to hike it.

Now you're a doctor with a patient whose medical problems are complicated. You don't know whether to use aggressive meds or surgery at this point in her care. Even after consulting other doctors, there doesn't seem any way to tell which option is best, all things considered. So, you choose meds and proceed accordingly.

There are many cases in life akin to the two just described. The hiker withholds belief from both "The left path is the correct one" and "The left path is not the correct one"; the doctor withholds belief from both "Meds are the right choice" and "Meds are not the right choice". But in each case, the person has to act. They don't have to *believe*, but they do have to *act*.

Most skeptics think they are in the same situation. They suspend judgment on virtually everything but choose the option they guess – not *believe* but *guess* – will turn out the best. They end up acting pretty much like how everyone else acts. I should know (or "know"): I am pretty close to being a skeptic myself.

But not exactly. For what it's worth, since I became a near-skeptic, I have found that I react to counterevidence differently from how non-skeptics react. We are all familiar with how people react in defensive and irrational ways when presented with solid evidence that shows that their fundamental convictions – such as those about religion, morality, or politics – are false or at least doubtful. Not surprisingly, if one no longer has fundamental convictions, then these instances of irrational behavior become rarer. But it's the type of skepticism tied to controversy that has had the most effect on me. We explore this view in section 4 of this chapter.

The skeptic does believe one particularly relevant thing: she believes the conclusion of premises 1–3. One might worry: doesn't that belief concern a claim about the world external to our minds, and isn't there some inconsistency in her having that belief but not having beliefs about whether she has hands or eats food?

But look closely at the conclusion of 1–3: it does not make any "positive", substantive claim about the world. It says something "negative": Jo doesn't know that her hands are frostbitten. Furthermore, if the skeptic believes 1–3, she still doesn't believe anything "positive" about the world outside her mind. Premise 1 says *if* someone knows she has hands, *then* she can know she's not a mere BIV. It doesn't say that anyone knows she has hands; it doesn't even say that there are any people in the world! Premise 2 is similar: it says that *if* someone can know she is not a BIV, *then* there is something that rules out BIVH. Again, it doesn't entail anything substantive about the world – not even the idea that there are any people in the world. Premise 3 is straightforwardly negative: nothing rules out BIVH. Hence, the skeptic's beliefs in 1–3, if she does indeed believe them, don't make any substantive claims about the world around us.

2.12 Can We Really Take Skepticism Seriously?

You might have the attitude that it's as certain as anything ever gets that skepticism is false, and the only task is to find out which of the three premises is false. You may think that no one who isn't severely mentally ill could really, truly, be a skeptic any more than one could look at an apple and in full sanity think that it is an alien intelligence plotting to take over the planet. After all, we know perfectly well that we eat food! I mean, *come on*! Let's not lose our minds as the result of getting imaginative about science fiction stories about BIVs! The true nature of knowledge might be puzzling, for sure, and the skeptic is definitely helping us probe that issue. That's great, but we know perfectly well that we eat food, for goodness sakes.

However, I suspect this attitude is mistaken: one can be completely mentally sane and truly think that no one knows that we eat food. Even so, there may be *something* true about the attitude expressed in the preceding paragraph, although it isn't obvious what that truth is. For what it's worth, I suspect that what's wrong about the attitude is this:

> The idea "I know I eat food" is certainly true.

But what's right about it is something along this line:

> The idea "I know I eat food" is well worth relying on in everyday life.

Just because some claim is well worth assuming to be true in everyday life (and even in more stringent contexts such as scientific research) doesn't automatically mean it's really true. Truth is harder than that. So, when the skeptical idea that you don't really know that you eat food seems insane to you, I recommend that you take seriously the idea that what's insane is not the alleged *truth* of "I don't know I eat food". Roughly put, the insanity belongs to the idea that "I know I eat food" fails to be worth relying on. The skeptic is saying that "I know I eat food" is false, but her view is rendered sane because she is free to admit that "I know I eat food" is still good in some practical manner (although to be consistent, she has to also admit that she doesn't *know* that "I know I eat food" is good in some practical manner!).

3 Subtle Skepticism: Consistency With Knowledge

There is a philosophical view that is midway between skepticism and realism. It's on the knife edge between the two, as it were. In my judgment, it is more in the spirit of skepticism than realism, so I call it "subtle skepticism" instead of "subtle realism'. In order to introduce this new view, we ask what is initially a peculiar question: what if knowledge isn't nearly as impressive as we thought it was?

In order to get an initial idea of what this question means, consider what may at first appear to be a very different case. Suppose someone tells you that he has three friends who are witches. You object that that's silly, since there are no witches. "There is no real black magic! That's just fiction and silly stories!" But then someone informs you that "witch" has always been synonymous with "a woman who is eccentric, is really into the dark arts, and identifies as a witch". Just for the sake of argument suppose she is right: that's what "witch" has always *really meant* in English.

Assuming she has convinced you of that linguistic matter, at this point, you have to admit that in English, your friend's remark "I have three friends who are witches" is straightforwardly true even though there is no such thing as black magic. In effect, *the term "witch" has a watered-down meaning so that it doesn't take much for someone to count as a "witch"*. It is watered down compared with what you thought it was; it is a helluva lot easier to be a "witch" than you thought.

One sees this situation show up with other words. For instance, people occasionally argue past each other when debating whether there are any "miracles". At one extreme, you have people who insist that every birth of a baby is a "miracle". At another extreme, there are those who insist that in order for a "miracle" to occur, it has to violate the so-called laws of nature, such as $E = mc^2$. Neither person is wrong. The term "miracle" can have different standard meanings in different linguistic contexts. More to the point, a particular event can count as a "miracle" according to one meaning but not according to another, more stringent, meaning.

Similarly, someone might say that *the term "knowledge" has a watered-down meaning so that it doesn't take much for a belief to count as "knowledge"*. By saying it's "watered-down", I mean to compare it to what many people, including but not limited to skeptics, would have thought before encountering the argument for skepticism. Somewhat paradoxically, perhaps the skeptic was closer to the truth than the realist was even though strictly speaking the Realist view is true! More exactly, perhaps the skeptic was *wrong* when she endorsed this thesis:

> Virtually all our best beliefs – the ones that are true, are reliably formed, satisfy all social measures of acceptability, and are not guilty of any irrationality such as wishful thinking – are *insufficiently justified for knowledge*.

Hence, skepticism as strictly defined is false. But she was *right* to implicitly suggest this thesis:

> Virtually all our best beliefs – the ones that are true, are reliably formed, satisfy all social measures of acceptability, and are not guilty of any irrationality such as wishful thinking – are *epistemically impoverished* even if justified enough for knowledge.

Let's say that **subtle skepticism** is the latter thesis. The immediate follow-up question is this: what does it mean to say that our beliefs are "epistemically impoverished" but good enough to count as knowledge?

We can't say they are impoverished in the sense of being inadequate for knowledge, as the subtle skeptic has admitted we have knowledge. She could say that they are impoverished in the sense of being inadequate for *epistemically impressive* knowledge, but that doesn't seem enlightening.

Let's approach subtle skepticism from a different angle. Since it says that skepticism is strictly speaking false, she has to reject at least one of 1–3, since the combination of 1–3 entails skepticism. Given that her core idea is that although we have plenty of knowledge of the world around us, that knowledge is significantly unimpressive, which of 1–3 is she rejecting? I see two at least initially plausible answers.

First, the subtle skeptic might be saying that knowledge is cheap in this sense: one doesn't need anything at all to rule out the BIV scenario in order to be able to know that one isn't a BIV. There is something weird about that scenario that means we don't need anything to rule it out in order to know that it fails to obtain. In contrast, in order for me to know that I have a bike in the garage, there has to be something that rules out the possibility that someone recently took the bike out of the garage. But perhaps knowledge is cheap in that in order for me to know that I'm not a BIV, I do not need anything that rules out the BIV scenario. So, *knowledge is cheap* in the sense that the "ruling out" principles don't apply to weird possibilities like the BIV one.

Second, the subtle skeptic might be saying that knowledge is cheap in this sense: although one does need something to rule out the BIV scenario in order to know that one isn't a BIV, the fact F – without one being able to know F – does the ruling out job all by itself. As to the question "What is F?", different subtle skeptics could give different answers. Here are three candidate Fs:

F1: the fact that one's belief-forming systems are reliable in producing true beliefs
F2: the fact that one can see and feel one's body parts other than one's brain
F3: the fact that there are no actual BIVs (at least on Earth!)

That is, the subtle skeptic might be saying each of the following. In order for Sherlock Holmes to know that the butler killed the maid, he needs to *possess some evidence* that rules out the possibility that the gardener killed the maid. But in order for Jo to know she isn't a BIV, she doesn't need to possess any evidence whatsoever. Instead, the mere fact that her belief-forming processes are highly reliable (for instance; that's F1) is enough to rule out the BIV scenario – even if she hasn't the faintest idea what belief-forming processes are, she doesn't know what it means for them to be reliable, and if we told her about these things, she would still be totally confused about them. Jo can know she's not a BIV not because she cognitively possesses something that rules out the BIV scenario but because something she is utterly clueless about does it on her behalf. So, *knowledge is cheap* in the sense that one can know that X isn't true (e.g., it's not true that Jo isn't a BIV) even though one has no evidence or anything similar that rules out X (Jo has no evidence or anything else that rules out the BIV possibility).

I suspect that this version of subtle skepticism will seem plausible to you provided you have certain ideas in mind – but it will strike you as implausible if you have quite different ideas in mind. Let me explain.

What you are *inclined* to think about knowledge – inclinations that serve as a powerful yet hidden guide to how you evaluate arguments, premises, and other ideas encountered when investigating skepticism – is mainly determined by the illustrations that come to your mind when you think about knowledge. These illustrations can serve as *definitive models* for what you implicitly think knowledge must come to. For instance, if you think of how someone like Sherlock Holmes or a careful scientist comes to know things, then you are going to be strongly attracted to the idea that knowledge is pretty special, a real *cognitive* achievement *of the knower* that has just about everything to do with truth, evidence, skill, and ability (and perhaps objectivity). You will think that in order to know that X doesn't obtain, one has got to *possess* something such as evidence that rules out X. So, you will reject both versions of subtle skepticism.

But if you change your illustrations, you can end up with a very different conception of knowledge – one that is more congenial to subtle skepticism. You might start with the idea that any two-year-old child knows that the blanket is warm, the cat is outside, and mommy is talking. The child knows these things automatically, without any cognitive effort at all. She knows these things in pretty much the same way she breathes and regulates her body temperature: it just happens without any thought at all; it's almost as though it happens on the level of biology, not cognition. Under this conception, much of what we know isn't so much a cognitive but a *biological* achievement. Illustrations involving non-human animals can reinforce the idea (e.g., the dog knows the cat ran up the tree). The idea that the toddler or dog needs to possess something that rules out the BIV scenario is silly.

Is skepticism true? Is subtle skepticism true? Well, I certainly don't *know*.

Summary

The previous section is about language more than epistemology. Is that odd?

I was tutoring a rich venture capitalist from San Francisco recently. He wanted to learn how to avoid stupidity and achieve advanced critical thinking skills. One thing that surprised him about our lessons was how much attention there was to language and meaning. It's almost as though when someone wants to study X, the philosopher responds with "Well, let's look at the word 'X' first."

This may seem annoying but there is really no way around it. And the need for a linguistic detour is essential outside of philosophy, too. Suppose you wanted to debate who the greatest actors of all time are. You won't get very far unless you decide on what you mean by acting greatness. Do you mean actors who are great at entertaining audiences? Or do you mean actors who give convincing, nuanced portrayals of emotionally sophisticated and complicated characters in dramas? These are different things. So, if you want to write an essay regarding the greatest actors of all time, your essay has to start by *ignoring acting entirely*. It has to be a linguistic-psychological investigation first, in order to figure out what the people you're engaging with mean by "great actor". After that, you can turn to considering Robert De Niro, Meryl Streep, Jim Carrey, and Lucille Ball.

Similarly, at various points in this book, we will need to examine the linguistic characteristics of words such as "know", just in case knowledge is similar to context-sensitive terms such as "is a great actor".

4 Controversy Skepticism

Odds are, you have some beliefs that you know full well to be fairly controversial. Perhaps you think God doesn't really exist, we do indeed have free will, socialism is better than communism, affirmative action is unjust, and global warming is going to be catastrophic. Or think of beliefs that aren't out there in the public eye but are controversial nonetheless: your belief that your father had an affair when you and your sister were ten years old (you believe it; your sister denies it) or your opinion that your son lied about stealing from the corner store (your spouse thinks he's innocent, while you disagree). In each case, you are well aware that there are people who disagree with you – and a good number of these people (which is not to say all of them) aren't foolish or evidentially challenged or any more biased than you are. And yet you think you're right and they're wrong, and you're holding fast to your view even though you know that the people who disagree with you have heard your side of the story, have understood it, and still think you're wrong. You're aware that your reasons, the ones that convinced you of the belief in question, have not impressed them enough to agree with you.

In such a scenario, your belief may well be the true one; good for you. But will it amount to *knowledge*? Will it be *wise* for you to stick to your belief in these circumstances? The **controversy skeptic** thinks that awareness of certain kinds of disagreement provides one with a reason to think one's belief is false – a reason often strong enough to make one's epistemic position impoverished in the event that one retains one's belief in the face of recognized disagreement.

Controversy skepticism (CS) is importantly different from traditional skepticism, not only with regard to the supporting argument, which will be obvious, but also with regard to what the conclusion comes to. It will turn out to be somewhat akin to subtle skepticism.

The phenomenon of disagreement supplies a kind of skepticism worth worrying about in a practical way because it generates an argument for the conclusion that many of your most precious beliefs are *false*. The traditional skeptic says that my most precious beliefs may be true, reasonable according to almost any social standard and not guilty of any irrationality such as wishful thinking. The controversy skeptic says none of that. This is a much more worrisome kind of skepticism.

In what follows, I examine the cases of disagreement that generate what I take to be *the best* arguments for skeptical conclusions that have some bite in the sense that they apply to a *large* portion of our actual beliefs – especially ones we really *care* about.

4.1 When Disagreement Does Not Ruin Knowledge

Clearly, just because you know of a bunch of people who disagree with you does not preclude you from knowing that they are wrong and you are right. A group of children might think that so and so is the most famous person alive, but you could easily know that they are wrong. Disagreement generates good skeptical arguments only when the disagreement meets more demanding conditions. However, it isn't easy to come up with an impressive skeptical argument based on disagreement.[1]

---

1. For an introduction to the epistemology of disagreement, see Frances 2014.

We begin with some stipulations. Suppose you're faced with the question "Is claim C true?" You have your view on the matter: you think C is true. If you are convinced that a certain person is clearly lacking compared with you on many epistemic factors when it comes to answering the question "Is C true?" – factors such as general intelligence, relevant evidence, time spent thinking the evidence through, amount of distractions encountered while thinking about the evidence, background knowledge – then you'll probably say that you are *more likely* than she is to answer the question correctly (provided there are no other factors that give her an advantage over you). If you are convinced that a certain person definitely surpasses you on many factors when it comes to answering "Is C true?" then you'll probably say that you are *less likely* than she is to answer the question correctly (provided you think there are no factors that give you an advantage over her). In general, you can make judgments about how likely someone is compared with you to answer "Is C true?" correctly. If you think she is more likely (e.g., the odds that she will answer it correctly are 90%, whereas your odds are just 80%), then you think she is your *epistemic superior* on this question; if you think she is less likely, then you think she is your *epistemic inferior* on this question; if you think she is about equally likely, then you think she is your *epistemic peer* on this question.

With these notions in mind, here is a simple rule to start us off looking at skeptical arguments from disagreement:

> **Rule 1**: Suppose that before the discovery of disagreement, you thought that a certain person is your epistemic peer or superior on the question whether claim C is true. Then you realize that the two of you disagree on C. You stick with your belief C, not even lowering your confidence level significantly. Your retained belief in C won't amount to knowledge.

The idea here in the case of peers is this: if you thought that the two of you were equally likely to judge C correctly, then when you find out she believes not-C while you believe C, you should conclude that there's a 50% chance she's right and a 50% chance you're right. So you're saying to yourself that there's just a 50% chance C is true. So you should suspend judgment on C. For the case of superiors, if you thought she was far and away your superior when it came to judging C, then you should probably move your opinion on C to be much closer to her view than your old view. If you don't give up your belief C or at least lower your confidence in it drastically, then in either case – peers or superiors – it won't be reasonable. And if it's not reasonable, then it won't amount to knowledge.

By this reasoning, if you discovered you had disagreeing peers or superiors on a *great many* of your beliefs, then a *great many* of your beliefs would fail to amount to knowledge even if they were true – or so says rule 1. This would be a limited but significant kind of skepticism.

But many cases show why rule 1 is contentious. Suppose Viktoriya is convinced that C is true, where C is "Smoking causes cancer." If asked, Viktoriya would say, "I am very confident that C is true." Viktoriya is highly confident C is true because she is very well aware that virtually all of the many experts on the topic have long thought that it's true. She has excellent testimonial evidence backing up her belief in C. She knows, of course, that there are many people who verbally deny the smoking-cancer connection, but she thinks such people are ignorant, foolish, lying, or caught in self-deception. Viktoriya is also convinced that Willard is her peer on knowing whether C is true. The basis for this belief in peerhood isn't anything fancy or involved; she just supposes that Willard is about as intelligent and scientifically literate as she is, since he is a software engineer like she is, and he seems generally knowledgeable about many scientific things in the news (e.g., he knew about the latest mission to Mars). Then she finds out that Willard genuinely thinks smoking doesn't cause cancer.

By my lights, when Viktoriya learns of Willard's opinion, she will have acquired little or no reason to give up her belief that smoking causes cancer. When she learned of Willard's opinion, she probably thought to herself, "Oh Jeez. He is one of *those* people, ones who have been brainwashed by the tobacco companies and their shills." She already knew about "those people"; actually running into one won't matter to her overall evidence regarding smoking and cancer. And even if she didn't already know of these people, she did know that there's almost never 100% agreement among intelligent and informed people. So Rule 1 looks dubious. If we are going to find a powerful skeptical argument from disagreement, we will need a better rule to use.

Things don't change if the person you disagree with is a recognized superior on C. Even if Viktoriya thought that Willard was her superior on the issue (e.g., he is a doctor or a medical researcher), she would be reasonable in sticking with C. She would just recall or perhaps conclude that even the experts are rarely 100% in agreement. She might think to herself, "He probably thinks he knows something all the many thousands of other experts missed. But the odds are really against him". She might conclude that Willard must be biased or somehow emotionally invested in denying the smoking-cancer connection – or maybe she will just think to herself, "Well, something is definitely going on with that guy on this topic" (so she is open to the possibility that he isn't saying what he appears to be saying). She will implicitly think that even though he's smarter than her, knows all about her good testimonial evidence for her view, has thought about the issue a lot more than she has, and so on, there must be some explanation of why he went wrong.

One thing we can do in order to find a better skeptical rule is focus on groups instead of individual people:

> **Rule 2:** You and many others believe C. But you realize that there are many people who disbelieve C. After reflection, you come to think that the group you're disagreeing with is in a better position than your group (the group of people who like you believe C) to judge C correctly (this is the superior case). Or you might think that the two groups are equally likely to judge C correctly (this is the peer case). In either situation, sticking with C will be unreasonable, and your belief in C won't amount to knowledge.

This rule is better in part because it matches well with the worrisome disagreements we find ourselves in: often the most intriguing disagreements hold among very large groups of people, many of whom are experts.

The smoking-cancer case isn't a counterexample to Rule 2 because Viktoriya did not think that when it came to judging C, the group of deniers of C was in a better or equal position than the group of affirmers of C. Indeed, it was precisely because her group contains almost all the relevant experts that she was reasonable in sticking with C.

However, rule 2 is doubtful as well. Suppose that in a college class, the students break into two groups of ten students in order to independently investigate some complicated matter. Student Stu thinks the groups are evenly matched based on his modest knowledge of their abilities and what he knows about how much work each group has put into the project (pretend this is a small college, and Stu knows a great many of his fellow students). After a week of work, the two groups have representatives give oral progress reports to the whole class. The representative from the other group says that her group has figured out several things regarding the topic of investigation, which is college resources. One claim in particular, C: there are about 113 student computers in the college's main library. But this strikes Stu as way too low. He was disposed to be 100% confident in his disbelief in C. He briefly wonders whether the student in question is accurately presenting the verdict of her group, but when he sees the members of her group nodding their heads, he knows his group definitely disagrees with their group. Stu is extremely confident the number is quite a bit more than 113, as he and his group members have scoured the library to count the computers. He sticks with his belief not-C and starts to doubt whether he was right to think the other group had done about as much work on the project as his group did.

I suspect that the factor that secures Stu's rationality (in an epistemic sense of "rational") is the fact that *Stu has much better overall evidence for his belief in not-C than for his belief in peerhood between the two groups of students*. That is, Stu has much better evidence for the belief that there aren't about 113 student computers in the college's main library than for the belief that the second group of students is the peer of his group when it comes to judging the number of computers.

In this story, Stu started out thinking the two groups were peers when it came to judging straightforwardly factual claims about the number of computers on campus. By altering the story a little, we can use it to cast doubt on the "superior" part of rule 2 as well – the clause that treats the case when you think the group of people who disagree with you is the epistemic superior to your group. Suppose Stu started out, before hearing their view on C, with *mildly* good evidence that the other group was *mildly better* positioned to answer "How many student computers are in the main library?" So, he thinks their group is the epistemic superior of his group but not by much. Suppose further that he learns that although the other group believes C, they do not do so with extreme conviction: they believe it, but not vehemently. Finally, suppose he and his group are extremely confident in not-C, as they counted the computers very carefully, multiple times, in order to be certain, since the number was crucial to their project.

For what it's worth, in my judgment, he is reasonable if he sticks with his belief not-C and concludes that despite their mild superiority, the other group just got things wrong this time around. Stu knows they were *more likely* than his group to judge C correctly, but this doesn't mean that they were *guaranteed* to judge C correctly. The main thing that secures his reasonability is his extremely powerful overall evidence for not-C coupled with his comparatively *mild* evidence for the other group's *mild* superiority and *mild* confidence in C.

Considerations like these show that it's no small matter to construct a worthwhile skeptical argument that centers on disagreement. So what are the troublesome cases, the ones that *do* generate a good case for a worrisome kind of skepticism?

4.2 When Disagreement May Ruin Knowledge

When one knows that one's belief is highly controversial, then one has *available* a good if potentially defeasible reason for serious doubt. However, again, it's tricky to formulate the skeptical argument, as there may be flaws lying in wait.[2]

For the sake of argument, I will assume that some controversial beliefs very often start out epistemically rational and even overall justified (in any of several senses of these terms). Roughly put, the controversy skeptic thinks that even if a controversial belief *starts out* as knowledge, once one appreciates the controversy, one's belief will *no longer* amount to knowledge.

Not all cases are the same, however. Just because someone learns that his belief is highly controversial doesn't *guarantee* that his belief will no longer amount to knowledge. For instance, he might be the only living soul who knows that Oswald assassinated Kennedy, as he is Oswald.

---

2. Fumerton 2010; Kornblith 2010; Goldberg 2009; Frances 2010, 2013, 2018b; andChristensen 2009 each address the epistemology of controversial belief. Feldman 2006; Frances 2021, 2018a; Kraft 2012; Oppy 2010; and Thune 2011 each address the specific case of religious controversy.

In my judgment, the cases of disagreement that generate powerful arguments for types of worrisome skepticism *typically* satisfy the following group of conditions.

You know that the controversial claim C in question has been investigated and debated (i) for a very long time by (ii) a great many (iii) very smart people, some of whom (iv) are your epistemic superiors on the matter, and (v) have worked very hard (vi) under the best available circumstances to figure out if C is true. But (vii) as far as you know, these people have not come to any significant agreement on C, and (viii) as far as you know, the people who agree with you are not, as a group, in a better position to judge C than those who disagree with you.

We typically come to know (i)–(vi) through testimony: these are just brute facts about society that we are well aware of. For instance, I might have some opinion regarding free will or capital punishment or affirmative action or spiritual experience or the causes of World War II. I know full well that these matters have been debated by an enormous number of really smart people for a very long time – in some cases, for centuries. I also know that I'm no expert on any of these topics. I also know that there are genuine experts on those topics – at least, they have thought about these topics *much* longer than I have, with a great deal more awareness of relevant considerations, etc. It's no contest: I know I'm just an amateur compared with them. Part of being wise is coming to know about your comparative epistemic status on controversial subjects.

The person who satisfies (i)–(viii) appears to be robbed of the reasonableness of several comforting responses to disagreement. She realizes that she can't reasonably say, at least with any reasonable amount of confidence, anything like the following remarks (or anything similar):

a) Well, the people who agree with me are smarter than the people who disagree with me.
b) We have crucial evidence they don't have.
c) We have studied the key issue a great deal more than they have.
d) They are a lot more biased than we are.

This phenomenon is particularly prevalent with regard to religion, politics, morality, and philosophy. Recall college student Stu. When he learned that the other group disagreed with him, he could easily say to himself, "Well, I guess they didn't do as much work on the issue as I thought" or "Maybe they aren't as smart as I thought" or "Perhaps they just screwed up the count of the computers or made some other slip, even though they're just as smart and thorough as we are." But when it comes to debates about free will, economics, abortion, the law, capital punishment, affirmative action, and many other standard controversial topics, a great many of us – not all of us, but many – either know that such responses are false or, if we do embrace them, we do so irrationally. If when it comes to the question of whether we have free will, you say to yourself, "The people who disagree with me just don't understand the issues", "They aren't very smart", "They haven't thought about it much", et cetera, then you are doing so irrationally in the sense that *you should know better* than to say that, at least if you're honest with your informed self.

Now for the argument for CS:

1. Suppose you believe C.
2. Then you become aware of the controversial nature of C: you know (i)–(vi) from before and (vii) and (viii) are true of you as well. You retain your belief in C, with no significant alteration in confidence level.
3. If (2) is true of you, then you are being unwise in retaining belief in C – and this is true even if C is true and you used to *know* C was true.
4. Thus, for any belief that makes (2) true, retaining this belief will be unwise.

This argument concludes that even if your belief C is optimal in key epistemic respects (true and previously known to be true), it's unwise to retain it.

Notice that the argument does not conclude that the retained belief is unjustified. This would be another argument, one that results from replacing "then you are being unwise in retaining belief in C" with "then your retained belief in C is unjustified". In this case, we have premise (3*):

> 3*. If (2) is true of you, then your retained belief in C is unjustified – and this is true even if C is true and you used to *know* C was true.

The first argument concludes that you *acted* foolishly in retaining your controversial belief; so the focus is on your cognitive action of sticking with your controversial belief. The second argument says your retained belief itself is not justified; so the focus is not on your action but the result of the action, so to speak. Both arguments are plausible and intriguing. But how good are they?

Summary

The argument for CS has just one key premise, (3). In this respect, it is simpler than the argument for skepticism.

However, there is an implicit premise in the argument regarding controversy: it's the idea that we are *often* in the situation described in premise (2). Maybe not statistically often but often enough that the conclusion of CS is worrying. You should think about how many of your beliefs satisfy premise (2).

4.3 Two Objections to the Arguments for Controversy Skepticism

The first objection starts out by reminding us that the two CS arguments have a very limited scope compared with the argument for traditional skepticism, since the former arguments only target beliefs that meet conditions (i)–(viii)! If we take out some of the conditions, we can increase the applicability of the argument – it will apply to many more of our beliefs – but then there will be more at least initially reasonable ways (3) and (3*) might be false (and (2) has to be modified). For instance, a person with a controversial belief may falsely think that she has some key evidence that the disagreers lack; this is response (b) from before. In such a case, she might have a fully justified belief in (b), which would probably make the retaining of the controversial belief in C reasonable, too. And even if she had an unreasonable belief in (b), there is the key question of whether the epistemic sin in unjustifiably believing (b) negatively affects the epistemic status of the retained controversial belief.

The second objection targets the two original arguments for CS and casts doubt on (3) and (3*). The objection can be expressed with a story.

Pretend that Pat thinks little boys are naturally more violent than little girls. He thinks this because he is father of two boys and two girls, he has run a daycare for little kids for 25 years, and he has talked about the issue with many other experienced daycare workers over many years. He is not, however, a child psychologist or anything related; neither has he read any studies on the issue. Suppose further that he's exactly right: little boys are definitely naturally more violent than little girls, no matter how you construe "natural", "little", "violent", "boy", or "girl". Assume that the experts on child behavior – at least, the ones doing the research with PhDs – have for a very long time been stubbornly divided on the question of whether little boys are naturally more violent than little girls. They are well aware of the observational evidence that has suggested that boys are naturally more violent – they know all about the kinds of evidence Pat has – but for a quarter century now, they have had studies that collectively strongly suggest the exact opposite. In this story, the question of natural violence and gender has long been one of the outstanding questions in child psychology.

Might Pat's retained belief "Boys are naturally more violent than girls" be justified provided (i) he obtained and holds the belief on the basis of his experiences, experiences that gave him plenty of justification for his true belief; (ii) the evidence the experts have that suggests otherwise is unknown to him; and (iii) although he is vaguely aware that there have been some studies that go against his view, he just shrugged his shoulders and never really dwelled on this fact? Would the epistemic sin involved in this shrug – if it is such – be so bad as to either make his retaining his controversial belief unwise (so (3) is false) or make the retained belief unjustified (so (3*) is false)?

I don't know. Perhaps it matters what knowledge and justification come to. Over the centuries, many philosophers have thought that knowledge is something pretty special, something that has to be fought for with real cognitive power. Others have thought that any two-year-old child knows an enormous number of mundane facts. It's not entirely clear that anyone is wrong in this debate. We went over some of these considerations when evaluating subtle skepticism. We use the words "know" and "knowledge" quite a bit in life, but perhaps "knowledge" is ambiguous, which would go some way toward explaining why we can never agree on the analysis of "the" notion *knowledge* (because there is no such singular notion).

Thus, even when one is aware that one's belief is controversial among the experts, aware that one is an amateur in many respects compared with them, and aware that one has no evidence that they have missed, it isn't clear that this will mean that one's retained belief fails to amount to knowledge or is unjustified.

The controversy skeptic may well protest that Pat was in an unusual situation: he started out knowing P because of his extensive experience with children over a quarter century; the experts had generated large amounts of misleading evidence; Pat had been exposed to none of that misleading evidence; and although Pat knew the issue was controversial, he didn't think about it much and it more or less slipped from his consciousness. The objection here is that even if Pat is in a position to have knowledge, for the vast number of controversial beliefs, this position is rare. So even if the objection succeeds in showing that (3) and (3*) are false, they are false only for a small percentage of beliefs that the controversy skeptic's argument applies to.

Chapter 2

The Reality of Knowledge

Michael Huemer

Contents

1 Introduction	54
1.1 Skepticism About What?	54
1.2 Certainty vs. Justification Skeptics	56
1.3 How to Phrase the Brain-in-a-Vat Argument	59
1.4 My Overall View	60
2 Some Responses to the Brain-in-a-Vat Argument	61
2.1 Is Skepticism Self-Refuting?	61
2.2 The G.E. Moore Shift	62
2.3 Can Brains in Vats Think About Brains in Vats?	65
2.4 Knowledge Without Justification?	70
2.5 Denying Closure	72
2.6 Does the Skeptic Beg the Question?	77
2.7 A Direct Realist Response to Skepticism	79
2.8 Indirect Realist Responses	82
3 A Theory of Justified Belief	86
3.1 Foundationalism	86
3.2 Phenomenal Conservatism	88
3.3 Phenomenal Conservatism Gets the Right Answers	90
3.4 Alternatives Are Self-Defeating	91
3.5 Internalist Intuitions	92
3.6 Phenomenal Conservatism vs. External-World Skepticism	94
4 Controversy Skepticism	95
4.1 The Obviousness of Controversy Skepticism	95
4.2 How Irrational Are We?	96

DOI: 10.4324/9781003434931-3

| 4.3 The Real Issue: Who Is Your Peer? | 99 |
| 4.4 A Defense of Opinion | 100 |

1 Introduction

I would like to start by thanking Bryan Frances for his extremely helpful and interesting discussion of philosophical skepticism. In section 1, I add some remarks to further clarify the kind of skepticism we are concerned with in this debate. I also briefly overview my own position. It may turn out that Frances and I have less disagreement than one normally expects from "debaters".

After that, I explain how non-skeptical philosophers have responded to the sort of argument for skepticism that Frances has laid out (see section 2). Then I explain my general view of how we know the things that we know (see section 3). And I conclude by specifically addressing the issue Frances has raised concerning how (if at all) we should form opinions about questions that are controversial in our society (see section 4).

1.1 Skepticism About What?

In philosophy, there are a variety of different *kinds* of skepticism. So if one wants to argue about skepticism, one should first clarify what kind of skepticism one is interested in and make sure that everyone is talking about the same issue.

The first point to clarify is *what subject matter* the skeptic is skeptical about. In the history of philosophy, there have been a great many things that philosophers have been skeptical about. Some, for example, are skeptical about *morality* (they hold that we don't know any moral facts), others are skeptical about *unobserved* facts, others are skeptical about other people's minds, and so on. A very small number of philosophers have been skeptical about *everything* – that is, they have doubted that we know any propositions at all. This position, of course, is open to the retort that, if it is true, then the skeptic does not know that his own thesis is true.

We're not going to talk about any of those forms of skepticism, though. I'm only mentioning them to tell you that they're not what we're talking about. (Philosophers like to do this sort of thing. It's one of the reasons people find us annoying.)

The form of skepticism that concerns us is **external-world skepticism**. This is the view that *no one knows any contingent facts about the external world*. The "external world" refers to all the stuff that is outside one's own mind. By the way, *other people's minds* are external *for you* but not external for them. For each person, the things going on in that person's own mind count as "internal" for that person, and everything else is "external" to them. So external-world skepticism denies that any person can know what is going on outside that individual's own mind.

Why did I insert the word "contingent" in the definition of external-world skepticism? Well, there are some truths that even most skeptics think we know that might be described as truths "about the external world". For example, I know for certain that there are no married bachelors, anywhere in the universe. That's a fact about the external world, right? But it would be hard to argue that I can't know that fact, since it just follows from the meaning of "bachelor". Similarly, I know that 3 + 3 = 6, that there are infinitely many prime numbers, and that no object is completely red and also completely green. It doesn't matter if I am a brain in a vat (BIV) – all of these things would still be true. And the BIV skeptic doesn't really want to deny this.

These propositions that I just listed –

> There are no married bachelors.
> 3 + 3 = 6.
> There are infinitely many prime numbers.
> Nothing is completely red and completely green.

– are called **necessary** truths (things that *must* be true; they could not have been otherwise). Other things – things that *could* have been otherwise – are known as **contingent**. For instance, it is a contingent truth that most bachelors are slobs (that didn't *have to be* the case; it just turns out that's how things are in this world of ours). The skeptic is not interested in questioning the necessary truths. The skeptic means to raise questions about the *contingent* truths. In other words, the skeptic thinks the only things we can know about the world around us are the things that had to be the way they are; for anything that could have been otherwise, the skeptic thinks we don't know how it actually is. We know bachelors can't be married, but we can't know whether bachelors are neat or sloppy. We know green things can't be red, but we don't know whether green things are ever more than a million miles long. And so on.

Why would someone hold this view? Well, this is explained by the argument that Frances discussed in his section 2 of Chapter 1. In brief, you *might* be a BIV, and if you are a BIV, then any of the contingent truths about the external world that you think you know *may* very well not be true.

1.2 Certainty vs. Justification Skeptics

External-world skepticism, so defined, is a strong claim, which some will find absurd. It implies, for example, that I don't even know what city I live in, that no one in the USA knows who the current U.S. President is, that astronomers don't know how many planets are in the solar system, and so on.

Now, if someone says things like that, you might start wondering just what exactly that person means by "knowledge". Is the skeptic assuming some incredibly demanding interpretation of the word "know"?

In fact, *some* skeptics assume an extremely demanding interpretation of "know": they assume that knowledge requires *absolute certainty*. I call these people **certainty skeptics**. There are a number of arguments for the claim that no contingent, external-world proposition is ever absolutely certain.

Aside: Arguments for Certainty Skepticism

How could one argue, for example, that it is not certain that I have two hands?

Here is one sort of argument: if X is absolutely certain, then nothing can possibly be *more* certain than X. But it is, for me, more certain that I *exist* than it is that I have two hands. Therefore, it is not *absolutely certain* that I have two hands.

Here is another sort of argument: if X is absolutely certain, then no evidence could possibly cast any doubt on X. But it is *possible* for me to acquire evidence that would cast some doubt on whether I now have hands. Therefore, it is not now absolutely certain that I have two hands.

But we're not going to talk about certainty skepticism further (beyond this paragraph). There are a few reasons for this. One is that certainty skepticism is either trivial or semantic. That is, *if* one grants the certainty skeptic's definitions of "know" and "certain", it then becomes simply *obvious* that there is no "knowledge" of contingent truths about the external world – so obvious that there is essentially no debate about the matter in philosophy. So this would not be an interesting thesis to discuss. The only disputes that philosophers would raise would be about the meanings of words: some philosophers would deny that "knowledge", as used in standard English, requires absolute certainty. Or they might deny that "certainty", in standard English, means what the skeptic thinks it means. But these would be semantic debates, which also are not very interesting. A second reason to ignore certainty skepticism is that, even if the certainty skeptic is right, this has no interesting implications. It does not, for example, imply that we ought to change our beliefs about the external world or that we ought to change our behavior in any interesting way. At most, perhaps we should stop using the word "know" as often as we have. (Then again, maybe we should keep using it and just change its meaning so that it no longer implies certainty.) Finally, I note that Frances has not defended certainty-skepticism in his opening chapter. He has, I believe, defended a much more interesting form of skepticism. (See Chapter 1, section 2.4, where he denies that the skeptic is demanding certainty.)

What is the alternative to certainty skepticism? The other main form of skepticism is **justification skepticism**. This is the view that we lack (contingent) knowledge of the external world because our (contingent) beliefs about the external world are never *justified*.

What is meant by a belief's being "justified"? Justification is something that philosophers discuss quite a lot, and a great deal has been written about it. Here we'll just try to get an intuitive grasp of the idea. The intuitive idea is that some beliefs *make sense* to hold, given all the information available to you, whereas other beliefs would not make sense to hold. Or, it is *rational* to think certain things, given your situation, whereas other things are not rational to think. "Justification" is a matter of what is rational, or what it makes sense, to believe. Some examples:

> In normal circumstances, if you look at the window and you see drops of water falling past the window and the sky is grey,

it makes sense (or it is reasonable, it is rational, it would be justified) for you to think that it is raining.

If you think about the statement "$1 + 2 = 3$", it makes sense for you to think that statement is true.

If you have a headache, which you are consciously aware of, it makes sense for you to believe that you are in pain.

In giving these examples, I'm assuming a commonsense view of what it makes sense to believe. Justification skeptics, however, take a revisionary view, which would reject the first example: they would say you are *not* justified in thinking that it is raining – because this is a contingent claim about the external world, and no such claim is *ever* justified, according to the skeptic.

Justification skepticism is much more interesting to discuss than certainty skepticism. This is for a few reasons. First, unlike the case for certainty skepticism, justification skepticism actually implies that we should radically alter our beliefs (at least, we should if we want to remain rational). If none of our contingent, external-world beliefs are justified, then we should give up these beliefs. Second, justification skepticism is far from obvious. Almost everyone, including both professional philosophers and ordinary people, even after agreeing about the meaning of "justification", thinks that we *have* justification for most of our contingent, external-world beliefs. But despite this, there are interesting arguments to the conclusion that we *don't* have such justification. Some of these arguments are quite difficult to rebut, and there is no general agreement on what exactly is wrong with them. I have in mind especially the BIV argument, which I will discuss at some length later. If there are difficult-to-rebut arguments for a highly controversial conclusion that would require a radical revision of our belief system, then it is, in general, a very interesting thing to discuss.

Now, I'm not certain that this is the form of skepticism that Frances meant to discuss in his opening chapter. That's partly because I'm not quite sure what Frances meant by such expressions as "epistemically impoverished" and "epistemically impressive" (see his section 3 in Chapter 1). But I think it is at least close to what he meant to discuss. (If not, then I don't understand what Frances meant well enough to address it usefully.) So, I am going to talk about justification skepticism.

1.3 How to Phrase the Brain-in-a-Vat Argument

Here is Frances' formulation of the main argument for external-world skepticism, the so-called BIV argument:

BIV Argument, Version 1

1. If you know you have two hands, then you can know you're not a mere BIV.
2. If you can know you're not a mere BIV, then there is something that rules out the mere BIV scenario for you.
3. There isn't anything that rules out the mere BIV scenario for you.
4. Therefore, you do not know that you have two hands.

(See Chapter 1, sections 2.2–2.4.) I am less than satisfied with this statement of the argument, though, for a few reasons.

The first problem I see is that the formulation doesn't make clear whether the conclusion is supposed to be certainty skepticism, justification skepticism, or something else. This depends on how we are meant to interpret the word "know", which is not entirely clear just from this formulation. It is similarly unclear to me how the notion of "ruling out" should be understood. If we take a strong interpretation of "ruling out" (which would actually be quite natural), then the consequent of premise 2 requires that one have absolute certainty that one is not a BIV, and premise 3 denies that we can be *absolutely certain* that we're not BIVs. In this case, the conclusion of the earlier argument would seem to be merely certainty skepticism, which we have already said is uninteresting. Finally, I do not see how introducing premise 2 was helpful. A simpler version of the BIV argument can be given with only two premises instead of three (see below).

For these reasons, I prefer to formulate the BIV argument as follows:

BIV Argument, Version 2

1. If I am justified in believing that I have two hands, then I have some available justification for denying that I am a BIV.
2. I have no available justification for denying that I am a BIV.
3. Therefore, I am not justified in believing that I have two hands.

Now, it is hazardous to rewrite someone else's arguments, as the other person does not always appreciate this. But this is intended as a friendly rewriting. I am not, for example, rewriting the BIV argument in order to make it easier to rebut (which would be bad behavior on my part). Rather, I am rewriting it to make it simpler and clearer and more clearly focused on the most interesting issue.

The motivations for premises 1 and 2 are still easy to see. Most people find premise 1 obvious on its face. And it's also easy to motivate premise 2. If you think you have a justification for denying that you are a BIV, what is that justification? It is really hard to say. If you *were* a BIV, everything would seem to you just the way it does now. So it doesn't look as if you have any evidence that you're not a BIV. (Granted, you have no evidence that you *are* a BIV, either. But absence of evidence should not be confused with evidence of absence.) Could you somehow be justified in assuming that you're not a BIV even though you have no evidence at all for this assumption? That would be pretty interesting if this were so, and we would need a good explanation of it. So, in brief, the BIV argument, version 2, is a good argument to discuss. So that is what I am going to discuss.

1.4 My Overall View

To preview the rest of this chapter, here is my view: I think we are justified in believing many (contingent) things about the external world, including things that we directly observe, such as the fact that one has two hands. I think the BIV hypothesis (BIVH) is unreasonable for two reasons. First, I think that it is, in general, reasonable to assume that everything is the way it appears unless one has specific reasons to think otherwise. BIVH contradicts the appearances, and we have no specific reason to suspect that we are BIVs. Second, as an independent point, I think BIVH is a bad theory because it is essentially unfalsifiable. But before I elaborate on these points, I will explain (see section 2) some other philosophers' responses to the BIV argument.

Summary

The form of skepticism to be discussed is external-world, justification skepticism, which holds that we lack knowledge of contingent facts about the world outside our minds because beliefs about such facts are never *justified*. The main argument for this view is that our contingent, external-world beliefs are justified *only if* we have a justification for denying that we are BIVs, but we do not in fact have a justification for denying that we are BIVs.

2 Some Responses to the Brain-in-a-Vat Argument

Very few philosophers are skeptics. Non-skeptical philosophers have devised many different responses to the BIV argument in order to defend our knowledge of the external world. I'm going to explain several such responses later. But first, I will briefly mention a bad response that some students might be tempted by.

2.1 Is Skepticism Self-Refuting?

In a typical classroom, within a minute of hearing about philosophical skepticism, someone in the class will think of the idea that skepticism is self-refuting: if we don't know anything, then we don't know skepticism itself! In this case, the skeptic has no business going around asserting skepticism.

Now, this might be a good retort to a universal skeptic. That is, if you meet someone who thinks that literally *nothing at all* is known, by anyone, then it might be a good retort to point out that this person's thesis entails that he himself does not know that very thesis.

But be that as it may, the "self-refutation" charge does *not* apply to the form of skepticism that we're discussing here. We're discussing external-world skepticism, which denies knowledge of contingent, external-world facts. Now, you might be tempted to say that this thesis is self-undermining because "No one knows any contingent fact about the external world" is, if true, a fact about the external world; hence, you might think, it applies to itself and implies that no one knows that very claim.

However, external-world skepticism is not a *contingent* truth, nor does anyone think that it is. If external-world skepticism is true, it's true because of something like the BIV argument – that is, it's true because we can't show that we're not BIVs. But if you think about it, *this* fact (if it's a fact) is not *contingent*. It's not as if there is some further investigation that we could do, some further evidence we could gather, to figure out whether we're BIVs, and we just haven't yet gathered this evidence. For example, if you interview some scientists to find out whether we actually possess the technology to keep a disembodied brain alive, it won't help because whatever the scientists say could just be part of the BIV simulation. No matter what evidence you gather, the evidence will be able to be explained as just another part of the simulation that the BIV is experiencing. So, *if* you agree that we presently have no justification for denying that we're BIVs, you should agree that we *could not* have any such justification. So the skeptical conclusion is not contingent: if it's true, it's necessarily true. So it is not self-refuting; it does *not* imply that no one could know that very conclusion.

2.2 The G.E. Moore Shift

Sometimes you hear an argument whose conclusion is so implausible that you can conclude, from this alone, that something is wrong with the argument. You need not know *where* the argument went wrong – which premise was mistaken, or which inference was invalid – in order to know that it went wrong *somewhere*.

For example, suppose you were given a problem in a science class. You were given some data about, say, lengths of shadows at different latitudes at different times of day, and from this, you are supposed to calculate the diameter of the Earth. (This is like how the ancient Greek scientist Eratosthenes actually figured out the rough size of the Earth.) You do some calculations and come up with an answer: the Earth is about 800 miles wide. Imagine that you check over your calculations several times and can find nothing wrong with them. What should you conclude? Should you, in fact, think that the Earth is only 800 miles in diameter?

If you have even a minimal knowledge of the world – even if you don't know what the *correct* answer to the problem is – you know that "800 miles" simply is not a reasonable answer. It is much too small to be plausible. Even though you cannot identify the error in your calculations, you can rationally assume that your calculations are in error (or the data you were given were in error).

Here is another example. The ancient Greek philosopher Zeno gave an argument that motion is impossible. Suppose an object wants to move from point A to point B. To do this, the object must first go half the distance. After doing that, it will need to go half the remaining distance (a quarter of the total distance). And after that, half the remaining distance again. And so on. This is an infinite series, one that has no end. It is not possible to complete a series that has no end. Therefore, the object can never reach point B. Since "point B" can be chosen to be any point you like, this allegedly shows that no object can ever move anywhere. Zeno, accordingly, concluded that all the motion we *seem* to see in the world around us is just an illusion.

Was this reasonable? I don't think so. A rational person would realize the conclusion ("motion is impossible") is absurd, so something or other has to be wrong with the argument. This is an interesting thing to investigate. But we surely should not just accept the conclusion, even if we can't right away see what is wrong with the argument. Indeed, even if years pass and we still haven't figured out what the problem is, it still would not be rational to endorse the argument, since obviously motion does occur.

There are many philosophers (myself included) who think that arguments for skepticism are analogous to the argument that motion is impossible or the calculation resulting in a figure of 800 miles for the Earth's diameter: the conclusion is so implausible that one can reject the argument for this reason alone, whether or not one can identify a specific flaw in the argument.

G.E. Moore (a famous 20th-century British philosopher) was one such person.[1] He noticed that logic alone only tells us that, when faced with a (valid) deductive argument, one cannot simultaneously accept the premises *and* reject the conclusion, but logic alone doesn't tell us whether we should accept the premises. Moore argued that when one encounters an argument for philosophical skepticism, it is more rational to reject a premise of the argument than it is to accept the conclusion. Hence, the maneuver of rejecting an opponent's premise on the ground that his conclusion is too implausible has come to be called "the G.E. Moore shift". To illustrate, consider the following three propositions, which I will label "(1)", "(2)" and "(J)":

1. If I am justified in believing that I have two hands, then I have some justification for denying that I am a BIV.
2. I have no justification for denying that I am a BIV.
J. I *am* justified in believing that I have two hands.

Logic alone tells us that (1), (2), and (J) are jointly incompatible – that is, at least one of them has to be false. But that's all that *logic* tells us. Now, the skeptic assumes that (1) and (2) are true and thus concludes that (J) is false. But we could, equally validly, assume that (1) and (J) are true and conclude that (2) is false. Or we could assume that (2) and (J) are true and conclude that (1) is

---

1. See Moore 1953.

false. In other words, all three of the following are logically valid arguments:

(1) is true.	(1) is true.	(2) is true.
(2) is true.	(J) is true.	(J) is true.
Therefore, (J) is false.	Therefore, (2) is false.	Therefore, (1) is false.

The first argument is logically **valid** (i.e., the conclusion follows from the premises), since (1), (2) and (J) are jointly incompatible. The second argument is valid since (1), (J), and (2) are jointly incompatible. The third is valid since (2), (J), and (1) are jointly incompatible.

Notice that this is a perfectly general point about deductive arguments. If (and only if) some set of propositions is jointly incompatible, then we can construct an argument against any proposition in the set, whichever one we choose, by assuming that all the *others* are true, and therefore the remaining one must be false.

All such arguments are equally *self-consistent*. But of course, not all such arguments are equally *reasonable*. What would make one of these arguments more reasonable than another? Well, if you notice that some set of propositions can't all be true, then presumably you should reject whichever one seems *least obvious* to you, or whichever one you were *least confident* of, prior to noticing the inconsistency. (What would be the alternative to this? Surely you should not reject a *more* plausible idea on the basis of a *less* plausible one, should you?)

Now, when it comes to skeptical arguments, the conclusion that the skeptic is arguing for is, as a rule, incredibly implausible on its face. It seems much less initially plausible, to almost anyone, than the denial of one of the skeptic's premises. Therefore, it would be irrational to accept the skeptic's conclusion based on those premises; it would be more rational, instead, to deny one of the skeptic's premises (whichever one seems least plausible). In the case of the BIV argument, it is more reasonable to say, "Actually, I *have* a justification for denying that I am a BIV" or even to say, "I *don't need* a justification for denying that I am a BIV in order to justifiably believe that I have hands" than it is to say, "I have no justification for thinking I have hands".

Now, G.E. Moore didn't say *which* premise of the skeptic's argument he thought was most likely to be mistaken (and he was not writing about the BIV argument in the first place but about a different skeptical argument that we don't have time to discuss here). Nor did he *explain why* the particular premise that was mistaken (whichever it was) would be mistaken. He just said that *one premise or another* must be mistaken, since they lead to an absurd conclusion. For this reason, even if (as I think) Moore's basic point is right, it still is not very *illuminating*. We should keep looking for philosophical accounts of *where* the skeptic went wrong.

Aside: David Hume's Argument for External-World Skepticism

Moore was responding to an argument for skepticism found in David Hume's works. (A similar one later appears in Bertrand Russell, and Moore responded similarly to that one, too.) Hume's argument was something like this:

During sensory perception, we are only *directly* aware of the experiences in our own minds, not the real, physical objects. Therefore, to acquire knowledge of the external world, we must verify that experiences of certain kinds are generally *caused by* physical objects of certain kinds. The way one verifies causal claims like this is by observing one type of event being followed by another on many occasions; one then infers that the event that normally comes first is the *cause* of the one that comes after. So in order to know what X causes, one has to be able to observe X. But as indicated earlier, one never really (directly) observes physical objects or events; one only directly observes one's own experiences. So one has no basis for making any inferences about what effects *physical objects or events* might cause. So one cannot in fact make justified inferences from one's experiences to claims about the physical world.

2.3 Can Brains in Vats Think About Brains in Vats?

Some philosophers think we can rule out the BIV scenario because the scenario is self-refuting, and it is self-refuting because if there *were* a BIV, that brain would not be able to talk or think about brains or vats.[2] Since the skeptic who advances the BIV argument

---

2. Putnam 1981, ch. 1.

cannot very well deny that he himself, at the time of advancing that argument, is thinking about BIVs, the fact that we can talk or think about BIVs rules out our actually being BIVs.

To understand this point of view, we first need to talk about an interesting phenomenon that philosophers call **intentionality**. *Note:* the word "intentionality", in philosophy, *does not* refer to the property of being intended by someone! Rather, there is a special, technical use of "intentional" and "intentionality" that is completely different from the ordinary English term "intend". "Intentionality" refers to the property of being *about, representing, standing for, referring to,* or *meaning* something. For instance, the word "dog" *refers to* a certain type of animal. You may also draw a picture *of* a dog. You may see a dog, in which case you will have a visual experience that represents the dog. You also have a concept of dogs, and you have various beliefs about dogs. All of these are examples of intentionality: we say that the word "dog", a picture of a dog, a visual experience of a dog, a concept of a dog, and beliefs about dogs all "have intentionality" since they all represent something (in this case, dogs).

Having drawn attention to the interesting phenomenon of intentionality, we can now ask: Under what conditions, in general, does x refer to y? More specifically, what does it take for a person's *thoughts* to refer to some phenomenon outside themselves?

It is plausible that the intentionality of our *thoughts* depends on the intentionality of our *perceptual experiences*. For instance, we can have concepts and beliefs about dogs because we have *perceived* dogs. Granted, we also have some thoughts that refer to things that no one has ever observed: we have an idea of a unicorn, though no one has ever seen one. But this is possible only because a "unicorn" can be *described* in terms of other things (horses and horns) that we *have* observed. So to think about x, it seems, we need to have either observed x or observed other things that x could be described in terms of.

Now, what about the intentionality of our perceptual experiences: what does it take for a sensory experience to represent some particular physical phenomenon? Take our visual experiences of color. There is a particular color experience, which you typically have when you observe ripe tomatoes, that we might call "the sensation of red". What phenomenon in the physical world does this sensation refer to? Of course, it refers to redness, but what is that?

Well, roughly (we don't need to be very precise here), when you see an object as red, what you are actually detecting is the object's disposition to reflect mainly light of around 700-nanometer (nm) wavelength, within the visible spectrum. For simplicity, let's just say that the sensation of red refers to 700-nm light.

Notice that there is no *intrinsic* connection between that particular sensation and this particular wavelength. There could just as easily have been a creature that had (what we would call) the sensation of red when viewing objects that reflect 460-nm light and had (what we would call) the sensation of blue when viewing objects that reflect 700-nm light. In other words, there could be creature for whom tomatoes looked about the way that the sky looks to us and for whom the sky looked about the way that tomatoes look to us (in terms of color). The other creature would not be radically misperceiving the world. (What could possibly make its perceptions any more or less "correct" than ours?) It would just have a *different way* of perceiving wavelengths of light. (Of course, it would be difficult or impossible to *know* that any creature had this different way of perceiving. For all we know, some people might actually perceive colors differently from each other, in just this sort of way!)

These points are all supposed to be intuitive. If you agree with all this, then it is plausible to hold that sensory experiences get their intentionality from how they are normally caused. For us, the sensation of red represents 700-nm light because 700-nm light is the actual external phenomenon that *normally causes* this particular sensation in us. The sensation of blue is normally caused (in us, normal humans) by 460-nm light, so the sensation of blue represents 460-nm light. But for a creature that normally has the red sensation when looking at the sky, the red sensation would represent 460-nm light. And so on.

If you buy this, it is plausible to generalize to all sensory experiences. It's not just color sensations, but *every* sensation that we have refers to whatever external phenomenon regularly causes this experience in us.

But now, if all this is correct, then what becomes of the BIV? If there *were* a brain whose experiences were all caused by electrical stimulation by some supercomputer, what would the brain's experiences refer to? They wouldn't refer to the same things that *our* experiences refer to when we see normal physical objects. If the brain's experiences represented anything, they would presumably represent states of the computer, since this is what normally causes the brain's experiences. Or perhaps they would represent "virtual objects" (whatever they are). Hereafter, I'll assume that the brain's experiences represent virtual objects. (Maybe a "virtual object" just *is* the state of the computer that causes the computer to simulate the type of object in question. I don't know, but it doesn't matter.)

So, for instance, when the brain has an experience qualitatively similar to your experience of seeing a dog, the brain's experience does not represent *a dog*. It can't represent a dog, since the brain has never had any experiences caused by dogs, nor by animals of any kind, nor by anything else that dogs could be described in terms of. The brain's visual experience would just represent a *virtual dog*.

Accordingly, when the brain formed a belief, the brain would not form the belief that a dog was present. The brain would form the belief that there was a virtual dog (because the brain's thoughts would refer to the same thing that its sensory experiences referred to). And the brain would be *right* to think this – there would in fact be a virtual dog. So the brain would not be at all deceived about this. More generally, the BIV's sensory experiences and its beliefs about its immediate environment would be *correct*, not mistaken.

(Of course, the brain would not think to itself, "There is a virtual dog". The brain would think to itself words that sounded like, "There is a dog". It's just that, in the BIV's language, the word "dog" would refer to what *we* call a *virtual* dog.)

It follows from all this that the BIV scenario should not cause us to become skeptical. Whether we were normal humans or BIVs, our main beliefs about our environment would be true, so there is no need for us to doubt our current beliefs.

Now, suppose the BIV entertains the hypothesis that it would express by, "Perhaps I am a brain in a vat". In the BIV's language, "brain in a vat" could not refer to real, physical BIVs; it would instead refer to *virtual* BIVs. So if the brain thinks, "I am a brain in a vat", it would actually mean "I am a virtual brain in a vat" – which of course would be false.

This creates a problem for someone advancing the BIV scenario as a reason to doubt our ordinary beliefs. One way to think of the problem is to say that the BIV scenario is self-defeating because the assumption that you are a BIV implies that you are not now thinking about whether you are a BIV; therefore, we can reject the BIV scenario. Another way to pose the problem is to say that "I am a BIV" is guaranteed to be false, whoever thinks it. Thus:

1. If a BIV thinks, "I am a BIV", that is false.
2. If a non-BIV thinks, "I am a BIV", that is false.
3. Therefore, if I think "I am a BIV", that is false.
4. Therefore, I am not a BIV.

Premise 1 is true because the BIV would mean that it is a virtual BIV, which it isn't. Premise 2 is true because the non-BIV would mean that it is a BIV, which it isn't. Step 3 follows from 1 and 2. Step 4 follows from 3 (with the implicit assumption: "I am a BIV" is true if and only if I am a BIV).

Is this a suitable response to the BIV argument? I see two ways for a BIV skeptic to respond. The first sort of response would be to reject the theory of intentionality given earlier. Perhaps we have at least some thoughts that do *not* just refer to whatever normally causes certain experiences in us. Perhaps, say, sensory experiences of spatial properties just intrinsically refer to properties in real, physical space. Or perhaps our concepts of what we call "physical objects" contain some built-in assumption that the objects exist on their own, not merely as simulations within some other objects.

The other sort of response would be to modify the BIV scenario so that it ceases to be self-refuting, *even if* we assume the theory of intentionality discussed earlier. In the traditional BIV scenario, one imagines a brain that has always (since its creation) been in a vat, so none of its experiences have been caused in the normal way. But suppose, instead, that your brain was taken out of your body and put in the vat *just last night*. In this case, you would still have the concept of a BIV (a real, physical BIV, not just a *virtual* BIV!), so there would be no problem with your being able to entertain the hypothesis that you are a BIV. (Frances actually introduced the BIV scenario in this second way to begin with, probably to pre-empt the objection discussed in this section.)

The "you were kidnaped last night" scenario avoids the charge that the BIV scenario is self-undermining. On the other hand, if the BIVH that you're supposed to consider is just that your brain was envatted last night, then you can use your background knowledge of the world – knowledge acquired long *before* last night – to cast doubt on this. I don't know about you, but based on *my* understanding of the current state of medical and computer technology (which I gained before last night), it is technically infeasible to keep a brain alive in a vat or to program a simulation indistinguishable from normal life.

The BIV skeptic faces a dilemma: if the BIV scenario allows that you have lots of past experience of the real world, then you can use that experience to construct arguments for why it is extremely unlikely that your brain was recently envatted. But if the scenario instead posits that *all* your past experience is part of the BIV simulation, then the scenario implies that you would have no way of thinking about (real) brains or vats, so the scenario is self-undermining.

That being said, this is not my favored way of responding to the BIV argument. That is partly because I am not sure that the theory of intentionality used earlier is correct (I'm not sure that sensations only refer to whatever normally causes them, nor am I sure that thoughts always derive their intentionality entirely from the intentionality of sensations). In addition, I would prefer a response to the BIV argument that could also apply to other skeptical hypotheses, like the hypothesis that I'm dreaming ("the dream scenario") or the hypothesis that all our sensory experiences are directly planted in our minds by God ("the deceiving God scenario").

2.4 Knowledge Without Justification?

Some philosophers argue that we can "know" things without having the sort of *justification* that we have been assuming is required. On one account, "knowing" something only requires having a correct belief that was formed by a reliable mechanism. The person with the belief need not have an argument for the belief, nor need they be able to defend the belief against criticisms or present reasons against alternative hypotheses.

This permissive view of knowledge seems plausible if you think about how small children or non-human animals are said to "know" all sorts of things. For instance, when you take a can of cat food out and start using the electric can opener on it, you might find that your cat runs into the kitchen. How would you explain why the cat comes to the kitchen? "Because he knows that he's about to be fed" sounds like a reasonable answer. But the cat probably can't formulate any argument for the proposition that he's about to be fed, nor could the cat cite evidence or reasons to rule out alternative explanations for the can-opener sound; indeed, your cat most likely never entertains alternative explanations. So it's a little bit difficult to ascribe to the cat "justification for believing" that he's going to be fed. Plausibly, what makes us say that the cat "knows he's about to be fed" is the following: (i) that the cat thinks he is about to be fed, (ii) he is in fact about to be fed, and (iii) he is reliable about this – he reliably forms the expectation of being fed only when he is about to be fed. (Of course, if he is unreliable – for instance, if he just always thinks he's about to be fed – then you would not say that he *knows* he's about to be fed.)

This particular view about knowledge is known as **reliabilism** (roughly, that knowledge is just reliably formed, true belief). There are a variety of other analyses of "knowledge" that philosophers have developed that similarly leave out "justification". We don't need to go into these here. The general point is that the BIV argument for external-world, justification skepticism can be stymied by claiming that we don't *need* justification in order to count as "knowing" things. (Aside: a related approach, which differs semantically from the foregoing, is to grant that we need justification but to claim that reliability is enough for "justification", even if one has no reason to believe that one is reliable. Thus, the cat's belief is "justified" simply in virtue of the fact that the cat is reliable about when it is about to be fed.[3])

Notice what this reply does not do. It does not provide an argument to prove that we aren't BIVs. Nor does it provide an argument to show that we actually know things about the external world. The only thing this reply is trying to do is *undermine* the *skeptic's* argument. That is, the reply claims that the skeptic *hasn't shown that we lack knowledge* of the external world. The skeptic (of the sort we're discussing here) claims that we lack knowledge of the external world because we lack *justification* for our beliefs about the external world; the reply just says that we don't need justification in order to have knowledge.

This is not my favorite way of responding to the skeptic. It is the sort of thing that helps you only if you have a very particular interest in the use of the English word "know". If, on hearing about the BIV scenario, your main concern was that you might have to stop calling your beliefs "knowledge", then you might be satisfied with the reliabilist response. If, however, you were worried about what you ought to believe about the world, the reliabilist response doesn't help you.

---

3. See Goldman 1979.

It *seems* as if our ordinary beliefs about the world are justified – for instance, that it makes sense, when you see your hands, to believe that you have hands. The skeptic has an argument that these beliefs are all unjustified. That would be a disturbing conclusion, one we should like to examine and find the flaws in, *whether or not* the English word "know" implies that one has justification.

2.5 Denying Closure

One response to skepticism that is popular among philosophers is one that normal people find incredibly counterintuitive; indeed, students are apt to mistake this response for a contradiction. (Philosophers often do this: respond to a crazy view by taking up a seemingly contradictory one instead. It's one of the charms of contemporary philosophy.) The response is to claim that one can *know* a thing to be true even if one cannot rule out some incompatible alternatives. In particular (some philosophers would say), for all you know, you might be a handless BIV; nevertheless, you still *know* that you have two hands and are not just a BIV. That probably sounds contradictory to you, but it is really not (not quite!) a contradiction.[4]

In philosophy, the following proposition is sometimes called **the Closure Principle for Knowledge** (or sometimes just "the Closure Principle"):[5]

> If a person knows P and knows that P entails Q, then the person can know Q.

This principle is very intuitive. You might even think it is a tautology. But it isn't; if you think it is a tautology, you are probably confusing the Closure Principle for Knowledge with the following

---

4. To symbolize this, let H = the proposition that you have hands, BIV = the proposition that you are a brain in a vat, and K(p) = the proposition that you know p. Then the claim is that one can have $\sim$K($\sim$($\sim$H & BIV)) but yet K(H & $\sim$BIV).
5. Why is it called "the Closure Principle"? Well, there is a technical use of "closure" in logic: a set is said to be "closed under" a relation R if, for every element that the set contains, the set also contains everything that stands in relation R to that element. Thus, we could say that the set of known propositions is "closed under entailment", provided that, for every proposition that one knows, one also knows everything *entailed by* that proposition.

principle (which we might call "the closure principle for truth"): "If P is true, and P entails Q, then Q is true". *This* is a tautology; it's just made true by the meaning of "entails". But, again, the Closure Principle for *Knowledge* (for short: "Closure for Knowledge") is *not* tautological, and some philosophers reject it.

Why would someone reject Closure for Knowledge? There are two sorts of reasons. One is that some philosophers have *analyses* of the meaning of "know" that imply that Closure fails. The other sort of reason is that some philosophers believe they have discovered *counter-examples*.

Let's start with the analysis of "know". Here is one account, sometimes called **the tracking account** of knowledge:[6] To *know* a proposition, P, requires (i) believing P, (ii) being right about P (i.e., P has to be true), and (iii) having formed the belief in such a way that, in the closest possible scenario in which P was false, you would *not* have come to believe P.

Example: I *know* that I have two hands. What does this mean? First of all, I certainly *believe* that I have two hands. Second, I do in fact have two hands. Third, I formed the belief that I have two hands in such a way that, in the closest situation in which I *didn't* have two hands, I *wouldn't* have come to think I had two hands. The way I formed my belief that I have two hands was by using my vision (I *looked* down and saw the hands). Now, the closest possible situation in which I *didn't* have two hands would be a situation in which one of my hands was missing – perhaps because it was amputated, I had a horrible accident, etc., but everything else about the world was normal. In such a situation, when I looked down, I would see the stump where a hand was missing, and I would thus *not* believe that I had two hands. So, all of this suffices (according to the tracking account) to say that "I know I have two hands".

But it is fairly easy to see that, on this same account of knowledge, I would *not* be able to know some of the things that *logically follow from* my having two hands. I cannot, for example, know that I am not a BIV. I can *believe* I am not a BIV, to be sure. And I can be correct in this belief. But however I formed this belief, if I *were* a BIV, I would have formed the same belief. That is, in the closest possible

---

6. Why is it called "the tracking account"? Because the idea is that, when you know something, your belief "tracks the truth" – if the thing were true, you would believe it, and if it were false, you would not believe it. The theory derives from Robert Nozick (1981, ch. 3).

situation in which I *am* a BIV, I could use the same way of forming beliefs, and I would (falsely) conclude that I wasn't a BIV. This is enough to prevent me from "knowing" that I am not a BIV (on the tracking account).

What this means is that, on the tracking account of knowledge, Closure is false. You can know something but be in no position to know some of its logical consequences. You can know that you have two hands but be in no position to know that you're not a BIV – even though "I have two hands" entails "I'm not a BIV".

Aside: The "Relevant Alternatives" Account of Knowledge

There are other analyses of "knowledge" that also reject closure. For instance, another theory holds that to "know" a proposition, you have to have evidence capable of ruling out the "relevant alternatives" to that proposition but not necessarily all the *logically possible* alternatives.[7]

What are the relevant alternatives? Roughly, the idea is that *only* the alternatives that are reasonably close to reality, or that had some significant objective chance of being the case, are relevant. For example, if you lived in a society that *actually had* BIV technology and in which people periodically got kidnaped and had their brains envatted overnight, *then* the BIV scenario would be a relevant alternative for you, and you would have to rule it out before you could know that you had hands. (Note: the question would not be whether you *believed* or *had reason to believe* that there was BIV technology. The *actual existence* of this technology, whether or not you had any awareness of it, would make the BIV alternative "relevant".) If, however, you live in a society that does not in fact possess BIV technology (again, whether or not you know this), then the BIV scenario is irrelevant, and thus you can count as "knowing" things about the world even without having any evidence against the BIV scenario.

---

7. Dretske 1981.

This is not one of my favorite responses to skepticism. One reason is that I am skeptical (pun intended) of the analyses of "knowledge" that require rejecting closure. Anyway, these responses are too tied to semantic debates about the meaning of the word "know". But the use of "know" is not what matters. We ought to be disturbed enough if it turns out that our external-world beliefs have *no justification*, whether or not justification is part of *knowledge*.

I said earlier that some philosophers claim to have discovered counter-examples to closure. Some of these are counter-examples that you can appreciate without having accepted any particular analysis of "knowledge". Here is one: you're at the zoo with your daughter. She points at some animals in a pen and asks what they are. You see that the animals have black and white stripes, that they are shaped like horses but a little smaller, and that there is a sign on the enclosure that says, "Zebras". Taken together, these things are excellent evidence that the animals in the pen are zebras. So that's what you tell your daughter. But suppose she then asks, "How do you know that they are not mules that were painted black and white by the zoo authorities and put in the zebra pen to trick us into thinking they are zebras?"[8]

Notice that the evidence that you had for thinking that the animals were zebras (their shape, their color, their location in the zebra pen) is not evidence *against* their being cleverly disguised mules. That's exactly what cleverly disguised mules would be like! When you think about it, it is hard to cite any evidence against their being cleverly disguised mules. So, it looks as if you have good evidence that they are zebras but no evidence that they are not cleverly disguised mules. Therefore, plausibly, you can *know* and be *justified in believing* that they are zebras, yet you cannot know nor be justified in believing that they aren't cleverly disguised mules. Yet their being zebras entails that they are not cleverly disguised mules. So, the Closure Principle must be false.

---

8. The example is from Dretske (1970).

> **Aside: Another Counter-Example to Closure**
>
> Suppose I am adding up a column of numbers. I'm pretty good at arithmetic, good enough that I can normally be justified in believing that I have correctly added such a column, although my wife is more reliable than me. I add the numbers and get 1,257. I form the justified belief, "The sum of these numbers is 1,257". Now, it logically follows from [the sum of these numbers is 1,257] that, *if* my wife says that the sum is not 1,257 then she is wrong. But it does not seem that I would be justified in believing [if my wife says that the sum is not 1,257 then she is wrong]. Rather, I should think that if my wife says the sum is not 1,257, then I am most likely wrong. (Fortunately, she has not said this, so I am presently justified in thinking the sum is 1,257.) So, it seems that I am justified in believing a proposition yet not justified in believing something that logically follows from it.[9]

The zebra example does not require denying that knowledge requires justification. In fact, it directly suggests that *justification* does not satisfy closure. (You can have justification for something but lack justification for some of its logical consequences.) If this is right, then perhaps we can be justified in believing we have two hands despite having no justification for denying that we are BIVs.

Here, I will just review one way that a skeptic could respond to the zebra example. Earlier I made the point that the evidence for thinking the animals were zebras is not evidence against their being cleverly disguised mules. One could agree with this but still embrace closure for justification. To see what I mean, consider the following three proposed principles:

(i) If P is justified and P entails Q, then Q is justified.
(ii) If E justifies P and P entails Q, then E justifies Q.
(iii) If P is justified and P entails Q, then P justifies Q.

---

9. The example is from Audi (1988).

Proposition (i) is the **Closure Principle for Justification** (for short: "Closure for Justification"). Now, there are at least two different *reasons why* you might think (i) is true. (i) might be true because (ii) is true, or it might be true because (iii) is true. In other words: one reason why Closure for Justification might hold is that whenever P is justified, *the evidence that justifies it* also provides adequate justification for anything that P entails. Another reason why Closure for Justification might hold is that whenever P is justified, *P itself* provides adequate justification for anything that P entails.

Notice how these are different. Notice also that the zebra example is a counter-example to principle (ii) but not to principle (iii). In the zebra case, the evidence that supports "these animals are zebras" does *not* support "these animals are not cleverly disguised mules". For example, the fact that they have black-and-white stripes doesn't justify denying that they are cleverly disguised mules. But nothing about the example explains why *the fact that they are zebras* would not be a good enough reason to deny that they are cleverly disguised mules. After all, you are (as the example grants) justified in thinking they are zebras, and you surely realize that being a zebra is incompatible with being a mule. Why can't you simply deduce that they are not mules?

This is to say that the Closure Principle for Justification can be most plausibly defended by appealing to (iii) instead of (ii). And this, by the way, is in fact how Frances defended it in Chapter 1 (see his section 2.2).

2.6 Does the Skeptic Beg the Question?

The preceding defense of closure, however, leads us right into the next response to skepticism. This response claims that, once the skeptic defends Closure for Justification as just suggested (see section 2.5), the skeptic's argument will have to commit the fallacy of begging the question.[10]

Background: **begging the question** is the fallacy in which one argues in a circle or takes some proposition for granted in the course of trying to prove that very proposition. An argument can also be

---

10. This response derives from Klein (1995). Klein leaves open that the skeptic's argument may not in fact beg the question; rather, the skeptic's argument *either* begs the question *or* succumbs to the counter-examples to Closure for Justification.

said to "beg the question" when the only way of justifying one of the premises would be by appealing to the argument's *conclusion*.[11] So if I argue "A; therefore, B", but there is for some reason no way for me to justify A except by appealing to B, then I could be said to have "begged the question", and this would render my argument useless.

How might the skeptic be accused of begging the question? Recall the skeptic's main argument:

1. If I am justified in believing that I have two hands, then I have some available justification for denying that I am a BIV.
2. I have no available justification for denying that I am a BIV.
3. Therefore, I am not justified in believing that I have two hands.

We just discussed how the skeptic could defend premise 1: premise 1 is plausibly true because if I have sufficient justification for believing that I have two hands, then, given that I also know that having two hands is incompatible with being a BIV, I could simply *deduce* that I am not a BIV *from the fact that I have hands*, and that would be an adequate justification for [I am not a BIV].

But if that's why premise 1 is true, then why should we think premise 2 is true? Given the defense we just gave of premise 1, it seems that there is a very obvious justification for denying that I am a BIV. Here it is:

H1. I have two hands. Therefore:
H2. I'm not a BIV.

(Or, to put the point in terms of Frances' original version of the BIV argument: the thing that "rules out" for me that I am a BIV is the fact that I have hands.) What could the skeptic possibly say against this? The skeptic *just told us* that this inference *would* provide justification for its conclusion, *if* we are justified in believing H1 – that is the reason why Closure for Justification is supposed to be true. So it seems as if the only thing the skeptic could say at this point is that this is not a good justification *because H1 is not justified*.

---

11. Klein (1995) actually refers to this as "*virtually* begging the question", as distinct from begging the question proper, in which one actually appeals to the conclusion to justify the premise. But this distinction is too subtle for the main text.

But the claim "H1 is not justified" is just the conclusion of the skeptic's overall argument. The whole point the skeptic was trying to prove was that we're not justified in believing things like that we have hands. So what we've just seen is that in order to defend one of the *premises* of the skeptic's argument (premise 2), the skeptic has to appeal to the *conclusion* of that very argument. So the skeptic's argument begs the question.

2.7 A Direct Realist Response to Skepticism

Now I'm going to explain how a skeptic could respond to the last objection (the accusation of "begging the question"). But it will turn out that this response will leave the skeptic vulnerable to yet another objection.[12]

The skeptic should reject the defense of closure that we suggested in section 2.5. The skeptic should say:

> No, that's not why my premise 1 is true. It's not that you could deduce "I am not a BIV" from "I have two hands". Rather, premise 1 is true because ruling out that you are a BIV is a *precondition* on justifiably believing that you have two hands. That is, you would have to *first* give an argument that you are not a BIV, *in order* to have any reason for trusting any of your supposed observations of the external world (including your ostensible visual observation of your hands).

Obviously, if this is the skeptic's position, then one cannot simply cite one's hands and use that to deduce that one is not a BIV.

But why would ruling out that you are a BIV be a precondition on knowing about your hands? It cannot be that in general, in order to know P, one has to first know every logical consequence of P. Here is an account that the skeptic might give:

> The only reason you have for thinking that you have two hands is that you have certain sensory experiences, and you take these sensory experiences to be best explained by your having actual hands and a reliable faculty of vision by which you can detect such things. But to conclude that this is the best explanation, you have to rule out all competing explanations of the same

---

12. Huemer 2000.

evidence. Here is one competing explanation: you are a BIV being fed electrical impulses to simulate life in the real world. So you have to have reasons for ruling out this explanation in order to be able to infer, from your sensory experiences, that you have actual hands.

This is a coherent view, which seems fair to the intuitions behind the BIV argument. It is worth noticing, however, that it assumes a particular view about why we believe in ordinary physical objects, which could be disputed.

Some background: in the philosophy of perception, there are traditionally two views about our knowledge, or justified beliefs, about the external world: direct realism and indirect realism.

Direct realism: in normal perception, we acquire *direct* knowledge (or justified beliefs) about some aspects of the external world.

Indirect realism: in normal perception, we acquire only *indirect* knowledge (or justified beliefs) about the external world.

What is meant by "direct" and "indirect" knowledge or justified belief? In this context, to know something (or be justified in believing something) *indirectly* is to know it (or be justified in believing it) inferentially, that is, *on the basis of something else* that one knows (or is justified in believing). To know (/be justified in believing) something *directly* is simply to know it non-inferentially, that is, in a way that is *not* based on something else that one knows (/is justified in believing).

Aside: Idealism

Direct and indirect realism are the most popular views about perception but not the only views. A third position is **idealism**, which holds that there *are no* objects that are external to all minds. The most famous proponent of this view was Bishop Berkeley, who held that there is no such thing as matter and that the sensory images we experience are directly implanted in our minds by God. Many other idealists have tried to get by without God, making everything dependent on human minds. Idealism was surprisingly popular in the 19th century, but it is very far out of favor today. For this reason (and because the view is completely insane), we do not discuss it further herein.

It is easy to give examples of things that we can only know about indirectly. For instance, no one can directly observe the gravitational field, yet we justifiably believe there is such a thing because this provides the best explanation for why bodies fall to the earth, why the planets orbit the sun, and so on. To take a more mundane example, I have never been to China, yet I am highly confident (and rationally so) that China exists because other people have told me many things about it, and it is highly unlikely that people would say all these things if the place did not exist. These are cases in which I have *indirect knowledge* (assuming, of course, that I have knowledge at all).

In ordinary life, we tend to think of our perceptual observations as giving us *direct* knowledge. We can't see the gravitational field, but we *can* see the movement of material objects. Hence, in our commonsense worldview, we would say that we have *indirect* knowledge of the gravitational field but *direct* knowledge of the material objects. Similarly, we normally think that we directly know about our hands when we look at them. And direct realists in the philosophy of perception agree with all this.

Indirect realists, however, disagree. Indirect realists think that even our knowledge of the things we see – our hands, the Earth, surfaces of tables, and all other physical phenomena – is only indirect. What we are *directly* aware of is always only *our experiences*, that is, the states of our own minds. You don't know directly that there is a hand in front of you; what you know directly is that you have a *sensory experience* as of a hand. You just unconsciously infer that there is a real hand, without noticing that this is an inference.

There is an ongoing debate between direct and indirect realists in philosophy.[13] In the history of the subject, most philosophers who weighed in on the issue have in fact been *indirect* realists. It would therefore be understandable for a skeptic to present arguments specifically aimed at indirect realists.

The reason I am bringing all of this up is that at this point, it looks as if the skeptic's BIV argument is indeed an argument directed solely at indirect realists. Our skeptic is saying that in order to infer that you have hands from the fact that you have sensory experiences of hands, you need to rule out the BIV scenario. You cannot rule this out by appealing to the fact that you have hands, since this would involve circular reasoning. Against an indirect realist, this is

---

13. See, e.g., Smythies and French 2018.

a forceful argument, since the indirect realist agrees that our knowledge of our hands depends on an inference.

However, the argument has no force against a direct realist, since the direct realist does not claim to *infer* that he has hands on the basis of anything else. The direct realist thinks that we are allowed to just *start from* the fact that we have hands (along with other physical facts that we observe during normal perception). From the fact that we have hands, it directly follows that we are not BIVs. So the BIV scenario is ruled out by (among other things) our actual hands. In the direct realist's hands (pun intended), this argument is *not* circular, because [I have two hands] is taken to be immediately, non-inferentially justified, and a linear inference from an immediately justified belief cannot be circular.

Of course, I have not so far given an argument for direct realism. I haven't told you why one should believe direct realism. My point is that the *skeptic* hasn't given us a good reason for skepticism. That is, if you started out with a commonsense view of the world (which would include being a direct realist), then the BIV argument does not give you any reason for giving up this view. The BIV argument cannot refute direct realism; it just *assumes* that we're not direct realists and gives an argument against indirect realism.

2.8 Indirect Realist Responses

As we have just seen, the direct realist has an easy way to avoid the BIV argument. But let's return to the indirect realist. What should they say? The indirect realist is going to have more work to do, but there are things that indirect realists can say against the BIV argument.

Just to remind the reader, we are discussing justification skepticism, not certainty skepticism. So the indirect realist's task is to explain why it is (much) more reasonable to think that you have real hands than to think that you are a BIV. This might seem obvious, but it is no trivial task to explain why this is the case.

Upon hearing of the BIV scenario, many people are tempted to say that the Real World Hypothesis (RWH) – namely, that we are reliably perceiving the real world – is "the simplest explanation" for our experiences. If so, this might explain why it is more reasonable to believe RWH than to believe BIVH.

Unfortunately, it is far from obvious that RWH is simpler than BIVH. Notice that if RWH is true, there are enormous numbers of things in existence, from the billions of other people to the hundreds of billions of other stars. There also are many *different types* of things (plants, animals, stars, quarks, black holes, and so on). By contrast, BIVH only requires there to be one brain, one vat, and the apparatus for stimulating the BIV. (BIVH does not *deny* that there are other things in the universe; it merely is *neutral* regarding all other things.) On the face of it, then, BIVH is *vastly simpler* than RWH.

Okay, here is another try. If we were BIVs, we should expect to see the effects of program errors. Any very sophisticated program that you can find has some errors in it. Sometimes they produce bizarre, unexpected results; more often, they simply result in the program's crashing and having to be restarted. But this never happens in our experience – we never see the equivalent of our world having to be restarted due to a program bug. So we're probably not living in a simulation.

I imagine the skeptic responding to this by arguing that all your expectations about how complicated computer programs behave are formed by your experiences *within this world*, which could be a simulation. Perhaps the people who programmed your simulation decided to make it *appear* to you that complicated computer programs usually have bugs, just so you wouldn't suspect that you're living in a computer simulation – but in the *real* world, outside your simulation, there are lots of complicated programs that are flawless and never have to be restarted. Computers and software in the *real* world are much more stable and perfect than the simulated computers and software in your simulated world.

Okay, here is a final try. What is wrong with BIVH as an explanation of our sensory experience is that it is an *unfalsifiable theory*.[14] This is illustrated by the observations in the preceding paragraph. No matter what evidence someone cites to try to refute the BIV theory, the BIV theorist can always say that that evidence was just programmed into the simulation by the scientists stimulating the BIV. So there's no way of refuting the theory. In modern science, it is widely accepted that unfalsifiable theories are bad. So this, perhaps, is why the BIV theory is worse than the real world theory.

Notice that the same complaint cannot be applied to RWH. RWH is *not* unfalsifiable in the way that BIVH is. If, for example,

---

14. This argument derives from Huemer 2016.

we had occasional experiences of the world "crashing" – say, an error message appears in your visual field; then your visual field goes black; then after a while, objects start reappearing as the world is rebooted – then RWH would be refuted. The proponent of RWH would not have a facile way of explaining away this sort of thing, in the way that the proponent of BIVH can easily explain away anything that happens.

So BIVH is unfalsifiable but RWH isn't. But so what? What's bad about an unfalsifiable theory? The basic answer is that a theory that is unfalsifiable is *also unsupportable*, whereas a theory that can be refuted by evidence can also be supported by evidence. (A more precise statement: for any given theory, it is possible to have evidence that *raises* the probability of the theory, *if and only if* it is possible to have evidence that *lowers* the probability of the theory.) In scientific reasoning (as well as other good empirical reasoning), the way a theory is tested is that the theory makes some specific predictions about what evidence should exist, and we see whether these predictions pan out. If the evidence *is* as the theory predicts, then the theory is *supported* (it is rendered more probable) by this evidence; if the evidence is *not* as the theory predicts, then the theory is *refuted* (or at least rendered less probable) by this evidence. If a theory makes *no* predictions, then it cannot be tested, which means we cannot gather evidence for or against it. That means that we in fact have no evidence for any such theory, which will generally mean that we should not believe it.

So, because BIVH is untestable, we have no reason to believe it. But RWH is *not* untestable; there is some possible evidence (as described earlier) that would refute RWH. Fortunately, the things that would refute RWH have not in fact occurred. This means that we have some reason to believe RWH.

In other words, if there *could* have been evidence refuting a particular theory but there in fact isn't, then this very fact is some evidence in favor of the theory. But if, on the other hand, there *couldn't* have been any evidence refuting a given theory, then the fact that there isn't any evidence refuting it is *not* evidence in favor of it. In the case of RWH and BIVH, there is no evidence refuting either one. But there *could* have been evidence refuting RWH, whereas there *could not* have been evidence refuting BIVH. So the failure to find any evidence refuting either one counts *in favor* of RWH but does *not* count in favor of BIVH. So RWH is better than BIVH. All of this reasoning, by the way, has a more precise, mathematical formulation within probability theory, which I have omitted here in consideration of math-phobic students.

Aside: Bayesian Reasoning

The following equation is a theorem of probability theory, known as Bayes' theorem:

$$P(h|e) = \frac{P(h) \cdot P(e \mid h)}{P(h) \cdot P(e|h) + P(\sim h) \cdot P(e \mid \sim h)}$$

("$P(h|e)$" is read "the probability of h given e" and refers to the probability that h would be true *if* e were true.) It is a consequence of this that $P(h|e) > P(h)$ if and only if $P(e|h) > P(e|\sim h)$. That is: e raises the probability of h if and only if e would be more likely to be true if h were the case than if h were not the case. Bayesian reasoning is reasoning in which a hypothesis is said to be supported because the evidence that we have would have been more likely to occur if the hypothesis were true than otherwise.

Bayesian reasoning supports RWH over BIVH. The fact that we have a generally coherent series of experiences, with nothing resembling program crashing, is evidence for RWH because it is more likely that we would have such experiences if we were reliably perceiving the real world than it is if we were not reliably perceiving the real world. Our coherent experiences do not support BIVH because it is *not* the case that we would be more likely to have coherent experiences if we were BIVs than if we were not.

Summary

There are many responses to the BIV argument. Some philosophers think its conclusion is so implausible that we should reject one or more premises for this reason alone. Some think the BIV scenario is self-refuting because it would be impossible for a BIV to have an idea that referred to physical brains or vats. Some think it does not matter that we can't refute the BIV scenario, either because knowledge does not require justification or because we can have justification for our beliefs even though we lack justification for some of the logical consequences of these beliefs (i.e., the Closure Principle for Justification is false). Some think that, once the skeptic defends it against the preceding objection, the BIV argument begs the question, since in order to argue that we lack justification to reject the BIV scenario, the skeptic would have to first prove that we lack justification for our ordinary beliefs about the external world. Some think that the BIV argument works only against indirect realists, not direct realists; the direct realist claims to have immediate (non-inferential) knowledge of physical facts about the external world, some of which just directly entail that the BIV scenario is false. Finally, indirect realists can argue that the BIV scenario is a worse explanation for our experiences than the RWH. One reason for this is that RWH makes testable (and correct) predictions, whereas the BIV scenario makes no predictions.

3 A Theory of Justified Belief

3.1 *Foundationalism*

When, in general, is it reasonable to believe something? Most people who think about this question come to a position known as **foundationalism**. Foundationalism is a philosophical view that holds that there are two kinds of justified beliefs: first, there are some beliefs that are immediately justified, that is, justified in a way that does not depend on other justified beliefs; these are known as "foundational beliefs". Second, there are beliefs that are justified, directly or indirectly, *on the basis of* the foundational beliefs. All justified beliefs are either themselves foundational or based on foundational beliefs.

What are the alternatives to foundationalism? One alternative is that there are *no* justified beliefs (the most extreme form of skepticism, which we will not discuss here; see section 1.1). A second alternative is that there is an *infinite series* of justified beliefs with no foundation: each belief depends on further beliefs in the series, and the series goes on forever. A third alternative is some form of circularity: that a belief can be justified by itself or two beliefs can be justified by each other or in general, that if you trace back the reason for a belief, and the reason for the reason, and so on, you at some point come back to the belief with which you started. Any of these would be ways of avoiding foundationalism. However, none of them sound plausible. It seems obvious that we have justified beliefs, that we cannot have an infinite series of reasons, and that, although we *can* reason in a circle, doing so does not result in justified beliefs.

This is the main reason why most people who consider this question wind up as foundationalists: each of the alternative views seems unacceptable, so foundationalism must be the correct view. (This is sometimes called **the regress argument**, due to the traditional emphasis on avoiding an infinite regress of reasons.)[15]

What sort of beliefs are foundational? Almost all foundationalists agree that certain beliefs about one's own present, conscious mental states count as foundational. For instance, when you are in pain, your belief "I am in pain" is foundational. When you see a table (under normal conditions), your belief that you are having a *visual experience* representing a table is foundational. Also, when you believe that *P*, and you notice that you believe this, then your belief *that you believe that* P is foundational. (Notice that this is not to say that the belief *that* P is foundational.) In addition, almost all foundationalists include some beliefs about simple necessary truths as foundational, such as the belief that 2 = 2, the belief that no bachelor is married, and the belief that no proposition is both true and false.

There is disagreement about some other candidate foundational beliefs. *Some* foundationalists (the "direct realists") include observations made by the five senses as foundational – for instance, when you look at a tomato, you might have the foundationally justified belief that there is a red, round object there in the external world. However, other foundationalists reject this, claiming that the only foundationally justified belief in this example is that one is having a *visual experience* as of a red, round thing, not that there actually is a red, round thing in the external world.

Not everyone accepts foundationalism. Each of the three alternative views mentioned (skepticism, infinite regress, circularity) has

---

15. The regress argument was introduced by Aristotle a long time ago (*Posterior Analytics* I.3).

defenders.[16] The critics of foundationalism usually have a problem with the idea of foundational beliefs (they almost never have a problem with the other part of foundationalism, namely, the idea of basing other beliefs on the foundations). Foundational beliefs, by definition, are *justified*, yet their justification does not depend on any other justified beliefs. *How* are they justified? Most of the time, if you believe something, that belief requires a reason; otherwise, it will be unjustified. For instance, if I think there are unicorns living on Mars, I need a reason for this; I cannot be justified in believing it without a reason. Yet in the case of foundational beliefs, allegedly, we need no reasons in order to be justified in believing them. (Alternately, perhaps we can have reasons that are not themselves justified beliefs?) Why is this? What is special about these "foundational" beliefs that lets them count as *justified* rather than being merely *arbitrary* assumptions?

Critics think that there is no satisfactory answer to this. Some argue that the only plausible answers to what makes foundational beliefs justified would have to be things that would provide the believer with *reasons to believe* that the foundational propositions are true – which would defeat the point of calling them "foundational". This is the central challenge for foundationalism: to explain what makes foundational beliefs justified, *without* resorting to *reasons* (in the form of other justified beliefs) that the believer would have for holding those beliefs.

3.2 Phenomenal Conservatism

Here, I will briefly explain my own view about which beliefs are foundational and why they are justified. My view is known as **Phenomenal Conservatism** (PC).[17] The basic idea is that we have justification for believing whatever *appears to us* to be the case, provided that we have no specific reasons for doubting this belief. That is:

> **PC** If it seems to S that P, then, in the absence of defeaters, S thereby has at least some justification for believing that P.

---

16. On skepticism, see Sextus Empiricus 1994. On the infinite regress, see Klein 2007. For something like the circularity view, see BonJour 1985; Davidson 1986.
17. I coined the term in Huemer 2001. I reformulated the principle, as written here, in Huemer 2006.

(where S is some person and P is some proposition). In this section, I explain what I mean by that.

Start with the notion of its seeming to one that P. In my view, there is a particular type of introspectible mental state one can have whereby things *seem* to one or *appear* to one to be a certain way. This type of mental state is known as an "appearance" or "seeming". There are several different species of appearance states, including sensory experiences, memory experiences, states of introspective awareness, and intellectual intuitions. For instance, when you look at a tomato in normal conditions, it will *look to you* as if there is a red, round object there; this "looking to you" is a matter of your having a sensory experience that represents there to be a red, round object, which is a species of its *appearing to* you (or *seeming to you*) that there is a red, round object. For another example, if you reflect intellectually on the proposition "The shortest path between any two points is a straight line", this should just *seem true* to you; this is an example of an intellectual intuition, which is another species of appearance.

Appearances are not to be confused with *beliefs*. It is possible to either believe or refuse to believe what seems to be the case. Suppose that, after a large dose of hallucinogenic drugs, you have a hallucination of a purple unicorn dancing on the table in front of you. In this case, it *appears* to you that there is a purple unicorn. But you may very well *not believe* that there is a purple unicorn, since you know that you have taken the drugs and that purple unicorns do not actually exist. There are also some cases in which a person *believes* a proposition that doesn't *seem* true to them – this is the case with self-deception or "taking a leap of faith".

That was all to explain the expression "it seems to S that P". Next, why did I include the clause "in the absence of defeaters"? Here, the term "defeater" essentially refers to reasons for doubting that one's (would-be) belief is true or reliable. We know that appearances are not infallible (of course, no human faculty is infallible). Sometimes appearances are misleading, and we may, on occasion, have information indicating that the appearance we are presently experiencing is either false or unreliable – as in the case where you ingest drugs and then hallucinate a purple unicorn. The clause "in the absence of defeaters" is needed to accommodate these cases. The principle of PC only says that we have justification in cases in which there are no reasons to doubt the appearance; of course, in cases in which there *is* a reason to doubt the appearances, we may not have justification for believing what appears to us to be the case.

Here is another way of putting the point: PC assigns a kind of *presumption* to the way things appear. That is, we ought rationally to proceed on the assumption that things are as they appear unless and until we acquire specific reasons not to do so. We do not in general need arguments in support of how things appear; rather, the person who *doubts* the way things appear has the burden of citing grounds for doubt.

Next, why did I write "at least some justification" in the statement of PC? Well, appearances come in degrees of strength. Some propositions are only *vaguely plausible*, whereas others are *completely obvious*. Justification also comes in degrees: propositions can be more or less justified. In general, *stronger* appearances provide *more* justification for belief. But any appearance provides *at least some* justification for belief, as long as it is not defeated by specific grounds for doubt.

Lastly, why do I speak of "specific" grounds for doubt? What I mean is grounds for doubt that have to do with problems or alleged problems with the particular appearance one is then having, as opposed to *general* skeptical doubts. In other words, an observation such as "Sometimes appearances can be misleading" does not count as a relevant defeater for a particular appearance – this is too general. To defeat the justification provided by an appearance, one needs to have reason for thinking *that appearance in particular* is likely to be misleading.

3.3 Phenomenal Conservatism Gets the Right Answers

Pre-theoretically (i.e., before we develop a philosophical theory), there are certain beliefs that we would expect to count as "justified" and others that we would expect not to count. This is why we have a concept of "justification" in the first place. When we go on to develop a philosophical theory of this thing we are calling "justification", it is good if the theory can explain why most of the things we think of as "justified" count as justified, and most of the things we think of as "unjustified" count as unjustified.

This, by the way, is a perfectly general point about philosophical theorizing. A philosophical theory of X should in general "get the cases right", which means it should explain why most of the things we think of as X are X, and most of the things we think of as non-X are non-X. A theory can, of course, lead us to revise *some* of our pre-theoretical beliefs. But to do this, the theory has to first prove its mettle by explaining a good range of other (what we take to be) facts. A theory that is too revisionary will simply be rejected via the G.E. Moore shift (see section 2.2).

One good thing about PC as a theory of justification is that it explains in a clear and simple manner a wide range of what we take to be justified beliefs: it explains why you are justified in believing that you have two hands, that 2 + 1 = 3, that murder is wrong, that you are in pain (when you are), and that you have existed for more than five minutes. (I take it that all of these things seem to you to be the case and that you lack specific grounds for doubting them.) It is difficult to think of any other theory that can so simply explain such a range of justified beliefs.

At the same time, the theory is not overly permissive – it does not, for example, license us in dogmatically clinging to our appearances, since the theory includes a clause recognizing the possibility of defeaters. Standard cases in which a person has an unjustified belief include cases in which the person refuses to revise their belief in the light of specific grounds for doubt – and PC, as formulated earlier, does not endorse such beliefs. Another paradigmatic kind of unjustified belief is a belief based on wishful thinking (in which a *desire* that P causes one to believe that P). PC also rightly avoids endorsing such beliefs, since they are not based on appearances. (Desires are not appearances.)

3.4 Alternatives Are Self-Defeating

How is it, in general, that we form beliefs? If you reflect, I think you are going to notice that you in fact form beliefs based on the way things seem to you. There are a few exceptions to this – as noted earlier, if you engage in wishful thinking or you form a belief through blind faith, this would not count as a belief based on appearances. But these exceptions are also obviously not what we would think of as justified beliefs. All of the *normal* cases – in particular, all of the cases that are on their face candidates for being justified – are cases in which you form beliefs based on what seems right to you. This includes – of particular interest here – when you are forming *philosophical* beliefs, about things like, say, justification. When you evaluate the things I'm saying right now, you are evaluating them based on what seems correct to you.

Admittedly, not everyone who thinks about PC accepts it. Who rejects it and why? The people who reject it are simply the people to whom it doesn't seem correct, and they reject it *because* something about it seems wrong to them. Now, you might think that people could reject PC because they found an *argument* against it and that this is different from appealing to appearances. But no argument would induce anyone to accept or reject anything *unless* the argument somehow seemed right to the person. So critics who think they have a good argument against PC are just people who have found an argument that to them *seems right* (the premises seem true, the conclusion seems to follow). There are exactly zero critics who have conducted an infinitely long chain of reasoning; 100% of critics started from at least one premise that they did not arrive at by reasoning. In general, they will have accepted the premise because it just seemed correct to them. (Again, there are alternative possibilities, but they wouldn't lead to the critics having justified beliefs; they could have accepted the premise by wishful thinking, based on emotion, or as a leap of faith.)

These reflections lead to what I call the **self-defeat argument** for PC. If what I've said is right, then rejection of PC is self-defeating: when one rejects PC, one does so on the basis of appearances. But if PC is false, then appearances are not a valid basis for justified belief; hence, one's belief in the denial of PC must not be justified.

3.5 Internalist Intuitions

Here is another argument. (By the way, of course this argument, *like all arguments whatsoever*, appeals to appearances. In this case, it appeals to intellectual intuitions.) Suppose we have some theory of justification that appeals to something other than appearances to explain why beliefs are justified. Whatever this other factor is, let's suppose it's something that can vary *independently* of appearances.

For the sake of concreteness, let's take the reliability theory mentioned in section 2.4. Some philosophers claim that a belief is justified if and only if the belief is the product of a *reliable* belief-forming method (a method with a robust tendency to produce true beliefs) regardless of whether the believer himself has any reason to think the method is reliable. So, for example, if you happen to have a reliable faculty of precognition, then even if you don't yourself have any *evidence* that it is reliable, you can form "justified beliefs" using your precognitive faculty. Notice (this is important to the argument) that reliability can vary independently of appearances. In other words, there can be one situation in which things appear to you a certain way, and your faculties are reliable, and another situation in which things *appear to you exactly the same*, but your faculties are *not* reliable. (Just think about the BIV compared with a normal person.)

Since this is possible, we can also imagine a situation in which a person has two beliefs, formed by different belief-forming mechanisms, and one of them is reliable and the other is not, even though everything *appears to the person* to be relevantly alike for these two beliefs. To illustrate the idea, consider the case of Sue the Psychic Brain in a Vat: Sue has a faculty of extrasensory perception (ESP), which tells her various things about the world. She also has sensory experiences that are qualitatively indistinguishable from those of a normal person. Unbeknownst to Sue, her ESP is highly *reliable*, but her sensory experiences are completely *unreliable* due to her being a BIV. Imagine that today, Sue has formed two interesting beliefs: using her ESP, she formed a belief that a plane crash was going to happen that day (assume that BIVs can form beliefs about the physical world, contra the theory discussed in section 2.3). Also, relying on her visual experiences, she formed the belief that there was a squirrel in front of her. These two beliefs *seem to Sue* relevantly alike: both seem to her equally true and equally reliable, she does not seem to herself to have any more reason for doubting one belief than the other, and so on. Nevertheless, as a matter of objective fact, unbeknownst to Sue, the ESP-based belief about the plane crash is reliable, while the visual belief about the squirrel is unreliable.

According to the reliability theory of justification, this means that Sue is *justified* in believing there will be a plane crash but *unjustified* in believing there is a squirrel in front of her. Presumably, a person should believe the things that are justified and not believe the things that are unjustified. So, on the reliability theory, Sue *should* think that there is going to be a plane crash but *not* think that there is a squirrel in front of her.

But this would be very odd. Suppose that Sue did this and suppose that someone in her BIV simulation world asked her to explain why she accepted the one belief but not the other. What could she say? "These two propositions seem equally true, equally reliable, and in all other ways equally worthy of belief to me. I just accept the one and not the other, for no apparent reason"? But this would surely be irrational. Therefore, it is false that Sue should hold this combination of attitudes. And therefore, it is false that reliability determines what beliefs are justified.

The point we just made about reliability can be generalized to *any* property that can vary independently of appearances. So the lesson is this: what it makes sense for a person to believe is a function of the way things seem to that person.

This lesson does not *entail* PC. But it is pretty close to PC. If we agree that justification cannot vary independent of appearances, it then becomes very plausible that this is because appearances are the source of justified belief because PC is true.

3.6 Phenomenal Conservatism vs. External-World Skepticism

PC makes short work of skepticism. According to PC, we are rationally entitled to presume that things are the way they appear to be until we have specific grounds for doubt. It appears that I have two hands; so, in the absence of grounds for doubt, this is what it makes sense for me to believe. I don't have to first prove that I'm not a BIV or refute any other weird scenarios of that kind. Rather, the skeptic would have the burden to produce reasons for thinking that I *am* a BIV or that my perceptions are unreliable for some other reason in order to defeat the presumption that things are as they appear. Since the skeptic cannot do this, we are justified in continuing to think that we have hands, that there are around us the kinds of physical objects that we seem to see, and so on.

Summary

Foundationalism holds that some beliefs are justified in a way that does not depend on *reasons*, that is, other justified beliefs that support them. This is necessary to avoid an infinite regress of reasons. According to PC, the foundational propositions are the things that *seem* true to one and that one does not have any specific grounds for doubting. PC gives a simple, unified explanation for a wide range of justified beliefs. Those who reject PC are in a self-defeating position since they reject PC only because it does not seem true to them. Alternative theories that make justification depend on something other than appearances imply (implausibly) that a person could justifiably accept one belief and reject another, even when the two beliefs appear to that person equally good in all respects. Accepting PC gives us an easy answer to skepticism.

4 Controversy Skepticism

4.1 The Obviousness of Controversy Skepticism

I turn now to a less radical and more reasonable kind of "skepticism", the kind that Frances dubs "controversy skepticism" (CS). I take this to be *something like* the view that most controversial beliefs are unjustified, or otherwise deficient, even when true (Frances uses the expression "epistemically second-rate"). (But see the discussion later on how to define CS.)

Frances also stipulates a number of conditions that we are supposed to imagine a believer satisfying before we can conclude that the controversial belief is deficient. These conditions essentially say that there are many people who are in at least as good a position as you are to judge whether C is true and who disagree with you about C. If, after learning of that disagreement, you hold on to your belief about C with undiminished confidence, then there is something defective about this. You should at least significantly diminish your confidence. This, I take it, is the basic idea of CS.

Thus formulated, CS might be *trivially* true. ("Trivial" is what philosophers say when a point is so obvious that it hardly needs stating.) *Obviously*, the conclusions that smart, well-informed, and generally reliable people have drawn about x are *relevant evidence* about x, other things being equal. Of course, experts are not *infallible* (sometimes they have been wrong), but neither are *you*, and the conditions that Frances has us imagine more or less entail that the experts are, as far as you can tell, at least as likely to get the right answer as you. So if you find out that many experts disagree with you about x, that is evidence against your opinion about x, and you must (if rational) lower your confidence in this opinion.

Here is an analogy. Suppose you want to know whether there is a unicorn in the forest. You have two unicorn-detecting devices, device A and device B. A is about 80% reliable, and B is *at least* 80% reliable. You activate device A, which tells you that there is a unicorn in the forest. Then you activate device B, and B tells you there is *no* unicorn. Now suppose that you just *ignore* device B and conclude, with 80% confidence, that there is a unicorn in the forest. In this case, you are obviously being irrational. You obviously have to reduce your confidence about the unicorn when you see device B's reading. Now, to arrive at CS, we only need to note that it does not matter if device A is actually a conscious being who, using his ordinary cognitive faculties, is 80% reliable, rather than a machine. It does not matter if device B is another human being who is at least 80% reliable. And, finally, it does not matter if one of the human beings is you. The fact that "device A" is actually one of your natural cognitive faculties cannot suddenly make it rational to ignore strong evidence that contravenes it.[18]

All of which is to say that I do not disagree with Frances' main point about CS. I think *traditional* forms of philosophical skepticism – notably, external-world skepticism – are crazy. But CS, as Frances formulates it, just seems obvious.

4.2 How Irrational Are We?

How *interesting* is CS? One might think it is so obvious as to be uninteresting. On the other hand, whether it is obvious or not, it appears that there are many cases in which people run afoul of CS – people form confident beliefs on controversial issues and seem unfazed by the information that there is no expert consensus and that many experts disagree with them. (Usually, we know of the controversy among experts *before* we form our own opinions, and this fails to deter us from forming confident opinions. This situation is problematic in the same way as the situation when we form an opinion first, then fail to revise it when we learn about controversy among the experts.) For instance, if you have an opinion about free will, or the existence of God, or the morality of abortion, then you probably also are well aware that there is no consensus on the issue among the experts and that many experts disagree with your

---

18. I made this argument in Huemer 2005.

opinion. You should know that these experts are not in general less intelligent than you, less informed, or less rational or in any other way less well-suited to form reliable opinions on the subject. And yet, a great many people continue to hold confident opinions in precisely this sort of situation. It seems that many people are thus being unreasonable. This makes it worthwhile to discuss CS.

All of this, I think, is basically right. Nevertheless, for the sake of discussion, I will mention some reasons why people may be less irrational, and CS may be less applicable to us, than it would at first appear.

First, it is not clear how confident people's beliefs really are. When we hold an opinion on an issue about which there is no consensus, do we really think our belief is as likely to be true as in the case where we hold a belief that corresponds to a well-established consensus of experts? For instance, when we think, "Humans have free will", do we typically think this with equal confidence as we would think that the Earth orbits the Sun? I don't think so. Maybe some people are that confident. But most people draw a distinction between settled issues (such as whether the Earth orbits the Sun) and unsettled issues (such as free will), and though we may feel free to hold opinions on the latter sort of issues, we do not think of those opinions as being of equal credibility to an established expert consensus. If one is a professor or other teacher, for example, one would have no hesitation about teaching, as fact, that the Earth orbits the Sun; yet even if one endorses free will, one will most likely hesitate to teach the existence of free will as a plain fact. Many people would say their belief about free will (or similar matters) is "just an opinion", which I suppose means that they have low confidence in it. This is to say that most people have already, to a significant degree, incorporated CS into their beliefs.

You may still think that most people have not incorporated CS *enough*: perhaps we should not hold beliefs on controversial subjects at all but should instead suspend judgment. I would like to suggest, however, that, when it comes to matters of philosophical or political controversy, "holding a belief" does not amount to very much and therefore does not require much justification.

To explain: beliefs are not all created equal. In particular, we can be *more or less confident* of a given proposition. When we say that a person *believes* a proposition P, this generally indicates that the person's level of confidence in P is above some threshold. But this threshold need not be the same for all propositions. Maybe for some questions, we have a high threshold for belief (one must have a high level of confidence before one counts as *believing* a proposition), but for other questions, we have a lower threshold.

When it comes to ordinary, mundane matters of fact, the threshold is usually pretty high. For instance, suppose it is the first day of class in a new semester, and I am wondering when my first class begins. I will not be satisfied if I am merely 75% confident that the class starts at 2:00 pm. I will gather evidence (e.g., by looking up the time in the university schedule of classes) until it is *extremely* likely that I have the correct time. I will want to be over 99% confident that I have the right time before I end my inquiry and rest satisfied with the belief that the class is starting at 2 pm or before I start telling other people that the class is at 2 pm.

Matters are different for disputed *philosophical* issues (including political issues), partly because we know that we can't generally get such strong evidence as we can in the case of ordinary practical matters. Since we don't expect to ever attain extremely high degrees of justification in this area, our threshold for "belief" is lower. That is, we can call a much lower level of confidence a "belief" if the question is a philosophical one. So, when a person "believes in free will", I conjecture, this does not mean that the person is extremely confident of the reality of free will. The person might be only 75% confident of it, perhaps even less. This level of confidence would not be enough for a mundane, practical belief, but it is enough for a philosophical belief.

In philosophical and especially political discourse, people often *sound* highly confident. But this may be misleading. It is misleading, first, because the people who are most confident are the ones who are most likely to speak and to speak for the longest time. It may be that *most* people actually have no opinion, or at most very tentative opinions, about controversial issues. It is also misleading because *part* of what people are doing in philosophical, and especially in *political* discourse, is putting on a performance. Partly, we're just trying to align ourselves with a faction and to display our loyalty to other members of that faction. We may not actually believe the positions that we advance with the sort of confidence that we appear to display. No doubt there are things about this that are problematic. But at least we are not as irrationally overconfident as it might seem at first glance.

4.3 The Real Issue: Who Is Your Peer?

Having said all this, I agree that many human beings are overconfident about many controversial matters. However, even so, I think Frances' defense of CS does not get to the heart of the matter. The reason is that too much of the real problem is stipulated away. (This is a frequent shortcoming of philosophers: when we come to discuss some topic, we define our theses in such a way as to avoid most of the hard problems.) Frances essentially asks us to *assume* a case in which we have no reason to believe, and we do not believe, that we are any better positioned to answer a given question than the people who disagree with us. We have no account of why *they* would go wrong and *we* would not go wrong. *Given this*, it seems irrational for us not to at least significantly decrease our own confidence in light of the fact that many people disagree with us.

That formulation of the issue, I think, avoids the biggest problems that arise in real cases. In most real cases of controversy, both sides do *not* grant that the people on the other side are equally well positioned to make judgments about the issue. Each side usually has an "error theory" about the other side. The most common thing to say is that the people on the other side are *biased* in a way that stops them from admitting the truth. (By the way, both sides may be right about this!) For instance, perhaps defenders of socialism are biased because they are hoping to get free money from the government under a socialist regime. Or perhaps defenders of capitalism are biased because they benefit from capitalist exploitation. A related type of error theory accuses one's opponents of moral deficiency. For instance, maybe people who support capitalism are just too selfish to care about the plight of the poor. Another type of error theory claims that the people on the other side of an issue are less intelligent or less educated than ourselves; academics and other intellectuals on the left often say this about those on the right of the political spectrum.

Now, my point is not to defend the practice of discounting opposing views in this way. My point is that Frances' defense of CS does not help with this large class of cases in which people hold overconfident beliefs. The parties to such disagreements will each just deny that the conditions for CS apply – each party will insist that the other side is in a *worse* position to answer the question and therefore that those on one's own side do not have to lower their confidence in light of the existence of the disagreement.

What we need is a stronger form of CS. We need an account that will tell us what to do in case of a controversy wherein each side regards the other as stupider, less informed, more biased, or more immoral than themselves. Unfortunately, I do not have such an account to offer.

4.4 A Defense of Opinion

In my own philosophical work, I have been known on occasion to defend controversial beliefs.[19] After reflecting on CS, I have not greatly diminished my confidence in most of my controversial beliefs. And yet despite all I have said earlier, I do not think that I am unreasonable in this. I don't know whether Frances would say that I am, nor whether Frances is in the same shoes as I am. But in any case, this seems like an appropriate place to comment on why my controversial beliefs might be reasonable.

In my view, appearances are the sole ultimate source for all justification. As almost everyone agrees, justification is relative to an individual believer: a given proposition is justified or unjustified *for* a particular person; the same proposition may be justified for one person but unjustified for another. What makes a proposition justified for a given individual, in my view, is always a matter of *that individual's* appearances, that is, how things seem to the individual. So two people can each be perfectly justified in believing completely different things if the world appears very different to them.

How, then, can the beliefs of other people affect what you are justified in believing? The answer is that your own appearances may support (i) the belief that another person believes some proposition *P* and (ii) the belief that this other person is likely to be reliable about *P*. You can then infer that *P* is likely to be true. Notice that condition (ii) is essential. If you learn that Don believes *P* but you do not believe, nor does it seem to you, that Don is reliable, then you will *not* thereby have any reason for believing *P*.

Fortunately, the vast majority of us have excellent reason to believe that the vast majority of people are highly reliable about a wide range of things. For example, I have excellent reason to think that most people have reliable visual appearances, since other people commonly report seeing the same things that I see, they navigate the physical world as successfully as I do, and so on. So, if another person reports having witnessed some event, I generally believe that the thing they claim to have seen happened.

---

19. See, e.g., Huemer 2013; 2019.

What about other people's *philosophical* beliefs? In this case, I do not seem to have any evidence for thinking that other people are very reliable. Here, there is nothing like the evidence that establishes the reliability of their vision. In fact, it seems to me that – quite unlike matters of observable, physical fact – other people are highly *unreliable* about philosophical matters, holding radically false views with alarming frequency. This is true even of the most brilliant and celebrated philosophers, the likes of Plato, Hume, and Kant, all of whom held some pretty wild views. Of course, I do not think people are *completely* unreliable about philosophy – that is, their opinions are not mere *random guesses*. I merely think they have *very low* reliability. So the knowledge that other people disagree with me about a philosophical matter provides only very small grounds for doubt about the correctness of my own opinion; I should make little adjustment to my confidence when I learn of the disagreement.

Aside: The Wild Beliefs of Philosophers

Here are some things that brilliant and celebrated philosophers have thought. Bishop Berkeley thought that there were no material objects, only minds and ideas in the mind. David Hume thought that there was no reason to believe any statement about the future, about anything unobserved, or indeed about the external world. Immanuel Kant thought that it was always wrong to tell a lie, even if the lie was necessary to save someone's life. Moving into the 20th century, J.M.E. McTaggart thought that time did not exist. W.V. Quine thought that meanings (in the sense of the meaning of a word) did not exist. Gilbert Ryle thought that thoughts, feelings, and other mental states were just dispositions to physically behave in certain ways. Karl Popper thought that there was no reason to believe any scientific theory. David Lewis thought that there were an infinity of alternate spacetimes, each equally real as our own, including one for every logically possible thing that might have happened. John Mackie thought that no action was ever right or wrong. Today, Daniel Dennett thinks that no one has any qualitative experiences (no experience has any subjective feel for the person having it). None of these are dumb or unimportant philosophers; these are all highly intelligent, famous, well-respected figures in philosophy.

Now, you might wonder: how can it be that even the most brilliant philosophers, even after decades of reflection and study, are extremely unreliable about philosophy? After looking at the field of philosophy for a few decades, it seems to me that the best explanation is that intelligence and long study are not enough for reliability in this field. Doubtless these things are *necessary* for reliability, and perhaps in *some* fields (mathematics, say) they are sufficient. But they are not sufficient in the field of philosophy. In addition, one needs something like *good judgment* or common sense – traits that are sometimes found together with high IQ but very often not. It appears that when human beings think about philosophical matters, many find themselves oddly attracted to the bizarre and revisionary, making them all too ready to embrace extremely counterintuitive ideas.

In saying all this, I am not disagreeing with the *letter* of Frances' CS. I do not think that most other philosophers (particularly those who hold bizarre and implausible views) are equally well positioned as I am to answer philosophical questions. I think they are less well positioned due to their shortage of good judgment. Of course, my assessment of their judgment is based in part on my substantive philosophical views, which those other philosophers dispute. And, of course, many of them would say that I am less well positioned to answer philosophical questions than they are, for one reason or another. But, again, what directly matters to what I am justified in believing is what *seems to me* to be the case. So, the conditions for Frances' CS do not apply, and I am not required to greatly reduce my confidence in my controversial philosophical beliefs – at least, not on account of disagreement with those philosophers who appear to possess poor judgment.

This raises an issue that Frances and I might disagree about: suppose I disagree with some other people about topic X. I ask myself whether these other people are in a good position to make reliable judgments about X. In assessing this, can I use my beliefs *about* X *itself* (perhaps along with other information) as a basis for downgrading my assessment of the other people's judgment? I say yes: if the other people appear to me to hold deeply implausible views about X, that is evidence that they aren't good judges of X. Example: suppose you go to a doctor for advice about an illness that you have. The doctor *initially* appears to you to be much better positioned than you are to speak on medical questions (he has a degree from a good school, years of training, and so on). Now suppose the doctor tells you that the best treatment for you would be to eat two Brillo pads and jump up and down; that, he thinks, will cure your illness.[20] In this case, I think you could justly conclude that this doctor is a quack, and you could discount his medical opinions. You could conclude this – despite your own lack of medical training – based solely on his holding a belief that you initially assign very low credence to. The same, I think, goes for some philosophical beliefs: if a philosopher *initially* appears equally well-positioned to judge philosophical matters as I am, but then I learn that the philosopher holds some seemingly crazy view, I think I may infer that this philosopher lacks reliable judgment.

Admittedly, not all philosophers with whom I disagree possess poor judgment. But of the remainder, many suffer from other disadvantages that are more straightforward. Many have unquestioned, quasi-ideological commitments that prevent them from viewing evidence impartially, such as a commitment to physicalism (the belief that everything in the world must be physical) or empiricism (the view that all substantive knowledge must come from observation). And a surprising number of philosophers simply *do not* in fact know the main arguments that persuade me of certain controversial positions. Others know the arguments and have no response to them. (A good example is my refutation of egalitarianism.[21] Most political philosophers have never heard it, and almost no one has tried to engage with it.) When I reflect on how many philosophers disagree with some philosophical position that I hold, I should not greatly reduce my credence in my own position – at least, not without a lot more information – since it is in fact very common for philosophers to be extremely unreliable about philosophical questions.

Now, while I have not contradicted the *letter* of CS as Frances formulates it, I seem to have contradicted its *spirit*. Perhaps a controversy skeptic worthy of the name ought to suspend judgment about a wide range of philosophical issues – not just under specified hypothetical conditions but *in the actual world*. This returns us to my earlier semi-complaint that Frances' formulation of CS is too weak (see section 4.3) – as he defines the view, even I count as a controversy skeptic!

---

20. I got this example from one of my undergraduate students many years ago.
21. Huemer 2003.

Summary

CS, as Bryan Frances formulates it, seems obviously true: if you learn that many people disagree with you about X and you judge them to be in an equally good position to make reliable judgments about X, then you should significantly lower your confidence in your opinions about X. This may seem to conflict with ordinary people's practices, but perhaps it does not: most people are already less confident in their controversial opinions than in uncontroversial beliefs. But CS, as formulated, doesn't help with most problem cases because people who hold overconfident beliefs about controversial matters (especially political issues) usually do *not* think that those on the other side are equally well positioned to make reliable judgments; they usually accuse each other of various biases and other failings. Also, in the case of philosophical beliefs, one can argue that most philosophers are highly unreliable about philosophical issues, and it is legitimate to use one's own philosophical beliefs in evaluating this. Thus, one can continue to hold many confident, controversial opinions, despite accepting Frances' CS. Frances may wish to strengthen his statement of the view to rule this out.

First Round of Replies

Chapter 3

The Skeptic's Response to the Realist

Bryan Frances

Contents

1 Understanding Skepticism Better	107
2 Some Advice on How to Approach the Debate	111
3 Where the Skeptic and Huemer's Realist Agree	112
4 Knowledge as an Achievement on the Part of the Knower	117
5 Can K-Justification Neutralize the Brain-in-a-Vat Scenario?	122
6 Can the Factual Lack of Brains in Vats Neutralize the Brain-in-a-Vat Scenario?	123
7 Externalist Neutralization and the Skeptic's Revenge	126
8 Brief Replies to Some of Huemer's Realist Criticisms of Skepticism	128
9 Making Excuses in the Face of Controversy	132

1 Understanding Skepticism Better

You wake up in pain. You are disoriented, confused, and starting to be alarmed. You quickly discover that you cannot move your head in the slightest. There is some metal device keeping your head and neck perfectly still. You can see the ceiling and wall opposite you, and you can move your eyes so that you can see around the room a little. It's obvious that you are in a hospital room, alone. You wonder, "What the hell is going on?!"

Then the memories start to come, in a flood. There was a horrific traffic accident. Crashes, screams, and fire. And blood. You remember being knocked off your motorcycle and flying into the windshield of a truck. You remember ending up on the pavement, listening to screams and smelling burning vehicles. You recall that you could not move a muscle while you lay there on the road. You remember seeing a nearby burning car. You remember seeing a severed forearm, just a foot or so in front of your face.

Returning your attention to your current predicament in the hospital, you find you can't move your hands in order to touch the metal contraption holding your head in place. In fact, to your surprise and horror, you realize you can't even *feel* your hands – it's as though they don't exist at all. You remember the severed forearm. You nearly panic at the thought: "Was that *my* forearm? Jesus Christ!"

You try to move your hands again. Just as before, not only does nothing happen but you also can't feel a thing below your bicep in each arm. You can shrug your shoulders, flex your quadriceps, and wiggle your toes and nose. But your hands? Nothing.

You start to panic. You laugh out loud, telling the walls, "Of course I have hands! How stupid this all is! I'm just . . . just a bit injured in my neck. My hands are fine, they're *fine*!" You're a jazz pianist, so your hands are your life. You start to outwardly calm down upon hearing your own seemingly confident assertions, even though slightly below the surface, your mind is racing in every direction.

Time marches on, with no one coming into the room. You continue to believe that you still have hands, despite the evidence that suggests you are now handless. The sun goes down, oblivious to your fears. But now you can see your reflection in the large hospital window. And, finally, you have your proof: you can see quite clearly a reflection of your hands in your lap. You still can't move or feel them, but you can see them very well in the window.

People who aren't skeptics think that *something epistemically crucial happened* when you saw the reflection of your hands. In fact, skeptics agree with them that something epistemically important happened at that time; the controversial issue is what that "something" is. Professor Huemer and other realists about knowledge side with common sense in holding that you went from not knowing to knowing that you have two hands. Skeptics deny this account while offering a competing account of the epistemically crucial thing that happened when you saw your hands: before you saw them, each of the following was true of you – but afterward, none of them were true of you.

- Your belief in your hands counts as premature and irrational, according to your society's standards, even though it was also excusable given your scary situation.
- Your belief was based on fear and panic.
- Your belief wasn't based on good overall evidence.
- Your belief was held even though you had good evidence against it, evidence you implicitly realized you could not rebut in any way.

You will remember from my initial chapter why the skeptic thinks we don't know ordinary things: this strange thesis is entailed by these four claims using as an example Jo the doctor with the frost-bitten hands.

> C1: If Jo knows that her hands are frostbitten, then she can know that she isn't a brain in a vat (BIV).
> C2: If Jo can know that she is not a BIV, then there is something that rules out or neutralizes for her the scenario in which she is a mere BIV.[1]
> C3: There isn't anything that rules out or neutralizes that BIV scenario for Jo.
> C4: If Jo doesn't know that her hands are frostbitten, then no one knows much of anything about the world.

Huemer examined a different argument for skepticism, one that also has four premises:

1. If I am justified in believing that I have two hands, then I have some available justification for denying that I am a BIV.
2. I have no available justification for denying that I am a BIV.
3. If am not justified in believing that I have two hands, then I do not know that I have two hands.
4. If I don't know that I have two hands, then no one knows anything contingent about the external world.

---

1. I include "for her" because it's arguable that different things neutralize the BIV scenario for different people. One thing neutralizes it for me, and another thing neutralizes it for you, assuming skepticism is false.

As you can see, Huemer uses "justification" in his construal of the skeptic's argument; I do not. As way of explanation of this term, he says the following:

> The intuitive idea is that some beliefs *make sense* to hold, given all the information available to you, whereas other beliefs would not make sense to hold. Or, it is *rational* to think certain things, given your situation, whereas other things are not rational to think. "Justification" is a matter of what is rational, or what it makes sense, to believe.

In order to understand how these two skeptical arguments are related, we have to tease apart some linguistic issues.

Under one natural interpretation, I think the skeptic *agrees* with the realist that we have "justified" beliefs. This is the familiar socio-epistemic notion of justification I discussed and set aside in my chapter: Jo's belief is "justified" when it is socially acceptable in the sense that she has met the epistemic conditions for believing that are standard in her community for being deemed "reasonable" and "rational" by just about everyone. Just about everyone who is familiar with Jo's situation and belief will agree, if they aren't being silly, that Jo has done an upstanding job in coming to believe that she has frostbitten hands. When it comes to praise and blame, any reasonable person – including a skeptic – will agree that Jo's belief is justified, reasonable, and rational in that sense because it's praiseworthy and not blameworthy *by society's epistemic standards for reasonable or rational belief*. There are actual standards that Jo's (fictional) society (and our actual society) goes by in assessing beliefs, and Jo's belief about her frostbitten hands meets these standards for justified-rational-reasonable belief. As noted earlier, Jo is a doctor very familiar with frostbite, she is highly reliable in detecting frostbitten hands, she got an excellent and thorough look at her own hands, she's not drunk or otherwise mentally incapacitated, and so on – and this is pretty much all it takes for her belief to meet the societal standards.

Huemer is using 'justified' in a different sense. He is assuming (at least on behalf of the skeptic), in his (3), that in order for a person to know something, she must satisfy some condition that the term "justified" *can* express, even if it's not quite the social one just articulated. So how are we to understand the relation between the skeptical argument Huemer investigates and the one I investigate, given their differences?

As I see it, both skeptical arguments have the same general structure (where X is something like the truth that one's hands are frostbitten):

- If person P knows X, then a certain epistemic condition C holds for them.
- If C holds, then there is something N that neutralizes the BIV scenario.
- Nothing neutralizes the BIV scenario.
- If P doesn't know X, then a colossal amount of alleged ordinary knowledge doesn't exist.
- Therefore, a colossal amount of alleged ordinary knowledge doesn't exist.

The comparison:
For Huemer:

- C = justification for believing X
- N = justification for denying BIV scenario

For Frances:

- C = can know BIV scenario doesn't hold
- N = item that rules out BIV scenario

C and N for Huemer are tied to the word "justification". I tried to use "rule out" and, what is even better, "neutralize" in order to (a) emphasize the fact that the skeptic *agrees* that many of our ordinary beliefs are "justified" in one ordinary epistemic sense of the term (as well as other senses), and (b) avoid debates about the semantics of "justification".

2 Some Advice on How to Approach the Debate

Some students wonder how to approach this debate. Should you approach it from the perspective of the skeptic, the realist, or a neutral party – and can one really even do the latter?

My recommendation is that one approach every issue involved in this debate as *both* a realist and a skeptic, alternating between them. For instance, when I am first trying to articulate the skeptic's argument, I let skeptical inclinations "flow through me", guiding my thinking. But after I'm finished with that task, I let the realist inclinations "flow through me", guiding my evaluation of the skeptic's argument. I go back and forth, more or less effortlessly, generating arguments, criticizing them, and then revising them in light of those criticisms. For what it's worth, I have found this approach fruitful.

One more question about how to approach the debate: who has the burden of argument in the debate? By my lights, they both do, although the lion's share falls on the skeptic. She's the one who is saying something odd ("Jo doesn't know that her hands are frostbitten"), and it's up to her to deliver a good argument for her odd conclusion. She cannot just say, "Well, you can't prove I'm wrong!" This is the response of a child; we demand better. However, once the skeptic has come up with a detailed argument with plausible-sounding premises – congratulations to her! – then the realist cannot just say, "Well, I don't think such-and-such premise is true" or "You haven't proven your premises beyond doubt." Instead, it's up to her to explain why the skeptic has a false even though initially plausible-sounding premise. In fact, it would be best if the realist could give a good argument that such-and-such premise P in the skeptic's argument is in fact false, but lots of us are tempted to think it's true because of our attraction to a *true* claim P* different from but closely related to P, one that we often confuse with P.

3 Where the Skeptic and Huemer's Realist Agree

In philosophical discourse, arguments are often, even usually, partial: philosophers leave out the defense of some premises. For instance, here is a famous argument from the philosophy of religion:

P1: If God exists, then he is omnipotent, omniscient, and perfectly good.
P2: If God is omnipotent, omniscient, and perfectly good, then he will eliminate all suffering that isn't outweighed by some good it's associated with.

P3: However, there is some suffering that has no outweighing good.
C1: So, God doesn't exist.

This argument is partial because the philosopher who advocates it has detailed reasons – arguments – for the three premises, P1–P3. I once wrote a whole book on that argument, and most of it was devoted to examining the arguments for the premises.

Similarly, the skeptic's argument C1–C4 is partial. In my opening chapter, I hinted at supporting arguments for C1 and C2 and even C3 (although the latter hints appeared in the context of a discussion of C6, discussed later). In this section, I present these supporting arguments for C1 and C2. I won't bother with much detail though, since as we shall see, C3 is the premise that Huemer challenges the most. I will ignore C4 since no one disputes it.

Here is my skeptic's defense of her premise C1:

- Assume for the sake of argument that Jo knows K1 that her hands are frostbitten.
- If she knows K1 that her hands are frostbitten, then she can know K2 that if her hands are frostbitten, then she isn't a BIV.
- In addition, if Jo knows K1 that her hands are frostbitten *and* can know K2 that if her hands are frostbitten, then she isn't a BIV, then she can know that she isn't a BIV.
- Hence, if Jo knows her hands are frostbitten, then she can know she isn't a BIV. That is claim C1.

The first premise is a provisional assumption, an "assumption for the sake of argument". It is dispensed with in the conclusion, so I don't think it is objectionable in any way.

I think Huemer agrees with the second bullet point: he thinks it's true. All it says is that if Jo knows K1, then she *can* know K2. It doesn't say that Jo knows K1, and it doesn't even say that if she knew K1, then she would *in fact* know K2. Furthermore, it doesn't say *how* she could know K2 if she knew K1. I suspect Huemer agrees with it because he thinks that Jo knows both K1 and *can* know K2 if she bothers to think about K2 at all. In fact, he probably thinks Jo can know K2 regardless of her knowledge of K1.

I also suspect he agrees with the third bullet point, since he agrees that if Jo knew K1 and K2, then she could reason to the conclusion that she isn't a BIV. This is because she *can*, if she tries, figure out that "I am not a BIV" follows with necessity from K1 and K2.

In sum, I suspect Huemer agrees with C1. One could offer detailed arguments in favor of the premises of the argument for C1, but since Huemer agrees with C1, I won't go over any of those arguments.

Here is my skeptic's defense of her premise C2:

- *Generalized C2*: if a person P can know that a scenario S doesn't obtain, then there is something that rules out or neutralizes for P the S scenario. That is, if you know that some situation doesn't occur, then there has got to be *something* that counts against it occurring!
- Hence, if Jo can know that she isn't a BIV, then there is something that rules out for her the BIV scenario. That is, C2 is true.

This argument is quite a bit shorter, and I offered no detailed defense of the first bullet point. The wise critic of it doesn't object that it's false; she objects that we need some guidance on what "rules out or neutralizes" means, so that we can start to evaluate it. In my initial chapter, I clarified it with two things: a short explanation of "rule out or neutralize" and examples:

- You can't know that your bike is in your garage unless there is something that rules out the scenario in which it has been stolen from the garage, your daughter took it out to ride it, and so on.
- Jasmine can't know that she isn't faking her toothache pain unless there is something that rules out for her the scenario in which she is lying to her doctors about her pain.

In many ordinary circumstances (and assuming for the sake of argument that skepticism is false!), you can know that your bike is in your garage. This is because you have *background knowledge* that sufficiently rules out the "It was stolen very recently" and "Your daughter took it out for a ride a few minutes ago" scenarios. For instance, you already know that bikes are virtually never stolen out of garages in your neighborhood, you have a good lock on the garage door, your daughter thinks she is too small to ride the bike well, and so on. With regard to the second example, as we saw in my opening chapter, Jasmine knows that she isn't faking her pain because her *awareness of her pain* sufficiently rules out the "She is lying to her doctors" scenario. Hence, both examples show that what does the ruling-out work need *not* be a piece of reasoning, an argument, that passes through your mind. The skeptic isn't saying that you must neutralize the BIV scenario via an inference. Thus, we are being open-minded about what can do "ruling-out or neutralizing" work.

Since we are being awfully open-minded about what can do "ruling out" work, as the examples show, I suspect that Huemer is willing to agree with C2. Thus, when it comes to Huemer's preferred way of challenging the skeptic, C3 is where the action lies. Other realists challenge C1 or C2, but since this book is a debate between me and Huemer (and not between me and those other realists), I will focus on just Huemer's criticism of skepticism.

With the agreement on C1 and C2 in mind and using "K-justified" in order to express Huemer's notion of justification ("K" for "knowledge"), the vital part of the skeptic's argument is this:

- If Jo's belief that her hands are frostbitten is K-justified, then something neutralized the BIV scenario for Jo.
- Nothing neutralized the BIV scenario for Jo. This is C3 again.
- Hence, Jo's belief that her hands are frostbitten isn't K-justified.

Huemer thinks the first premise is true but the second is false; the skeptic thinks both are true. Who is right?

Summary

When one is locked in a disagreement, it's often the case that it's hard to know where the disagreement really lies – and where the parties agree as well.

Every day at work, Gwen has lunch with a male colleague. They have incredibly intimate conversations, talking all about their respective sex lives, sexual pasts, and sexual fantasies. Nothing is held back. This goes on for months. Eventually, Gwen's husband Abdul finds out all about it. He angrily accuses Gwen of cheating on him.

Gwen adamantly denies cheating. She and her colleague have never even touched each other, she says. Neither one has ever even seen a photo of the other one nude. All their interactions were purely conversational.

Abdul doesn't care. He still says it's cheating. You can't talk that way to someone of the opposite sex who is attracted to you, as the colleague is. The argument goes round and round, endlessly, with no chance of resolution.

Part of the reason for the frustrating debate is that there is confusion on multiple levels. For starters, they are disagreeing on two separate matters. She says she didn't cheat; he says she did. She says she didn't do anything morally wrong; he says she did. The first disagreement concerns the application conditions of the concept of marital cheating: does it apply to what Gwen did or not? The second dispute is a moral one: is what she did morally permissible in her marriage? For this second dispute, it doesn't really matter whether what she did counts as cheating. Even if it doesn't amount to cheating, that doesn't automatically mean it's morally okay.

There are two hurdles that Gwen and Abdul face – ones that they need to sort out before actually getting to the important threat to their marriage. First, they need to separate the linguistic-conceptual issue of what "cheating" amounts to from the moral issue of whether Gwen's behavior, however you conceptualize it, is morally okay in their marriage. They need to tease apart these separate issues. Second, if they want to continue with the linguistic-conceptual issue, then they need to realize that "cheating" has multiple meanings that are subtly different and easy to confuse – and they might be talking past one another because they are focusing on different meanings. Clearly, one can use "cheating" so that only sexual touching is involved. But there is an expanded meaning to the term as well. If Gwen and Abdul are sufficiently reflective, they will eventually realize that the linguistic-conceptual isn't anywhere near as important as the moral one.

Huemer and I need to make sure we know where we agree and disagree. In philosophy, this task can be quite difficult, since key terms – such as "justified" or "knowledge" or "rule out" – can have several meanings which are difficult to tease apart. That's a big part of the rationale for sections 1–3 of this chapter.

4 Knowledge as an Achievement on the Part of the Knower

What the skeptic needs is a good supporting argument for C3, her pivotal premise according to Huemer's realist. Huemer is right, in my opinion, to demand a good argument for C3. In this section, we begin to explore one.

Here is a quick summary of the basic idea behind my supporting argument for C3. First, in order to have ordinary knowledge or K-justified beliefs, the BIV scenario has to be neutralized. Second, if it's going to be neutralized by Jo herself, then the neutralization must come from, in some sense, her nervous system since that's basically the basis for what we are. Third, the BIV scenario is not neutralized by anything that comes from her nervous system (as she would have that same nervous system even if she were a BIV, for which there is no neutralizer of the BIV scenario). Hence, it's not neutralized by Jo herself. Fourth, if it's neutralized by something external to Jo, then K-justification isn't an individual epistemic achievement creditable to Jo, and hence, K-justification and knowledge are diluted or impoverished compared with what we have thought they were.

This is the general idea. Now let's go into the details.

Contrast Real-Jo, who is as a matter of objective fact a normal person in a normal world and not a BIV, from BIV-Jo, who is the BIV version of Real-Jo.

Real-Jo and BIV-Jo live lives that are exactly the same "from the inside". That is, all the thoughts, emotions, sensory experiences, and other mental phenomena that they have their whole lives seem to them exactly the same even though their external worlds are very different. Their entire lives "feel" exactly the same to them every second of their lives, as this is precisely the situation the mad scientists deliberately engineer by perfectly manipulating BIV-Jo's nervous system. Each sensory experience, each emotion, and each thought seems exactly the same to each of them, throughout their entire lives. Indeed, the fact that this scenario is conceivable is in my opinion the central, mind-blowing insight of the skeptic; the debate concerns what its epistemic impact is, skepticism or something else.

There are two other important ways Real-Jo and BIV-Jo are the same, which come from the same fact: they have the exact same nervous system their whole lives. In my opening chapter when I said that a BIV is a BIV, I was being brief. Instead, the idea is, or easily can be, that a BIV has the same entire nervous system as a normal embodied person (so it's not just the brain but the whole nervous system that is included in the vat). BIV-Jo is nothing more or less than Real-Jo's entire nervous system, including her brain. The mad scientists then simulate it so that BIV-Jo has all the same experiences as Real-Jo.

Hence, BIV-Jo not only experiences exactly everything Real-Jo experiences, but she also has the same *unconscious* mental processes as well. In cognitive science, the guiding idea for most research is that mental operations involve *processing information*, processes that occur in the nervous system. According to this idea, we take in information about our environment via our senses and "process" it, and this process leads to the formation of ordinary beliefs such as "My hands are frostbitten." Roughly put, it's Jo's sensory experiences that encode that initial information, and it's her nervous system that processes it and ends up generating the belief that her hands are frostbitten. Most of this information processing is unconscious. Even if this information-processing idea of cognitive science is exaggerated or otherwise limited, this thought about the role of the nervous system is true: Real-Jo and BIV-Jo have the same unconscious mental processes.

So, Real-Jo and BIV-Jo don't *just* experience their very different worlds in the same way. Even at the level of unconscious mental processes, they are identical. We would characterize the information differently for the two of them – for instance, only Real-Jo has light waves incident on her retinas that come from a bowl of fruit on a kitchen table – but the processing inside her is the same as that for BIV-Jo. A neuroscientist examining their nervous system processing wouldn't detect any differences in them.

These observations are important for figuring out the conditions (requirements) that N must fulfill in order to neutralize the BIV scenario. The skeptic thinks there are three such conditions.

Condition 1 says that K-justification is (i) an *epistemic achievement*, of some kind, which is (ii) an achievement *on the part of the person justified*. For instance, if you are K-justified in thinking that the butler murdered the maid, well, then that means that *you* – that's part (ii) – did something *epistemically right* – and that's part (i). Maybe the butler didn't in fact murder the maid, so your belief is factually false, and the evidence you relied on was ultimately misleading (since it "leads" a person away from the objective truth). But if you are K-justified in thinking the butler did it, then there is something good about that fact about your belief (that's part (i) again) that is to *your* credit (that's part (ii) again). The fact that your belief is true is not a result of you but something external to you (the butler's actions), but the alleged fact that your belief is K-justified is an epistemic achievement *on your part* and not on the part of something external to you. Or so the skeptic thinks; that's her first condition on N.

Condition 2 says that because during their entire lives Real-Jo and BIV-Jo have the very same mental life, both conscious and unconscious, if Real-Jo gets epistemic credit for something, then so does BIV-Jo. That's because anything that Real-Jo gets epistemic credit for, such as having a K-justified belief, has got to come from her sensory experiences, how things seem to her, and her other mental processes. That's who Real-Jo really boils down to, for goodness sakes! Since BIV-Jo has all those things too, if Real-Jo has some epistemic achievement, then BIV-Jo has it too.

In order to understand condition 3 that N must satisfy, consider the admittedly odd question, "If Real-Jo's hands belief is K-justified, and N neutralizes the BIV scenario for her, which came first?"

The skeptic thinks that if Real-Jo's belief were K-justified and N really existed, then it would be partly in virtue of N's neutralizing that Real-Jo's belief gets K-justified; it would not be the case that it is partly in virtue of Real-Jo's belief being K-justified that N does its neutralizing job. That is, the hands belief is K-justified partly *as a result* of N doing its work; it's not true that N does its work partly *as a result* of the belief's being K-justified. The idea is that N does its neutralizing thing *before* her belief gets K-justified.

This can be clarified with analogies. In order for a person to be a bachelor, several conditions have to be satisfied. For instance, one has to be male, adult, unmarried, and (arguably) living in a time and place in history when marriage is available. Hence, part of what paves the way for Mo to be a bachelor is the fact that he is unmarried; it's *not* the case that part of what paves the way for him to be unmarried is the fact that he's a bachelor.

True

- Mo is a bachelor partly in virtue of Mo's being unmarried.
- Part of the reason why Mo is a bachelor is that he is unmarried.
- Part of what makes it the case that Mo is a bachelor is that he isn't married.

- Real-Jo's belief is K-justified partly in virtue of N's neutralizing the BIV scenario.
- Part of the reason why Real-Jo's belief is K-justified is that something N neutralizes the BIV scenario.
- Part of what makes it the case that Real-Jo's belief is K-justified is that something N neutralizes the BIV scenario.

False

- Mo is unmarried partly in virtue of his being a bachelor.
- Part of the reason why Mo is unmarried is that he is a bachelor.
- Part of what makes it the case that Mo is unmarried is that he is a bachelor.
- N neutralizes the BIV scenario partly in virtue of Real-Jo's belief being K-justified.
- Part of the reason why something N neutralizes the BIV scenario is that Real-Jo's belief is K-justified.
- Part of what makes it the case that something N neutralizes the BIV scenario is that Real-Jo's belief is K-justified.

There are other examples of the same or similar phenomena. What *made it the case that* the baseball team won the World Series is the fact that it won four games in the series (it's a best-of-seven series of games); it's not true that what *made it the case that* the team won four games in the series is the fact that it won the series. One is prior to the other: winning four games is prior to winning the series, even if this isn't a temporal use of "prior".

Summing up, here are the skeptic's three conditions on any candidate N for neutralizing the BIV scenario:

- Condition 1: N's neutralizing is an epistemic achievement on the part of Real-Jo.
- Condition 2: If N's neutralizing is an epistemic achievement on the part of Real-Jo, then N comes from how things seem to Real-Jo, her sensory experiences, and/or her nervous system's mental processes (conscious and unconscious) – and it does not come from anything else, anything external to Real-Jo's mental processing.
- Condition 3: Real-Jo's belief is K-justified partly *in virtue of* N doing its work; it's not true that N does its work partly *in virtue of* the belief's being K-justified.

The Skeptic's Response to the Realist 121

These claims lead to the skeptic's defense of C3. It begins with these three premises that the skeptic and the Realist agree upon:

a. There isn't anything that neutralizes the BIV scenario for BIV-Jo. (The BIV scenario is *true* for BIV-Jo; so obviously it isn't ruled out.)
b. Real-Jo and BIV-Jo live lives that are exactly the same from the inside, have the same sensory experiences, and have the same nervous system's mental processes.
c. If Real-Jo and BIV-Jo live lives that are exactly the same from the inside, have the same sensory experiences, and have the same nervous system mental processes and for Real-Jo but not BIV-Jo, something N neutralizes the BIV scenario (all of which the realist agrees to), then N is fixed (determined, made to exist) by something other than how things seem to Real-Jo, her sensory experiences, and her nervous system mental processes. Clearly, if N was fixed by these aspects of Real-Jo, then since BIV-Jo has those aspects too, BIV-Jo would have N just like Real-Jo has N, but BIV-Jo doesn't have N, so N isn't fixed by those aspects of Real-Jo.

It follows from (a)–(c) that *if* something N neutralizes the BIV scenario for Real-Jo, *then* N is fixed by something external to Real-Jo's mental processes, conscious and unconscious. That is, if the Realist is right that something N rules out the BIV scenario for Real-Jo, then N lies "outside" her mental life, both conscious and unconscious. So far, the skeptics and (at least some) realists are in agreement. Disagreement occurs over the last premises of the skeptical argument:

d. If something neutralizes the BIV scenario for Real-Jo (as the Realist thinks), then this epistemic neutralizing is an epistemic achievement on the part of Real-Jo. This is condition 1.
e. If this epistemic neutralizing of the BIV scenario is an epistemic achievement *on the part of Real-Jo*, then this neutralizing is made to exist by some combination of how things seem to Real-Jo, her sensory experiences, and her nervous system mental processes. This is condition 2.

It follows from (d) and (e) that that *if* something N neutralizes the BIV scenario for Real-Jo, then N *is not* fixed by something outside her mental life. But from (a)–(c), we said that that if something *N* neutralizes the BIV scenario for Real-Jo, then *N* *is* fixed by something outside her mental life. Well, the "is not" and "is" statements make a contradiction! So, the assumption that something *N* neutralizes the BIV scenario leads to a contradiction. We draw the inescapable conclusion from (a)–(e):

f. Hence, nothing neutralizes the BIV scenario for Jo. This is premise C3.

5 Can K-Justification Neutralize the Brain-in-a-Vat Scenario?

The Huemer realist and skeptic agree on several important matters: (a)–(c) are true, and *if* (d) and (e) are true as well, then the skeptic's key premise C3 is true. The only way the realist can avoid that final result is to undermine the case for either (d) or (e).

My guess is that Huemer would agree with (d): Real-Jo's hands belief is an epistemic achievement on her part. It's not as though God or other supernatural beings do it for her. The Huemer realist will reject (e) by claiming that the neutralizer *N* is external. But what is this external *N*?

I take it from Huemer's opening chapter that his Realist will say that Real-Jo's K-justified belief in her hands can serve as *N*: according to him it exists and neutralizes the BIV scenario for Real-Jo. More exactly, this realist does not think that the mere fact that Real-Jo *believes* she has hands does the neutralizing. Neither is it the fact that her hands belief is *true*.[2] Instead, the key fact is that her belief is *K-justified*. It's in virtue of it being K-justified that it can do the neutralizing work; it is the K-justification that does the neutralizing job.

However, the skeptic won't buy this. As we saw earlier, she thinks that if *N* exists, then Jo's belief is K-justified partly in virtue of *N*.

---

2. Clearly, it's not the mere *fact* that she has hands that does the neutralizing (at one point, Huemer said this, but I don't think he meant it literally). She is unaware of the fact that she has a blob of cancer cells in her pancreas, but it would be bizarre to think that the BIV scenario is ruled out by the fact that she has a blob of cancerous cells in her pancreas. The only reason her hands are key, while the cancerous blob is not, is that she allegedly has an experienced-based K-justified belief that she has hands.

N paves the way for K-justification, not the other way around. This is the idea behind condition 3. Obviously, N can't just be her K-justified belief: it can't be true that Jo's belief is K-justified partly in virtue of itself. For the skeptic, the neutralizing would have to be done *prior* to the K-justification. Let's make the skeptic's reliance on condition 3 explicit:

> *Priority*: If something N neutralizes the BIV scenario for Real-Jo, then her hands belief is K-justified partly in virtue of N. Further, no belief is K-justified partly in virtue of itself.

If follows from priority that if something N neutralizes the BIV scenario for Real-Jo, it's not the fact that her hands belief is K-justified. That rules out Huemer's candidate for N.

Again, the intuition that motivates (the first part of) priority is that the *means* for her belief to be K-justified is to *first* neutralize the BIV scenario. To put it metaphorically but suggestively: one of the entrance requirements into the land of K-justification is to have *already* neutralized the BIV hypothesis (BIVH); N paves the way for K-justification. As indicated earlier, the "already" should not be interpreted temporally, just as it shouldn't be interpreted that way in claims such as "In order to win the World Series, a team already has to have won four games", "If someone is a bachelor, then he already has to be unmarried", and so on.

6 Can the Factual Lack of Brains in Vats Neutralize the Brain-in-a-Vat Scenario?

Some people are tempted to think that Real-Jo's justification for her hands belief, if such justification really existed, would be intimately connected to her *sensory experiences* of her hands: she sees them, she feels them, she can hear them when she claps, and she could even smell or taste them! So, could it be these sensory experiences that do the neutralizing job?

Well, as pointed out earlier, *all these sensory experiences could be happening even if she were a handless BIV*, as the mad scientists would create sensory experiences in her that seem exactly in every detail like the ones she really has when looking at her real hands. So, pointing out that she has sensory experiences of her hands doesn't seem, at first glance anyway, to do much of anything to rule out the BIV scenario.

The realist has an initially reasonable response to this move by the skeptic, which leads to a different candidate N. This realist may well agree that nothing *100%* rules out the BIV scenario. But, she says, it is ruled out *enough* if you combine Real-Jo's sense experiences with the cold, hard fact that there are no BIVs who have sensory experiences that seem to be perceptions of hands! This fact has to count for something! So, sure: the skeptic is right that it's *possible* that Real-Jo has the sense experiences without having hands. But the BIV possibility is extremely unlikely given Real-Jo's sensory experiences that seem to call out for hands, and this duo of facts (about the sensory experiences and lack of actual BIVs) is all it takes to *sufficiently* rule out BIVH for Real-Jo.

Here is one way of converting the realist's idea into a relatively precise argument:

- Here is truth T: there aren't any BIVs with sensory experiences like the ones Real-Jo has when she sees her frostbitten hands (at least, there are no such BIVs *yet*).
- If T is true, then all by itself – without its being known or even knowable by Real-Jo – it neutralizes, for Real-Jo, BIVH *enough*.
- Hence, BIVH is ruled out *enough* for Real-Jo. So, C3 is false.

I see five problems with the second bullet point of this realist argument against C3.

- It's not clear that a truth (such as T) can rule out an alternative scenario for a person *without the person being in a position to know the truth*. In most cases, in order for a truth or group of truths to rule out a scenario for someone, she has to *at least* be in a position to *know* these truths. But Real-Jo can easily be an intelligent person and be so confused about T that she isn't even disposed to believe it let alone know it.
- Even if a truth can rule things out for a person who isn't in a position to know this truth (so the first problem is dodged), it's not clear that there are degrees of ruling out. There are degrees of *evidential support* – for example, although you and I both believe something, your evidential support for it might be better than mine – but this doesn't mean there are degrees of *ruling out*.

- Even if an unknown truth can rule things out and there are degrees of ruling out (so the first two problems are dodged), it's hardly clear that knowledge or K-justification requires something less than 100% ruling out.
- Even an unknown truth can rule things out, there are degrees of ruling out, and knowledge and K-justification need not require 100% ruling out (so we get around the three problems already mentioned), it seems that Real-Jo's knowledge that her hands are frostbitten is about as strong as knowledge ever gets. (Remember, she is a doctor extremely familiar with frostbite, she has examined her own hands very thoroughly several times, her hands really are definitely frostbitten, it isn't at all difficult for an experienced doctor to spot frostbite, and so on.) So, one would think that she must have ruled out alternatives to "My hands are frostbitten" to the maximum extent – 100%. If this is not convincing for "My hands are frostbitten", then surely it is for something even more certain, such as "I have hands".
- Finally, even if all those four problems are overcome and C3 is *successfully* defeated, now it seems that the defense of realism has rendered knowledge impoverished, in the sense captured by C6 from my opening chapter: if at least one of the skeptic's premises (such as C3) isn't true (and realism is true), then Real-Jo's belief is epistemically impoverished despite amounting to knowledge. After all, now we are saying that a truth T that *Real-Jo knows nothing about and might even reject if she encountered it* is doing all the epistemic work for her, paving the way for her hands belief to be K-justified. And this means the realist has only a Pyrrhic victory, akin to "dumbing down" knowledge to something comparable to mere true belief or merely evidentially backed belief (as discussed in my opening chapter).[3]

The realist who rejects C3 would need a convincing response to these challenges. Can you think of one on her behalf?

---

3. In addition, if T is the *only* N that is neutralizing the BIV scenario, then if in the future scientists do create lots of BIVs or very similar things, then T will be rendered false and we will no longer know we have hands. Hence, Skepticism will become true.

7 Externalist Neutralization and the Skeptic's Revenge

Remember back in my opening chapter when I talked about impoverished skepticism and impoverished realism? That discussion might have seemed pretty separate from the discussion of skepticism itself. The former seems somewhat "meta" to the latter. However, the claims about epistemic impoverishment are crucial when assessing some realist responses to the skeptic's argument for C3.

For what it's worth, when I let realist tendencies "flow through me", then I object to premise (e) from the skeptic's argument for C3. My realist agrees with the skeptic that knowledge, K-justification, and epistemic neutralizing are epistemic achievements. And she agrees that at least some of them are partly due to Real-Jo's doing things right, so they are *partly* "on the part of Real-Jo". But why think they have to be *entirely* on Real-Jo's part? Why can't there be a helpful assist from something external to her? Why does Real-Jo have to do all the work in order to be K-justified?

Roughly put, **externalism** in epistemology is the view that important epistemic notions such as K-justification, evidence, and rationality are partly "external" notions in the sense that they hold external to the epistemic agent, since there could be two people who are perfect duplicates in how things seem to them their whole lives (plus their entire mental processing, conscious and unconscious) but only one who has K-justified belief, evidence, and rational belief. On this view, being K-justified is a bit like being an uncle: it's not entirely a matter about the person himself who is an uncle. At 11:32 am, Matt is not an uncle; at 11:33 am, his sister gives birth, and now he's an uncle despite the fact that he didn't do a damn thing from 11:32 to 11:33 except watch football. Whether he counts as an uncle is partly determined by matters external to him (in this case, whether he has a sister who gives birth). Similarly, whether your belief is K-justified can be a matter partly external to how things seem to you from the inside plus your mental processes.

Premise (e) says that epistemic neutralizing isn't even partly external; it's up to Real-Jo alone, her mental life both conscious and unconscious. Is (e) right? Or is the externalist right?

Amazingly enough, it might not matter all that much (at least, it doesn't matter much to me). To see why, let's very generously assume for the sake of argument that the realist *successfully* shows that either (d) or (e) is false. By my lights, this plays into the skeptic's hand. The reason is this: if either (d) or (e) is false, then *knowledge is impoverished*, so impoverished realism instead of full-blooded realism is true. That is, if either (d) or (e) is false, then knowledge is not nearly as epistemically impressive as we have been thinking for hundreds of years. This is because N, the neutralizer of the BIV scenario, lies external to Real-Jo; *she didn't rule out the BIV scenario at all*. If externalism about neutralization is true, then knowledge is external not just in requiring truth but even in the notion of K-justification. We foreshadowed this point in my opening chapter, when we looked at the reasons for believing C6, "If at least one of C1–C4 isn't true (so realism is true), then Real-Jo's belief is epistemically impoverished despite amounting to knowledge." I won't repeat the discussion here.

The gist is this: if (d) and (e) are true, then as we saw earlier, skepticism is true, and full-blooded realism is false; if either (d) or (e) is false, then since C6 is true, impoverished realism is true, and full-blooded realism is false. Either way, though, full-blooded realism is false. This is why I am tempted to think that full-blooded realism is probably false.

Summary

We are now into the most difficult, and detailed, parts of the debate over skepticism. This is philosophy at its best but most challenging. A student might want a *rough idea* of this portion of the debate. But at this point, there is no such thing to offer. This is the hard part, folks.

It's also the point at which philosophers frequently say to one another, "Well, you've misunderstood me here." The accusation of misinterpretation is often accurate. Huemer and I are pretty good at writing clearly (believe it or not). But this doesn't mean we will avoid misinterpretation. If you really, really want to engage someone fruitfully in a debate – philosophical or not – it's a good idea to try to state your opponent's argument and position so accurately that they say in response "Yeah, that's exactly what I meant."

8 Brief Replies to Some of Huemer's Realist Criticisms of Skepticism

Huemer's realist has several replies to skepticism or the skeptic's premises, either my C1–C4 or Huemer's (1)–(4). I will respond to just four of them here:

I. The skeptic is begging the question: "in order to defend one of the *premises* of the skeptic's argument . . . [premise C3 in particular, the claim that nothing neutralizes the BIV scenario for Real-Jo], the skeptic has to appeal to the *conclusion* of that very argument [the claim that Real-Jo's belief in her hands isn't K-justified]. So, the skeptic's argument begs the question".

II. "If there *could* have been evidence refuting a particular theory, but there in fact isn't, then this very fact is some evidence in favor of the theory. But if, on the other hand, there *couldn't* have been any evidence refuting a given theory, then the fact that there isn't any evidence refuting it is *not* evidence in favor of it. In the case of the Real World Hypothesis (RWH) and BIVH, there is no evidence refuting either one. But there *could* have been evidence refuting RWH, whereas there *could not* have been evidence refuting BIVH. So the failure to find any evidence refuting either one counts *in favor* of RWH but does *not* count in favor of BIVH. So, RWH is better than BIVH."

III. "Phenomenal Conservatism (PC) [which Huemer endorses] makes short work of skepticism. According to PC, we are rationally entitled to presume that things are the way they appear to be until we have specific grounds for doubt. It appears that I have two hands; so, in the absence of grounds for doubt, this is what it makes sense for me to believe. I don't have to first prove that I'm not a BIV or refute any other weird scenarios of that kind. Rather, the skeptic would have the burden to produce reasons for thinking that I *am* a BIV or that my perceptions are unreliable for some other reason in order to defeat the presumption that things are as they appear. Since the skeptic cannot do this, we are justified in continuing to think that we have hands, that there are around us the kinds of physical objects that we seem to see, and so on".

IV. Skepticism is crazy.

My skeptic responds to (I) with her (a)–(f) argument for C3 – plus her priority thesis.

Realist reply (II) rests on some claims I don't see much reason to accept. But never mind this. The pivotal point is this: Huemer's realist accepts that that if C1–C4 are true, then skepticism is true; that C1, C2, and C4 are true; that if (a)–(e) are true, then C3 is true; and that (a)–(c) are true. Hence, this kind of realist has to find a way to convincingly criticize either (d) or (e). It's not clear to me how (II) supplies the materials for this.

Regarding (III), the skeptic has three primary doubts.

First, she sees inadequate reason to accept PC. As far as I can determine, the *main* argument for PC is the alleged fact that it fits our pre-theoretical judgments about when beliefs are, and are not, K-justified. This may be true, and philosophically significant, but the skeptic has an argument that our pre-theoretical judgments are massively mistaken. We should not be confident in theories built on data that are being seriously challenged. PC looks good if you have already assumed that skepticism is wildly false; if you haven't, then it looks like question begging.

Second, the skeptic never said that in order to be K-justified in believing I have hands, I need to "prove" I'm not a BIV, as Huemer wrote. Instead, she said that the BIV scenario has to be neutralized; she never said anything about proving anything. She was explicit that neutralizing need not involve anything like proving.

Third, I don't see why the skeptic has "the burden to produce reasons for thinking that I am a BIV or that my perceptions are unreliable for some other reason in order to defeat the presumption that things are as they appear." Instead, she has the burden of formulating a logically valid argument for her thesis, an argument with plausible premises. She did exactly this. As far as I can tell, there was never any reason for her to "produce reasons for thinking I am a BIV or that my perceptions are unreliable."

Regarding (IV), I disagree, and I think it's an important point despite not targeting any of the skeptic's premises (for one thing, I suspect it matters to Huemer's reply to controversy skepticism (CS), examined later). If we *mistakenly* think that a view is crazy, then we will be too willing to ignore evidence for it, and we will be too ready to bite bullets in order to avoid it. There are several overlapping reasons why I suspect the skepticism-is-crazy idea is mistaken.

First, if we have learned much of anything about the universe, we have learned that it is a *bizarre* place. Scientific advances very strongly suggest that reality is staggeringly odd. The size of the universe (or just a galaxy or even our puny solar system), Einstein's general relativity theory, his special relativity theory, transfinite mathematics, the biology of various strange creatures, quantum mechanics, the Big Bang, black holes, the stunning nature of cellular structure, and so on–all these things and more are profoundly counterintuitive in many ways, even though we often learn enough about them, over sufficient time, that the feeling of counterintuitiveness slowly dissipates. In some ways, it's unfortunate that the feeling of oddity diminishes.

The same holds for many topics in philosophy. For instance, a great many color scientists and philosophers think that the patches of color you can focus your attention on as you look around your environment are really not located where you think they are. The redness you can vividly focus on when looking at a tomato is not on the surface of the tomato. Pretty crazy! In addition, standard issues involving truth, meaning, free will, the composition of ordinary material objects, the relation of consciousness to neurological activity, and much else can be used to rigorously prove that reality is exceedingly odd – even if we have yet to figure out *which* of the odd theories is correct.[4] Skepticism is really not that exceptional.

Second, the connection between truth and usefulness might not be very tight. As I put it in my opening chapter (Chapter 1, section 2.12), skepticism would be crazy if it included the idea that "I know I eat food" *fails to be worth relying on*. But it's not including this idea. The skeptic is saying that "I know I eat food" is false, but her view is rendered sane because she is free to admit that "I know I eat food" is still good enough to rely on in any practical or even scientific context. I have never seen a decent reason for thinking that a claim's being useful, even in scientific contexts, means it's highly probable to be true. The point made in the previous paragraph even casts doubt on the inference.

Third, the skeptic can allow that we have *justified true beliefs* – as long as the notion of justification is the social-epistemic one

---

4. I offer these proofs in Frances 2022. In another research monograph in progress, I give a proof that the truth regarding the locations of colors – whatever it turns out to be – is similarly exceedingly odd.

I described in section 1 and my opening chapter. She is not powerless to find epistemic notions that rightly distinguish silly beliefs such as "Aliens rule the USA" from wise beliefs such as "My hands are frostbitten." This shows, again, that one intuitive objection to skepticism – the one that runs "But you're saying that even our best beliefs are no better, epistemically, than really silly beliefs!" – falls flat.

Fourth, the advocates of the skepticism-is-crazy view sometimes say that if you became convinced of skepticism, then this would require a massive number of unreasonable changes in your behavior. Suppose you are walking in a park and see a stranger walking their dog. The dog seems *very* friendly, in the ordinary way you have seen a million times, you adore dogs, and you want to stop and pet it. You implicitly take yourself to *know* that the dog won't try to rip your arm off. If someone, such as the dog's owner, convinced you that you don't know the dog won't try to rip your arm off, well, shit: you probably will no longer want to try to pet the dog. Going from implicitly believing "I know the dog won't try to kill me" to consciously accepting "I don't know the dog won't try to kill me" has enormous implications regarding what you should do regarding the dog!

However, with skepticism, the usual behavioral implications don't hold. When a *non*-skeptic says, "We don't know the dog won't try to kill you", she is saying (in an expansive sense of "saying") that you should change your behavior of approaching the dog. But when the skeptic says the same sentence, she isn't saying you should behave any differently. When it comes to the vital question "How should I live my life?", the skeptic is not saying you should no longer rely on how things appear to you. Rather, she is saying that knowledge turned out to be nearly nonexistent, but she never said that we should act much differently as a consequence (although this doesn't mean there are *no* behavioral consequences at all to accepting skepticism). The common link between "We don't know X" and behavior regarding X is significantly altered if we accept skepticism. The skeptic agrees that if your implicit "The dog won't try to kill me" belief is justified in the social-epistemic sense articulated earlier, then you can pet the dog.

The last three points collectively tempt some of us to say, "Well, ok, but then you are really diluting the significance of the skeptical thesis". I suspect that's right! That's why one might be tempted to endorse Impoverished skepticism, as discussed in section 2.7

of Chapter 1. The observations about virtual reality and virtual knowledge are directly relevant there.

9 Making Excuses in the Face of Controversy

The basic argument for skepticism, in either my form or Huemer's, is pretty standard in philosophy. Skepticism itself is also standard. The same cannot be said of either CS or its supporting argument. Discussions of the epistemology of controversy have been around for centuries, but no rigorous, thorough investigation even started until around 2005. This means that it is difficult to take the vague, ambiguous, and yet interesting worries about the epistemology of controversy and put them into the form of a sharp argument. At least it's difficult for me!

I want to approach the topic in a way different from how I did so in my opening chapter.

1. Suppose you believe B.
2. You are aware of the controversial nature of B:
   (a) You know that there is a large group of people *each* of whom is generally very smart and has investigated B for a long time, quite thoroughly. (Of course, there are people who have opinions on B who aren't at all smart or who haven't put much thought into B. We aren't considering them here.)
   (b) As far as you know, these people have not collectively come to any significant agreement on B. You know that a significant percentage think it's true, another significant percentage think it's false, and yet a third group of people hasn't made up their minds. But as far as you know, it's not as though one group is three times as large as the other groups combined, for instance.
3. In the face of all this, you retain your belief in B, with no significant alteration in confidence level.

The controversy skeptic makes two claims:

CS1 If (1)–(3) are true of your belief B, then in the majority of cases, your reaction to the controversy over B is unwise.

CS2 For the vast majority of us, (1)–(3) are true of many of our beliefs.

Most of us, when in the situation described in (2), offer some *explanation* (perhaps to others, perhaps just to ourselves) of the controversy surrounding B that allows us to be psychologically comfortable (if not epistemically reasonable) in retaining belief in B with no significant change in confidence. Here are four such explanations.

> E1. The specialists who are most expert on B – the super-specialist-experts, if you will – endorse my belief B much more than they reject it.
> E2. The vast majority of specialists who appear to disagree with B don't really disagree with it.
> E3. There is some prejudice, selection effect, bias, or similar problem that is pervasive in the relevant community of specialists and has radically warped its evaluation of B away from what it should be given the evidence widely available to them regarding B.
> E4. When it comes to B, I am an epistemic superior to almost all of those specialists who reject my view. Perhaps I have crucial evidence they lack (e.g., I know some fact, or argument, that they don't know about). Or maybe although I don't have crucial evidence they lack, I've evaluated our common evidence much better than they have.

The controversy skeptic is saying, with CS1, that *these excuses are usually unwise* – and the same holds for closely related excuses (e.g., "I am generally smarter than all the people who disagree with me"). Of course, you might be the world's smartest person and even know that fact about yourself. In this case, there is nothing unwise about your reaction to the controversy. But let's be realistic: in the vast majority of cases, not only is each of these excuses false, but they are pretty *obviously* false. Or so the CS advocate says.

Here is a real-life case that (1) and (2) are intended to capture. When I was a beginning PhD student in physics (before switching to philosophy), I had a certain belief B about "string theories" in theoretical physics. It was highly controversial at the time. But I didn't know about the controversy at all. I was under the mistaken impression that the physics community who investigated string theories agreed with B; they had reached consensus on it. Because of this, my belief in B was reasonable (at least in the sense of not being blameworthy). Both (1) and (2a) were true of me, but (2b) was false of me.

But then I found out, during a conversation with two of my professors in the hallway after a class in quantum mechanics, that there was vociferous disagreement over B. At that point, I was in the situation described in (2b). As a consequence of this realization, I suspended judgment on B. If I had given any of E1–E4, that would have been unwise of me, since I had no good reason to believe any of them – and for most of them, I had excellent, even overwhelming, reason to *disbelieve* them.

In my experience, when people encounter CS they respond to *how it affects them*, and they ignore what the argument says about anyone else. In one respect, this is understandable, since CS is correctly viewed as an attack on one's own beliefs. One feels compelled to defend *one's own* beliefs first.

However, I think that attitude often causes one's responses to CS to be implausible. My advice, for what it's worth, is to first set aside one's self and evaluate CS applied to others only. Then, after one has done that task, one can think about how it applies to one's own life.

Huemer focuses on his disagreements with a special subset of people: those who hold "deeply implausible" views.

> [S]uppose I disagree with some other people about topic X. I ask myself whether these other people are in a good position to make reliable judgments about X. In assessing this, can I use my beliefs *about X itself* (perhaps along with other information) as a basis for downgrading my assessment of the other people's judgment? I say yes: if the other people appear to me to hold deeply implausible views about X, that is evidence that they aren't good judges of X.

I have four things to say about this.

First, I agree with Huemer's thesis about evidence. Suppose I start talking with Jon about baseball, and he seems to be quite informed and perceptive about it. Then he says that Dave Kingman is the greatest home run hitter in baseball history. You can be forgiven for never even hearing of Kingman! The point is that Jon's view about

Kingman is "deeply implausible" – and I am aware of this fact. I now have *some evidence* that he isn't a good judge of baseball.

Second, however, in many cases, the evidence in question is defeated by other evidence. As I pointed out in the previous section, we have excellent evidence from science and philosophy that the truth about *some* topics is deeply counterintuitive – even when we can't be sure what that truth is. If I find I disagree with each of a large group of people about a certain topic and I know that these people hold deeply counterintuitive views on the topic, then although this gives me some evidence E that their "judgment" on the topic is unreliable, E is often defeated (significantly diminished in force) by (i) the fact that I already have excellent evidence that the truth about the topic – whatever it may come to – is deeply counterintuitive and/or (ii) the fact that I have oodles of evidence that many if not all of these people have good judgment on this topic.

Regarding (ii), it's often the case that there is no disagreement-independent evidence that the people I'm disagreeing with have bad judgment. That is, when I look at them independently of this disagreement, I find not the slightest reason to think that their judgment is any worse than mine. In fact, when it comes to many controversial topics, I am very often in the position of having to admit that many of them are obviously significantly *better* than I am at judging the topic! I'm not so foolish to think that I am among the best experts in the world when it comes to finding the truth about the topic in question! And the excuse that runs "But they haven't seen my argument for B!" is foolish, since I know quite well by induction on past arguments that it's not as though people will agree with me once they understand my amazing new argument for B.

Third, it's usually the case that I know that although people disagree with me about some controversial topic, their views are hardly "deeply implausible". I think that the people who disagree with B are wrong about B, but I have the wisdom to admit that their views on B are hardly "deeply implausible". This is often the case with debates about civil rights, censorship, free speech, abortion, capital punishment, affirmative action, the future impact of climate change, the future impact of the loss of biodiversity, the distribution of health care resources, the extent of racism, fascism, and misogyny, religious freedom, the proper extent of governmental welfare, labor unions, the Electoral College in the USA, vaccine mandates, gun control, foreign aid, and so on. These are large-scale controversies, but of course there are many small-scale ones, too:

- Should we put Grandma in a nursing home or have her live with us for a while?
- Should we raise the kids Catholic?
- Am I an above-average driver?
- Did Grandma love Mom as much as she loved Uncle Jared?
- Should we move in together now or wait until our relationship matures a bit more?
- Should we get an apartment in Manhattan or go with somewhere cheaper and just deal with the annoyances of the commute?
- Is our next-door neighbor paranoid or just nasty?

Fourth and finally, if I find myself *often* concluding, when faced with disagreement over some controversial topic, "Well, they have poor judgment on this topic", then I am coming very close to saying that my judgment is among the best in the world on a large body of controversial topics. But this is an unwise position to be in. I may be an expert about the statistical history of baseball and capital punishment, but I am not so wildly clueless to think I'm significantly more reliable than most people when it comes to the large-scale controversies mentioned earlier.

Chapter 4

The Realist's Response to the Skeptic

Michael Huemer

Contents

1 The Skeptic's Argument Again 137
2 Three Interpretations of "Ruling Out" and How the Skeptic's Argument Goes Wrong on Each 138
   2.1 Infallible Justification 138
   2.2 Fallible Justification 140
   2.3 External Conditions 141
3 Observations About Philosophical Method 143
   3.1 The Need to Accommodate Pre-theoretical Beliefs 143
   3.2 On Begging the Question 145
   3.3 Some Truths Are Weird 146
   3.4 Misunderstandings 148
4 How Crazy Is Skepticism? 151
   4.1 Socio-Epistemic Justification 151
   4.2 Distinguishing the Silly from the Wise 152
   4.3 Acting on Skepticism 153
5 Controversy Skepticism 156

1 The Skeptic's Argument Again

I would like to thank Bryan Frances for another interesting discussion of the argument for skepticism. It is becoming clearer where we agree and disagree; however, I continue to find some things about Frances' argument unclear.

Frances imagines two characters, Real-Jo (a normal person perceiving her hands normally) and brain-in-a vat Jo (BIV-Jo, a BIV hallucinating hands). Obviously, BIV-Jo lacks knowledge that she has hands. Frances argues that *Real*-Jo also lacks knowledge that she has hands because in order to know this, she would have to first be able to rule out (or "neutralize") the hypothesis that she is a BIV, and she has no way of doing that.[1]

Why think Real-Jo can't rule out that she is a BIV? As I understand it, the main argument is roughly this: Real-Jo and BIV-Jo have the same internal evidence available to them (where "internal evidence" is evidence that depends entirely on one's own experiences and other mental states). But surely BIV-Jo's internal evidence does not rule out that she is a BIV, since she *is* a BIV. Therefore, Real-Jo's internal evidence also fails to rule out that she is a BIV. Furthermore, only internal evidence counts because knowledge must be an achievement on the part of the subject, and it can only be an achievement on the subject's part if it is based on internal evidence.[2]

I think this argument is mistaken, but exactly what is wrong with it depends on what "ruling out" means, which I continue to find unclear. If "ruling out" P requires having infallible justification for denying P, then the error is the assumption that one needs to rule out the BIV scenario at all. If "ruling out" P only requires having *fallible* justification for denying P, then the error is the assumption that BIV-Jo hasn't ruled out that she is a BIV. If "ruling out" requires something more than (or other than) justification, then the error is the assumption that ruling out is an achievement attributable (solely) to the subject.

I'm going to explain all that in section 2. After that, I'll discuss some points about philosophical methodology and how one should evaluate philosophical theories. Then I'll revisit the question of how crazy external-world skepticism is (I still find it crazy). And then I'll return to controversy skepticism (CS), where I think Frances and I are in substantial agreement.

2 Three Interpretations of "Ruling Out" and How the Skeptic's Argument Goes Wrong on Each

2.1 Infallible Justification

Infallible justification is justification that cannot possibly go wrong. In other words, if you are infallibly justified in believing something,

---

1. In his response (this volume, Chapter 3), see premise C2 in section 1, condition 3 in section 4, and the priority principle in section 5.
2. See Frances' premises (d) and (e) in Chapter 3, section 4.

then it is *logically impossible* that you're mistaken, given that you have that justification. By contrast, fallible justification is justification that *can* go wrong. If you are fallibly justified in believing something, that thing is *probably* true (given your evidence), but it remains *possible* for it to be false.

On the face of it, "ruling out" a hypothesis *sounds* like it means having infallible justification to reject it. I've been assuming, nevertheless, that this is *not* what Frances intends. In his opening statement, he writes:

> I occasionally encounter students who complain that the skeptic is implausibly assuming that ordinary empirical knowledge has to be based on *absolutely conclusive evidence*. I don't think that is accurate. . . . There's no requirement that the ruling-out item has to be absolutely conclusive evidence, whatever that might mean. . . . I don't think there's anything about super-high standards of evidence there.[3]

So it seems that "ruling out", as Frances uses the term, *isn't* supposed to require infallible justification.

However, I am revisiting the issue here because at least two remarks in Frances' response suggest the contrary. First, he treats it as obvious that the BIV hypothesis (BIVH) isn't ruled out for BIV-Jo: "The BIV scenario is *true* for BIV-Jo, so obviously it isn't ruled out".[4] This remark appears in parentheses, as if it were almost unnecessary to even state it. He gives no further explanation or justification of the point. Now, if "ruling out" requires infallible justification, then this would be understandable. *Obviously*, if you have infallible justification, you can't be mistaken. But if "ruling out" can involve mere *fallible* justification, then by definition, things that are thus "ruled out" can still be true. So it is far from obvious why BIV-Jo can't "rule out" that she is a BIV. If that sounds odd, this oddness shows only that "ruling out", in English, does not normally refer to fallible justification.

Second, after entertaining the possibility of *degrees* of "ruling out", Frances writes: "Even if an unknown truth can rule things out and there are degrees of ruling out . . ., it's hardly clear that knowledge or K-justification requires something less than 100% ruling

---

3. Chapter 1, section 2.4.
4. Chapter 3, section 4, premise (a).

out". What could "100% ruling out" mean, other than infallible justification? Fallible justification is by definition less than maximal.

These remarks thus revive the suspicion that perhaps Frances' argument requires us to have infallible justification for denying that we are BIVs, in order to know anything about the external world. So now I will simply state my view of the skeptic's argument on this interpretation. *If* "ruling out" requires infallible justification, then I think that the BIV scenario *cannot* be ruled out but that ruling things out is *not required* for knowledge. No one has to rule out the BIV scenario, or any other alternative, in order to know that they have hands. This is because I think knowledge, in general, does not require infallible justification. (So premise C2 in Frances' formulation is false.)

Now, why do I think knowledge can be fallibly justified? Because this is just how the word "know" is used by normal English speakers. We ascribe "knowledge" all the time to people who obviously have only fallible justification. However, if you disagree with me about the use of "know" in English, I don't want to argue about that. As I noted in my opening statement (Chapter 2, section 1.2), I don't find semantic debates interesting, so I propose to leave this subject here.

2.2 Fallible Justification

So now let's assume that "ruling out" the BIV scenario only requires having fallible justification for denying it. In this case, I think both BIV-Jo and Real-Jo *can* rule out that they are BIVs – because all this means is that both have fallible justification for denying that they are BIVs. Since the justification is fallible, it leaves open the possibility of the subject being mistaken, as BIV-Jo in fact is by stipulation. In fact, I think it's *obvious* that BIV-Jo is justified in denying that she is a BIV, since for her, everything appears exactly the way it does to a normal person. If you started to seriously entertain that you were a BIV, you would be crazy – we would say you were having a psychotic break. Similarly, if BIV-Jo seriously entertained that she was a BIV, she would be crazy. (In terms of Frances' formulation, this means that premise (a) in the sub-argument for C3 is false.[5])

How are BIV-Jo and Real-Jo justified in denying that they are BIVs? I gave two accounts of this, each of which I regard as

---

5. See Chapter 3, section 4.

sufficient. First, in my view ("PC"), one is (fallibly) justified in believing that things are as they appear, unless and until one has specific reasons to doubt the appearances. Both Real-Jo and BIV-Jo appear to themselves to be normal people living in the real world, and neither of them has any reason to doubt this or to suspect that they are BIVs. So it's rational for them to assume they are in fact normal people living in the real world.

Now, why do I hold this theory of justification? Well, it accounts for our pre-theoretical judgments about what is and isn't justified, it is suggested by the internalist intuitions I discussed in my opening statement, and alternative views are self-defeating. See again my opening statement (Chapter 2, section 3).

Here is the second account of how BIV-Jo and Real-Jo can be justified in denying that they are BIVs: BIVH is an inferior theory because it, unlike RWH, is unfalsifiable. Unfalsifiable theories are bad because they (unlike falsifiable theories) cannot be supported by evidence, since they make no predictions. See section 2.8 in Chapter 2. In his response, Frances mentions this account, but all he says about it is that it fails to refute his premises (d) or (e), so he deems it irrelevant to the skeptic's argument. It is on its face counterintuitive that an account of how we're justified in rejecting the BIV scenario should be irrelevant to the BIV argument. He does not consider the possibility that this account rebuts his premise (a).

2.3 External Conditions

Lastly, let's consider the possibility that "ruling out" P requires something *other than* or *in addition to* justification for denying P. Perhaps, for example, ruling out P just means *knowing* (or being in a position to know) that P is false. It is generally accepted that, to know something, one must not only be justified in believing it, but one must also be *in fact correct* (plus some other stuff that we won't go into[6]). This could explain why Frances finds it obvious that BIV-Jo can't rule out that she is a BIV. Note that to explain this, we have to suppose that "ruling out" requires some condition, other than

---

6. For example, maybe one also has to be in general reliable; maybe one's cognitive faculties have to be functioning properly; maybe one's belief must be true in all the nearby possibilities; maybe there have to be no facts out there that, if you knew about them, would undermine your justification; and so on.

justification, that *entails being correct* – that is, *P* only counts as being "ruled out" if *P* is in fact false.

If this is how we interpret "ruling out", I think the mistake in Frances' argument is his premise (d):

> If something neutralizes the BIV scenario for Real-Jo . . ., then this epistemic neutralizing is an epistemic achievement on the part of Real-Jo.[7]

("Neutralizing" is used interchangeably with "ruling out".) Given that "ruling out" refers at least in part to something *other than* Jo's justification for her belief, I think the ruling out of an alternative is *not* an epistemic achievement attributable solely to Jo. Rather, it is at least partly attributable to the world.

To explain this a bit more: there are multiple distinct conditions for knowledge (things that have to happen for you to count as "knowing" something). Some of these are *internal* conditions – they depend solely on what is going on inside your mind. Other conditions are *external* – they depend on things going on outside your mind. Examples of internal conditions would be that you have to *believe* the proposition in question and that you have to *be justified* in that belief or hold it for rational reasons. Examples of external conditions are that your belief has be *in fact true* and that your belief-forming method has to be generally *reliable*. (Note: philosophers do not agree on exactly how "knowledge" should be defined. But these are examples of things that philosophers often say about it.)

Knowledge occurs when both the internal and the external conditions are satisfied. The satisfaction of the *internal* conditions is attributable to you, the knower. You get the credit for that. But the satisfaction of the *external* conditions is attributable to the external world – the world, so to speak, had to cooperate with you to enable you to know stuff.

Now, on the present interpretation of "ruling out", one's ruling out of an alternative is an (at least partly) *external* condition. We know that it's (partly) external because it entails the actual falsity of the thing that is "ruled out", whereas the subject's justification does *not* entail this (since we're allowing fallible justification).

---

7. Chapter 3, section 4, premise (d) in the sub-argument for C3.

By definition, this condition isn't attributable to the subject; it is dependent on the external world.

For example, suppose that ruling out the BIV scenario means *knowing* that one isn't a BIV. Knowledge requires truth, so ruling out the BIV scenario involves (among other things) *not in fact being* a BIV. But the fact that you aren't a BIV is not an achievement attributable to you. Rather, it's attributable to a hospitable world, one that doesn't actually contain scientists who would have kidnapped you, removed your brain from your body, and so on.

On the present interpretation of "ruling out", Real-Jo but not BIV-Jo can rule out the BIV scenario. This is because, while both satisfy the internal conditions for knowledge, only Real-Jo satisfies the external conditions.

Summary

The skeptic's argument, as Frances formulates it, draws plausibility from the ambiguity of the phrase "rule out". Depending on how it is interpreted, the argument claims either (i) that we need infallible justification for rejecting the BIV scenario, (ii) that we need fallible justification for rejecting the BIV scenario, or (iii) that we need to satisfy some external condition for knowing that we aren't BIVs. In the first case, the argument errs in assuming that knowledge must be infallible. In the second case, it errs in assuming that a BIV can't rule out that she is a BIV. In the third case, it errs in assuming that ruling out the BIV scenario is an achievement by the subject.

3 Observations About Philosophical Method

3.1 The Need to Accommodate Pre-theoretical Beliefs

I think Frances and I agree on the following: the skeptic needs to give positive, non–question-begging arguments for skepticism.[8] It's not enough for the skeptic to merely refuse to accept normal beliefs and then insist that we can't refute her. A skeptic *could* do this,

---

8. See Chapter 3, section 2.

but it would make her position uninteresting, and there would be little point in the discussion. Obviously, a skeptic could maintain her position by simply refusing to accept any premises that might be used to refute it. But we are not born skeptics; we come to philosophy starting from a commonsense belief system. What makes skepticism interesting to us is that the skeptic appears to be giving us some *reason to change* our beliefs.

Here is a related methodological point: as a general rule, a theory about any given subject is better if it predicts and/or explains most of the things that we pre-theoretically (before hearing about the theory) thought were true about that subject. If the theory contradicts the things we pre-theoretically thought were true, that is bad for the theory. For instance, if you were giving a theory of ethics, you would want it to explain such things as why breaking promises, robbing banks, and killing people are generally wrong. If you were giving a theory of aesthetics, you would want it to explain such things as why music counts as art, why Michelangelo's *David* is a good artwork, and why Virginia Woolf is a better writer than Cardi B. If you were giving a theory of biology, you would want it to explain such things as why trees, dogs, and people are alive. And so on. The reason for this is obvious: you want a theory that you have some reason to embrace, and *you* have no reason to embrace a theory if it doesn't explain anything that you take to be true.

I am not saying that one can never be justified in rejecting something that initially seemed obvious. One *can* be justified in rejecting something that seemed obvious, but this requires finding *other* obvious things that conflict with the first obvious thing. An argument against a pre-theoretical belief can succeed only if its premises are *more obviously correct* than the belief that they are being used to overturn. (See my opening statement, section 2.2.)

Suppose that someone advances a theory that blatantly fails on this point – it can't explain almost any of the things we pre-theoretically believe about its subject matter. In this case, the theory should almost certainly be rejected (unless it has some absolutely amazing argument in its favor); at any rate, this is certainly a major mark against the theory. But suppose that the person who thought of the theory, instead of giving it up, digs in his heels and insists that all these pre-theoretical beliefs are false *because* they conflict with his theory. Does it now become rational to embrace the theory?

Surely not. Surely the problem with the theory does not go away merely because one chooses to deny every apparent fact that conflicts with it. Whether the theorist chooses to accept them or not, the pre-theoretical beliefs give us reason to reject the theory.

Now apply all of this to epistemology. Just as with every other subject matter, if you are trying to develop a theory about knowledge, you're going to want your theory to explain most of the things that we think are knowledge. If you come up with a theory and it turns out to imply that no one knows where China is, that is bad. It continues to be bad even if you choose to insist that really no one knows where China is – your taking this dogmatic stance does not neutralize the problem with your theory. This is what the skeptic is doing. The skeptic starts from some set of theoretical claims about knowledge (e.g., "Knowing P requires ruling out every alternative to P", "Whatever is ruled out can't be true", and "Ruling out must be an epistemic achievement on the part of the subject"). We can consider the combination of these claims as a theory about knowledge. This theory turns out to conflict with nearly all of our pre-theoretical beliefs about what we know – that is, nearly everything that we thought we knew before hearing that theory turns out to be ruled out by this theory of knowledge. This is a pretty awful kind of theory. It is like an ethical theory that says that the most praiseworthy action is torturing children, an aesthetic theory that says that Cardi B is the world's greatest artist, or a biological theory that says that dogs aren't alive.

All this is closely related to Phenomenal Conservatism (PC), since our pre-theoretical beliefs are normally the things that initially *seem* correct to us.

3.2 On Begging the Question

Frances says that we can't rely on our pre-theoretical judgments about knowledge because the skeptic is challenging these judgments; to rely on them, he thinks, would beg the question against the skeptic.[9] Surely this isn't right; it can't be that easy to avoid problems with a theory. It can't be that you render a piece of apparent evidence impotent and unable to be used against your theory merely by denying it. Yet this is what is implied in Frances' argument that we can't rely on pre-theoretical judgments merely because the skeptic denies them.

---

9. Chapter 3, section 8.

Note that my goal here is not to *convince a skeptic*. My goal is to convince reasonable, ordinary people that the skeptic has not given *us* any reason why *we* should give up our commonsense beliefs. If you start out with ordinary, commonsense beliefs – including, for example, the belief that you know you have hands, that some people know where China is, and so on – the skeptic hasn't given you a good reason to change your beliefs. The skeptic has presented an argument, but this argument starts from a theory of knowledge that it would be irrational for you to accept, since the theory conflicts with nearly all of your pre-theoretical beliefs about knowledge. It would be more rational for you to accept PC, since this theory, besides being plausible in its own right, fits with nearly all of your pre-theoretical beliefs about justification.

Granted, the skeptic's theory may have *some* appeal – perhaps when you hear the skeptic's theoretical claims, they sound generally plausible. For instance, it sounds plausible to say that in order to know P, I have to rule out the alternatives to P. If (and only if) you find these claims plausible, then the skeptic succeeds in giving you *some* reason to revise your beliefs about what you know. But this reason is only as strong as the intuitions that it appeals to. It would be irrational to give up something that seems *more* obvious to you on the basis of something that seems *less* obvious. When you find a conflict among initially plausible propositions, you should reject the least plausible one. Doing so is not *begging the question*; it is just being rational.

3.3 Some Truths Are Weird

Frances goes on to argue that many truths about the world are "staggeringly odd", "profoundly counterintuitive", and so on, and he lists several of these. I don't find all of the examples convincing. Some of the examples I just don't find counterintuitive (e.g., the size of the universe). Other examples are controversial and may in fact just be surprising *falsehoods* (e.g., the view that colors are not on the surfaces of objects). In accord with his own view about CS, Frances probably should not be confident of these controversial claims.

But I take it that Frances doesn't need all of his examples to succeed; I take it that his point only requires that there be *some* genuine examples of very counterintuitive truths. And this is surely the case.

What follows from this? I take it that this is supposed to show that one should not reject skepticism merely due to its counterintuitiveness or apparent "craziness", since some crazy-sounding things are true. But how does this argument go?

Here is one gloss: assume that all justification must be infallible. Now, we can see that our intuitions are not infallible, and our sense of what is "crazy" isn't infallible, since there are *at least some* cases in which a "crazy", counterintuitive proposition is true. Therefore, our intuitions provide no justification at all, and there is no reason for rejecting seemingly crazy propositions.

The problem with this reasoning should be obvious. Not all justification is infallible. Indeed, virtually no justification is infallible. But *not being infallible* isn't equivalent to *being worthless*. We could still have *very strong reason* to reject skepticism due to its seeming craziness, even though the sense of craziness isn't infallible.

Okay, here is another try. Suppose we accept the notion of fallible justification. Perhaps the argument is that seemingly crazy beliefs turn out to be true *so often* that we don't even have any *good reason*, going forward, to reject things that seem crazy.

If this is the idea, I think the premise is factually false: seemingly crazy things turn out to be true *extremely rarely* at most. Frances lists a handful of allegedly crazy-sounding propositions that are allegedly true. But how about listing crazy-sounding propositions that *aren't* true? The latter list would be orders of magnitude longer (e.g., "The world is run by lizards", "All birds are robots", "The moon is made of cheese", "7 = 9", "The population of the Earth is six", "No one believes anything", "The sky is red", "I do not exist").

Here is a third try. Perhaps the idea is that the list of "crazy" truths shows how it is possible to have adequate justification for believing something that *initially* seemed obviously false, and perhaps skepticism could become justified in a similar manner.

If this is the idea, I think the problem is that the justification for skepticism is *nothing like* the justification for most of the counterintuitive theories that people accept today. Most of the counterintuitive theories that are widely accepted are accepted because there is either compelling scientific evidence or a mathematical proof. The case for skepticism, by contrast, turns on vaguely plausible but highly disputed philosophical intuitions about the nature of knowledge. Skeptics don't have anything remotely like a compelling scientific case or a mathematical proof. In fact, the skeptics are committed to rejecting all scientific evidence, since they think observations can never produce knowledge.

Now, here is what I think we should conclude: our intuitions are fallible. What seems obvious to us is not *100% guaranteed* to be true. We are sometimes justified in rejecting something that seemed obvious if it turns out to conflict with other obvious things. But we should not give up seemingly obvious truths *without a good reason*. When there is a conflict among seemingly obvious propositions, we should resolve the conflict in the most plausible way – by giving up the least obvious proposition. We should not adopt needlessly implausible resolutions, such as rejecting the *most* obvious proposition.

As far as I can tell, Frances has said nothing that counts against this view. In particular, all of this is perfectly compatible with, and not at all disconfirmed by, the observation that we have discovered some counterintuitive truths about the world.

How does all this apply to skepticism? The skeptic discovers a conflict among several initially plausible claims about knowledge, such as:

- Knowing P requires ruling out every alternative to P.
- Whatever is ruled out can't be true.
- Ruling out must be an epistemic achievement on the part of the subject.
- Some people know something about the physical world.

The skeptic chooses to resolve this conflict by rejecting the last proposition. This is irrational since the last proposition is, on its face, the *most* plausible of the four; it would be more rational to reject any of the others.

3.4 Misunderstandings

There were a couple of places where I think Frances misunderstood my point. These are not crucial to the overall dialectic; nevertheless, I'd like to clarify these points.

First, Frances writes:

> [T]he skeptic never said that in order to be K-justified in believing I have hands, I need to "prove" I'm not a BIV, as Huemer wrote. Instead, she said that the BIV scenario has to be neutralized; she never said anything about proving anything. She

was explicit that neutralizing need not involve anything like proving.[10]

In response, Frances definitely said things about "ruling out" BIVH. "Ruling out" a hypothesis sounds to me a lot like "disproving" it. If there is a semantic difference between these, I don't know what it is. Admittedly, Frances might be using a non-standard sense of "rule out". But then I don't know why we shouldn't use a non-standard sense (in fact, the *same* sense) for "disprove". But even if there is some semantic difference between ruling out a hypothesis and proving that the hypothesis is false, my point is not tied to the specific word "prove" – you can substitute "rule out", "neutralize", "have justification to reject", or whatever term you prefer. My point is that [disproving, ruling out, neutralizing, having reason to reject, or whatever] the skeptical scenario is not a precondition of knowing that you have hands. I don't care which expression you use in the brackets.

Obviously, Frances disagrees with that point, but I still am not sure why. In his chapter, he advances the priority principle, which is essentially exactly what I am denying.[11] But I did not see an argument for that principle, nor do I find it obvious. It seems more plausible to me, on the face of it, to say that one *doesn't* need a justification for *rejecting* the BIV scenario; one only needs to *lack* any reason for *believing* the BIV scenario. This strikes me as the more commonsense view, so I need to hear an argument for giving it up.

After the above passage, Frances continues:

> I don't see why the skeptic has "the burden to produce reasons for thinking that I am a BIV or that my perceptions are unreliable...". Instead, she has the burden of formulating a logically valid argument for her thesis, an argument with plausible premises. She did exactly this. As far as I can tell, there was never any reason for her to "produce reasons for thinking I am a BIV or that my perceptions are unreliable" (this volume, p. 126).

The reason for the skeptic to do that is that that is necessary to show that we lack knowledge of the external world, which is what the skeptic is trying to show.

---

10. Chapter 3, section 8.
11. See his condition 3 in Chapter 3, section 4, and the priority principle in Chapter 3, section 5.

Of course, the skeptic's argument *claims* that the skeptic *doesn't* have to do this. The skeptic has an epistemological theory according to which, in order to know P, you have to first rule out every alternative to P. But I am not about to grant the skeptic's epistemological theory. I am rejecting the skeptic's theory for the reasons discussed earlier and advancing a different, better theory (PC). This better theory says that you are justified in believing that things are as they appear unless you have specific grounds to doubt it. This theory avoids skepticism and rebuts the skeptic's argument. It is not apt to respond to this alternative view by simply saying there is no reason for the skeptic to give grounds to doubt our appearances.

Perhaps Frances did not see how my epistemological view can be used to rebut the skeptic's argument. I hope I have made this clear above. Again, PC explains how ordinary people are (fallibly) justified in believing the things they seemingly observe about the external world. Given this, we can reject the BIV scenario on the grounds that it clashes with these observations and we have no reason for suspecting that the scenario is true.

Summary

The skeptic's task is to give us a reason for changing our minds about what we know. The skeptic tries to do this by appealing to certain theoretical epistemological principles that entail that we lack knowledge of the external world. In general, however, one should not adopt a theory that accommodates almost none of one's pre-theoretical beliefs, nor should one reject a more plausible proposition in order to preserve a less plausible one. So it is more reasonable to reject the skeptic's epistemological principles than to reject all knowledge of the external world.

A more plausible epistemological principle is PC, which holds that a belief is justified if it seems correct and one has no specific grounds for doubting it. On this view, we are justified in thinking that we are perceiving the world normally unless we have specific grounds for doubting this. BIVH provides no such grounds since we have no grounds for suspecting that we are BIVs.

All of this is entirely consistent with the fact that there are some counterintuitive truths.

4 How Crazy Is Skepticism?

Earlier I touched on why I view skepticism as a crazy position. Frances, however, has made some valiant efforts to make skepticism seem less crazy. I think these efforts either fail or render skepticism uninteresting.

4.1 Socio-Epistemic Justification

First, Frances introduces a skeptic-friendly interpretation of "justification", the "socio-epistemic" notion. In the socio-epistemic sense, we can say a belief is "justified" provided that it satisfies the standards prevalent in one's community for being considered reasonable.[12] Call this "S-justification".

Notice how S-justification differs from *my* notion of justification (which Frances calls "K-justification"): in my sense, a belief must be *in fact* reasonable in order to be justified. But in the socio-epistemic sense, the belief need not actually be reasonable; it need only satisfy *the standards of one's community*. If one's community has crazy standards, then one can be "justified" in believing something completely unreasonable. For just about any norm of epistemic rationality, you can imagine a community that rejects that norm. So S-justification per se needn't satisfy any of the norms of rationality. Someone could be S-justified in believing contradictions, in believing empirical claims on no evidence, in holding credences that violate the laws of probability, and so on.

Frances tries to use this notion to soften the skeptic's apparent extremism: despite rejecting *knowledge* of the external world, the skeptic is free to concede that we have plenty of *justified beliefs* (i.e., S-justified beliefs) about the external world. This makes the skeptic's position sound less radical.

But this appearance is an illusion generated by the non-standard usage of the word "justified". In the *ordinary* sense of "justified", justified beliefs have something going for them: they are things that it is rational or reasonable to hold. But this is not true of mere S-justified beliefs; they need not have anything at all going for them. S-justification is a purely descriptive, not a normative condition;

---

12. Chapter 3, section 1: "Jo's belief is 'justified' when it is socially acceptable in the sense that she has met the epistemic conditions for believing that are standard in her community for being deemed 'reasonable' and 'rational' by just about everyone."

calling a belief S-justified is not, as such, to endorse the belief to any degree. So if *all* the skeptic can say on behalf of our ordinary beliefs is that they are S-justified, then the skeptic's position remains as radical as ever.

You might be tempted to say that although S-justification would be of little value in a community with crazy standards, S-justification is still pretty good in *our* society, since we in fact have pretty reasonable standards. I would be happy with this – but notice that this move defeats the point of introducing the notion of S-justification. The *reasonableness* or *correctness* of our standards could not itself be explained in terms of our standards, on pain of circularity. So we would have to adopt some objective notion of reasonableness. Once we do that, we might as well just say that our ordinary beliefs are objectively reasonable – that is, they are K-justified. (If they are justified according to norms that are objectively reasonable, this is very close to, if not the same thing as, simply being K-justified.)

Now, if the skeptic grants that our ordinary beliefs about the external world are K-justified, while continuing to insist that they are not *knowledge*, then I think the skeptic's position devolves into an uninteresting semantic point. That is, the skeptic and I would agree *substantively* on the assessment of our external world beliefs (they are K-justified but not infallible), while simply disagreeing about how the word "know" is to be used (e.g., we might disagree about whether "knowledge" requires infallible justification). I take it that Frances would reject this route.

4.2 Distinguishing the Silly from the Wise

Any decent epistemological theory should be able to distinguish ridiculous beliefs from reasonable ones. If the skeptic winds up saying that all beliefs are on a par, that would be a crazy-making feature of the view. Frances tries to show that the skeptic's view is not crazy in this respect:

> [T]he skeptic can allow that we have justified true beliefs – as long as the notion of justification is the social-epistemic one ... She is not powerless to find epistemic notions that rightly distinguish silly beliefs such as "Aliens rule the USA" from wise beliefs such as "My hands are frostbitten." This shows, again, that one intuitive objection to skepticism – the one that runs

"But you're saying that even our best beliefs are no better, epistemically, than really silly beliefs!" – falls flat.

I disagree. As noted earlier, S-justification as such has no normative force; to call something S-justified is not to endorse it in any way to any degree. Again, being S-justified is compatible with being thoroughly irrational. True, the skeptic can identify *some* difference between the belief "Aliens rule the USA" and the belief "I have hands" – the latter is widely accepted, while the former is not. But this isn't really what we wanted. We didn't want merely to say there is *some difference* between the two beliefs. (One could just as well say that the former belief mentions the USA, while the latter mentions hands – this is *a difference* between them.) Rather, we wanted to say that there is a *normatively relevant* difference, that is, there is a difference that makes one of the beliefs *better* or *more rational* to hold than the other. If the skeptic can't acknowledge any normatively relevant differences, then the skeptic really is saying that our best beliefs are no better than really silly beliefs.

What the skeptic seems to need is an *intermediate* notion of justification: she would like to say that some external-world beliefs (such as "Aliens rule the USA") are completely unjustified, while others (such as "I have hands") are justified to *some* degree, yet none are justified *enough* to count as knowledge. But the skeptic nevertheless wants to avoid saying that knowledge requires *infallible* justification. Perhaps knowledge requires a *high* degree of justification, though not infallible justification, and we possess only a *low* degree of justification for our ordinary beliefs.

This is all *coherent*. But I just don't see the argument for this combination of views. I see how one might use the BIV scenario to argue that our ordinary beliefs lack infallible justification. I also see how one might use it to argue that our beliefs have no justification at all. But I don't see how one might conclude from reflecting on the BIV scenario that our beliefs merely have a *low* degree of justification.

4.3 Acting on Skepticism

Let us next consider the practical implications of believing external-world skepticism. Normally, our beliefs about what we know have an impact on our behavior. As Frances notes, if you think that you *don't know* whether a certain dog will try to rip your arm off, then you are unlikely to try to pet that dog. So on the face of it, we would expect that people who think they don't know anything about the external world at all must behave very differently from those who think they *do* know things about the external world. For instance, perhaps skeptics would never pet dogs. Perhaps a true skeptic would simply lie inert all day since she would place no trust in any of her perceptions.

This, Frances assures us, is not the case:

> [W]ith skepticism the usual behavioral implications don't hold. When a non-skeptic says, "We don't know the dog won't try to kill you", she is saying . . . that you should change your behavior of approaching the dog. But when the skeptic says the same sentence, she isn't saying you should behave any differently. When it comes to the vital question "How should I live my life?", the skeptic is not saying you should no longer rely on how things appear to you. Rather, she is saying that knowledge turned out to be nearly nonexistent but she never said that we should act much differently as a consequence (although this doesn't mean there are no behavioral consequences at all to accepting skepticism).[13]

What is missing from this passage (and Frances' chapter in general) is an explanation of why this would be true. *Why* would the skeptic's denial of knowledge lack the practical implications of ordinary denials of knowledge?

I can think of at least two plausible answers to this, but I don't think Frances will like them. The first explanation is that avowed skeptics do not genuinely believe what they say. Skepticism is a position one takes in an intellectual debating game, not something one takes seriously in real life. That is why, upon adopting the "philosophical belief" in skepticism, one doesn't change one's behavior in the ways typical of those who consider themselves ignorant of particular external-world facts.

The other explanation is that although skeptics are perhaps sincere, they are using the word "know" differently from the rest of

---

13. Chapter 3, section 8.

us. When skeptics conclude that "you don't know whether the dog will try to rip your arm off", they don't behave the way ordinary people would behave on drawing this conclusion because the skeptics *do not mean the same thing* that ordinary people mean by this sentence. From here, there is an obvious argument that skeptics are simply misusing the word "know", that is, using it outside the standard English sense.

As I say, I don't think Frances will accept either of these explanations. Perhaps there is some other explanation that I have missed. My point is that *some* explanation is needed if Frances is to convince us that skepticism isn't a crazy view. The closest he comes to explaining it is another allusion to S-justification: "The skeptic agrees that if your implicit 'The dog won't try to kill me' belief is justified in the social-epistemic sense articulated earlier, then you can pet the dog".[14] Bearing in mind, however, that S-justification has no normative force and that the skeptic presumably does *not* hold that our epistemic standards are themselves justified in any meaningful sense, it remains unclear why the skeptic would say that you should plan your behavior according to S-justified beliefs. Why would this make any more sense than planning your behavior according to the assumption that aliens rule the USA, or any other arbitrary assumption?

Summary

Socio-epistemic justification lacks normative force and is compatible with any degree of irrationality. It thus does not enable the skeptic to distinguish silly from wise beliefs or to avoid a radical clash with common sense. It remains to be explained why skeptics should not behave in the manner typical of people who think they lack knowledge of practically relevant information. This could be explained if skeptics are insincere or are misusing the word "know".

---

14. Chapter 3, section 8.

5 Controversy Skepticism

Now to conclude on a note of agreement. In my previous chapter, I tried to find some things to disagree about regarding controversy skepticism. But I really agree with Frances' main points on the subject. I think a great many people are very overconfident about controversial questions, *especially* political questions. Frances mentions such issues as

> civil rights, censorship, free speech, abortion, capital punishment, affirmative action, the future impact of climate change, the future impact of the loss of biodiversity, the distribution of health care resources, the extent of racism, fascism, and misogyny, religious freedom, the proper extent of governmental welfare, labor unions, the Electoral College in the USA, vaccine mandates, gun control, foreign aid, and so on.

All of these are controversial issues, and most are issues about which people tend to be extremely overconfident. In my view, this is very different from external-world skepticism – there is no real controversy about whether there is an external world, in the way that there is a huge controversy about, say, whether abortion is wrong.

In my experience, it often seems that people hold their controversial opinions with little knowledge of or interest in the opposing arguments, which seems to me a pretty sure sign of irrationality. I don't think it is *impossible* to have justified beliefs about these things, but I think it requires a lot more effort to engage with opposing perspectives than most partisans appear ready to make. Often, we lazily dismiss reasonable views as crazy or evil without a serious effort to see others' points of view.

Why do we do this? I think the main reason is that we do not care very much about the truth. We know that our own individual political beliefs won't make any difference to how society actually functions (it's not as though *my* becoming a socialist would cause the USA to turn to socialism), so we have little stake in making sure that we get things right. Perhaps we care *a little* about getting to the truth, but we also care about such things as which beliefs make us feel good, which beliefs will be approved by the people we like, and which beliefs will annoy the people we dislike. Scrupulously attending to the evidence and trying to understand opposing perspectives doesn't make us feel good, it doesn't help us bond with our chosen tribe or defeat the opposing tribe, and it doesn't get us any tangible, material benefits. So we rarely do it.[15]

All of this is terrible for society, of course. Your *individual* political beliefs have negligible impact on society, but the collective impact of many people forming beliefs irrationally can be disastrous. It leads to political polarization, intolerance, and just plain bad policy. So I am on board with Frances' efforts to encourage a more skeptical attitude about politics and other matters of controversy.

Summary

Frances and I agree that we should generally be skeptical about highly controversial opinions, especially about politics. We are often overconfident about such matters because we care more about things like how our beliefs make us feel than about the truth.

---

15. For elaboration, see my 2015.

Second Round of Replies

Chapter 5

When Will It Ever End?
Response to Huemer's Reply

Bryan Frances

Contents

1 The End of the Debate? 161
2 Straightforward Linguistic Ambiguity 164
3 Subtle Linguistic Complexity 164
4 Controversy Skepticism, Knowledge, and Wisdom 169
5 Controversy Skepticism and the Phenomenology of
 Confident Belief 172

1 The End of the Debate?

The movie *The Lord of the Rings: The Return of the King* came out in 2003. It was a huge success, winning 11 Academy Awards. It grossed more than one billion USD. The movie had just about everything people love to see in movies.

At the end of the movie, the One Ring, which was the key to the evil Sauron's power, disintegrates in the lava of Mount Doom. As a consequence, Sauron dies, and Aragorn and the other heroes and heroines defeat the remaining supporters of Sauron. Evil has been decisively defeated. The end.

Not quite. This wasn't the ending, although it seemed like it at the time. After Sauron's death and Aragorn's victory, the surviving good people are reunited, and Aragorn is crowned King of Gondor and marries the love of his life, Arwen. He gives a moving speech, honoring Frodo, Sam, and the other pivotal Hobbits. Everyone is happy. The end.

Nope. It still wasn't over. The Hobbits return home to the Shire, where they get on with their lives. Sam marries the love of his life, Rosie Cotton. The end.

DOI: 10.4324/9781003434931-8

Sigh; it is *still* not over. After a period of several years, Frodo leaves Middle-Earth for the Undying Lands with Bilbo, Gandalf, and the remaining Elves. He leaves Sam the book he has written about their experiences together. *Now* the damn movie is over, although the movie folks couldn't resist throwing in a last scene of happy Sam with his happy wife and happy kids.

Philosophical debate is usually much worse than this: in most cases, it *never* ends, even when it seems like it has. There is a seemingly endless parade of pseudo-endings. Philosopher P1 comes up with what he or she genuinely thinks is a *conclusive* argument that settles the debate at hand. Trumpets blare through the glorious sunshine, announcing the end of the debate. But no: philosopher P2 pops up and shows that P1's argument has serious flaws, at least apparently. And not just that: P2 offers her own apparently conclusive argument for a view that in some sense is the *opposite* of P1. Trumpets blare once more. Then philosopher P3 comes along and upsets the consensus on P2's view. Then P4 shows up. And so on. If you think you have found the decisive argument that settles the matter, just wait a bit: someone will show that the argument has a significant weakness. The trumpeters grow weary and give up, moving over to sporting events.

The debate over skepticism keeps going. It is unresolved, at least in a community sense: the community of people who study the debate the most have not reached a stable consensus about it. Sure, for a period of a few decades or even a century, one side might be significantly more popular than the other side. But if you wait long enough and are too stubborn to die, you'll eventually see the consensus change. The direction of consensus has been akin to an unpredictable see-saw.

We started this book with some of the basics about skepticism and realism about knowledge. Then we moved on to more detailed arguments, back and forth. We ended up with some pretty advanced material, the kind that generates passages of the form "Frances' premise *X* can be challenged with argument *Y*, but then again, the second premise of *Y* can be challenged with further argument *Z*." I probably don't have to tell you that I, playing the skeptic's advocate, have responses to Huemer's criticisms of my defense of skepticism. Sometimes the disagreement is illusory since he misinterprets me, despite our efforts of communication. (Sometimes I am at fault, since I wasn't clear in my previous chapter; other times it's him; yet other times it's both, I suppose; but who cares, really, other than him and me?) Other times he offers arguments against my claims, arguments I respect but suspect don't establish their conclusions. And let's be honest: he will have fully intelligent, challenging responses to my responses. And so on, until he and I run out of patience, insight, or heartbeats.

Instead of adding to the debate, I will step back and pretend that I have the wisdom to address a question that many students ask about philosophical debates such as this one. Since this is a book for students and not professors, it makes sense to address this question. Here it is: given that the debate has been going on for centuries and shows no good sign of ending (in the community consensus sense), what does this mean? Is the debate just super hard, like trying to figure out what the average temperature in Times Square will be, to one degree Celsius, exactly 1,000 hours from now? Or is it not resolvable at all? If it's the latter, what does *this* mean? Is there something wrong with the issue itself perhaps?

Upon being introduced to the debate over skepticism, a significant percentage of students suspect that *there are two notions of knowledge*, and skepticism is true for one but not the other. If this is right, they say, then perhaps a main reason for the seeming endlessness of the debate is that we repeatedly, and confusedly, go back and forth between the two concepts. When we suspect skepticism is true, we are operating with one concept; when we think realism is true, we are operating with the other; and the only reason we think the two views conflict is that we mistakenly assume they concern the same concept of knowledge. Not all students have this suspicion, but I think a sizable portion do.

For comparison, if a student asks me, "Do you think we have free will?", then like any competent philosopher, I will start by saying, "Well, it depends." I'm not responding this way to be annoying! Instead, I know that different students have different notions of free will in mind, and although humans have some of those kinds or notions of free will, it's not at all clear that they have all of them. Before I can answer in a helpful manner, I need to have at least a rough idea of what the student means by "free will." Responding to "Do you think we have free will?" is a little bit similar to responding to "Is that a good restaurant?" or "Was your date enjoyable?" Or, as I mentioned in a previous chapter, we need linguistic clarification before tackling a question such as "Who are the greatest actors of all time?" In each case, some clarification is often (not always) needed before you can give an answer.

There are several ways to develop the idea that both realism and skepticism are, in some relevant respect, true. But the core idea is this: (a) there is some linguistic or conceptual confusion going on so that (b) the central assertions of the skeptic are true, (c) the central assertions of the realist are true, and (d) the debate continues because we fail to see that the two groups of assertions don't really conflict. I will say a bit about these ways in sections 2 and 3.

2 Straightforward Linguistic Ambiguity

Abdul's religion is football. For many years now, he has watched it virtually every day without fail, kept track of many different teams and players, attended football matches every week, worn the jerseys of his favorite teams and players, and so on. Then again, Islam is the religion he grew up with, that he practices every single day, and that is the one he would say he is devoted to.

Even so, it would be odd to say "Abdul is devoted to two religions". The term "religion" has multiple meanings, and we shouldn't throw them together haphazardly. All one has to do is consult a good, thorough dictionary to get a taste of the multiplicity of meanings of "religion".

However, you will find no such solution to the skepticism debate here. If you look up "know" in dictionaries, you won't find two meanings such that it's plausible that skepticism is true for one but not the other and we have been confusing them, so that (a)–(d) from the end of the previous section are satisfied.

I am not saying that there aren't multiple notions of knowledge! Maybe there are, and perhaps we confuse them and it leads to endless debate over skepticism; so, (a)–(d) might well be true. But the hypothesis that this is a *straightforward linguistic ambiguity matter* is not promising.

3 Subtle Linguistic Complexity

A story condensed from philosopher Keith DeRose (2009) is a fine starting point into seeing a more sophisticated way to argue that both sides are correct.

Thelma, Louise, and Lena work in the same office. Today is their day off, but before getting an early dinner together, they decide to drop by the office to pick up their paychecks. (This is the old days, when many things weren't done electronically.) Thelma and Lena are also interested in finding out whether their colleague John was at work that day, since they are involved in a small office bet with a couple of other workers over whether John would show up at work today. As they pass the door to John's personal office, they see what is obviously his hat and coat hanging on hooks right outside his door, which they know to be a reliable sign that John was in fact at work. So, they are convinced he was at work that day. Thelma and Lena bet that he would be at work that day. They conclude that they should collect their winnings from the coworkers who bet he wouldn't be at work that day. Louise didn't have anything to do with the bet.

Thelma, Louise, and Lena leave the office. Thelma goes to a local tavern to meet other friends from the office, and Louise and Lena each head home in different directions.

At the tavern, Thelma meets a friend who bet against John's being at work. Thelma says, "Hey, John was at work today. Pay up!" When her friend asks, "How do you know he was at work?" Thelma describes the facts about John's coat and hat. Then Thelma says, "Lena knows too, as she was with me. So she'll be asking for her money too."

The key point: when Thelma says "Lena knows", it is an entirely *appropriate* thing to say in the conversation in the tavern. Given that Lena saw the hat and coat, it would be weird to say that she didn't know that John was at work.

At the same time as the conversation in the tavern, Louise is stopped by the police on her way home. The police are conducting a very important investigation and are seeking to determine whether John was at work that day, since this piece of information is crucial to their inquiry. When the police ask Louise whether she could testify that John was at work, she replies, "Well, no, I never saw him. I could testify that I saw his coat and hat hanging in the hall, which is a reliable sign that he's at work. But I suppose John could have left his coat and hat on the hook when he went home yesterday, although that's really unlikely". When the police ask Louise whether her colleague Lena might know whether John was at work that day, Louise replies, "No. She has the same reasons I have for thinking John was there, but, like me, Lena doesn't know that John was there."

The key point: when Louise says, "Lena doesn't know", it is an entirely *appropriate* thing to say in the conversation with the police.

Hence, it seems that when Thelma says at the tavern "Lena knows", her claim is true. But it also seems that when Louise tells the police "Lena doesn't know", her claim is true. But that looks impossible, as they seem to be asserting obviously contradictory claims!

We all have the task of explaining why Louise's "Lena doesn't know" and Thelma's "Lena knows" are both conversationally appropriate even though they certainly appear to be inconsistent with one another.

Contextualists adopt a simple explanation: the reason the two assertions are conversationally appropriate is that they are both *true*. That means that for at least some sentences of the form "*S* knows *C*" and "*S* doesn't know *C*" (in this case, *C* is "John was at work today", and *S* is Lena), there are uses of these sentences that concern the same *S* and *C* (and time) even though both are true. So "*S* knows *C*" is linguistically complex.

Let **Partial Contextualism** be the idea that uses of "*S* knows *C*" and "*S* doesn't know *C*" can both be true even though they concern the very same *S* and *C* (and time), and "knows" is being used literally. The story from DeRose is intended to motivate this view.

Contextualists need an explanation of *how* Louise's assertion "Lena doesn't know" and Thelma's assertion "Lena knows" can both be true despite seeming to be in conflict with each other. In response, these philosophers hypothesize that (i) in different conversational contexts, there are different *epistemic standards* a belief has to meet in order to satisfy "*S* knows *C*"; (ii) in Louise's context with the police, the standard is high; (iii) in Thelma's in the tavern, it is low; and (iv) Lena's belief meets the low but not the high standard. So, "Lena knows" is true relative to the low standards but false relative to the high standards.

Let **Full Contextualism** be the combination of Partial Contextualism plus the idea in the previous paragraph, the idea being the proposed epistemic-standards *explanation* of how both "*S* knows" and "*S* doesn't know" can be true.

Full Contextualism motivates the following intriguing idea that is relevant to the skepticism debate. Perhaps in an ordinary conversation, "Jo knows that her hands are frostbitten" comes out true because the epistemic standards Jo's belief has to meet are pretty ordinary. But in a philosophical conversation that focuses on the epistemic relevance of brain-in-a-vat (BIV) scenarios – like the conversations we are having in this book – "Jo knows that her hands are frostbitten" comes out false because the epistemic standards are very high, and Jo's belief doesn't meet them. So, "Jo knows" is true relative to ordinary standards but false relative to the high standards.

If this is right, then when Huemer and other realists insist that "Jo knows that her hands are frostbitten" is true, they are right to this crucial extent: in virtually any normal conversation, the Jo sentence is true. But when I and other skeptics say the Jo sentence is false, we are right to this crucial extent: in a philosophical conversation that includes certain comments on BIV (and similar) scenarios, the Jo sentence is false. Hence, we skeptics and realists end up confused.

Let **Debate Contextualism** be Full Contextualism plus the idea presented in the previous two paragraphs – the application of Full Contextualism to the debate over skepticism.

Let me try to motivate these contextualist ideas with a similar idea, one I have gestured at before.

Former pro wrestler Dwayne Johnson has appeared in many movies over the past 20 years or so. Some of these movies made a fortune. Millions of people saw these films. He is beloved around the world. But is he a *great actor*?

It depends what you mean: is he great at entertaining people in his acting roles? Certainly. So if that's what you mean by "great actor", then he's a great actor. But if you mean can he give artistically great performances in dramas, convincingly conveying complex emotions and thoughts from a multi-dimensional character, then, no, he is not a great actor. Even he would probably admit this.

Notice that there are two ways "great actor" can cause problems in our interpreting one another in a debate. First, we need to know what *standard* is meant: great at entertaining, great at gaining awards for acting, and so on. This is the problem we noted in the previous paragraph. But then there is a second problem: even *after* we have settled on a standard (so the first problem is solved), how good does Dwayne Johnson have to be at the standard in order to be "great" relative to it? For instance, how entertaining does he have to be in order to be correctly judged great at entertaining? This shows that linguistic complexity can have multiple aspects.

It's easy to see how in a conversation, two people could appear to be disagreeing over whether Johnson is a great actor even though in reality they aren't disagreeing at all. Instead, they are merely using different conceptions of what it is to be a "great actor". When one person says, "He is definitely a great actor" and the other person responds with "No way. His movies are fun, but there's no way he's a great actor", they could easily be talking past one another: they *think* they are disagreeing with each other, but they really aren't at all. If they managed to make their meanings clear, then they may well realize that they agree completely in their assessments of Johnson's acting ability.

Could it be that knowledge = great true belief, and the two factors mentioned earlier – the relevant *standard* and *degree of goodness* on the standard – apply to "great true belief" just as they apply to "great" in "great actor"? This would mean that whether "Jo knows that her hands are frostbitten" is true depends on both what standard is in play and how good her belief is regarding the standard.

Keep in mind that when it comes to addressing skepticism, it isn't enough to show that "know" is linguistically ambiguous, there are multiple kinds of knowledge of truths, or that there are multiple conceptions of knowledge. That's all fine but not enough for our purposes here. If we are going to seriously defend the idea that *skepticism is both true and false depending on differing conceptions of or standards for knowledge and the debate is seemingly endless because we confuse these conceptions or standards*, then the four conditions mentioned at the end of section 1 have to be met: (a) there is some linguistic confusion going on so that (b) the central assertions of the skeptic are true, (c) the central assertions of the realist are true, and (d) the debate continues because we fail to see that the two groups of assertions don't really conflict.

We could just *create*, through linguistic stipulation, two notions of knowledge that fit the "knowledge = great true belief" idea so that skepticism is true for one and false for the other. Let knowledge$_S$ = true belief that is so great that the believer has evidence for her belief that is about as strong as one's evidence that one is conscious, and let knowledge$_R$ = true belief that isn't stupidly arrived at or maintained ("S" for skepticism and "R" for realism). Well, then it's arguable that skepticism is true for knowledge$_S$ but false for knowledge$_R$. But so what? I don't think there is any evidence that condition (d) is satisfied here. In other words, there's no good reason to think we keep debating skepticism because we are confusing knowledge$_S$ with knowledge$_R$.

Returning to Contextualism, many but not all epistemologists today think Partial Contextualism is true. Many of these epistemologists accept Full Contextualism as well. But people are more hesitant about accepting Debate Contextualism. For my own part, I doubt that a majority of skeptics would be happy with the thesis that *only in fairly bizarre conversational contexts* (such as some of the ones we have in philosophy) is "Jo doesn't know her hands are frostbitten" true. Instead, the skeptic thinks that even in fairly ordinary conversational contexts, like when your brother says to you "Mom knows you were riding on your boyfriend's motorcycle late last night. You're going to be in real trouble!", claims of the form "S knows C" are false even though they are worth relying on for practical or even scientific purposes. If a person has strong sympathies with skepticism but is willing to admit that the "Mom knows" assertion was literally true (and many other, similar, positive knowledge assertions are true in ordinary life), then she might think that impoverished realism (as defined earlier) is true. That's fine, but it's not skepticism.

Even if Debate Contextualism is false, the suspicion that there is something wrong with the debate over skepticism so that (a)–(d) are true despite the failure of Debate Contextualism might be correct anyway. It's a good exercise to creatively brainstorm the possibilities.

4 Controversy Skepticism, Knowledge, and Wisdom

Unfortunately, I agree with almost everything Huemer says about controversy skepticism (CS). Hence, there doesn't seem to be that much debate material! In these two concluding sections, I will discuss two issues about it.

CS's thesis is that when you are significantly aware of intelligent prolonged controversy over claim C, in the vast majority of cases, you would be *unwise* to have a belief about C's truth or falsity. The type of controversy matters, however. A claim is often controversial in some but not all relevant communities. For instance, in some benighted intellectual communities, there is controversy regarding the belief that Hell is a real physical place at the center of the earth, and bad people go there after death. I don't have any problem being quite confident that that belief is mistaken. But for an enormous number of other beliefs, which I sometimes care about a great deal, I realize that the people in the relevant intellectual community are about as sharp as I am with respect to this very belief.

The CS thesis doesn't mention knowledge; it mentions wisdom. What is the relation between the two, and how does it matter to CS?

I suspect that virtually everyone will agree that wisdom is pretty awesome, epistemically. One important question is that of what that awesomeness involves: even though we agree that wisdom is epistemically awesome, in what particular epistemic respect(s) is it awesome?

In response to that question, I do not think it means that one has super-high amounts of overall evidence or justification for a certain important set of beliefs. Although wisdom is epistemically great, its greatness doesn't come from that particular epistemic feature. I'm not sure what the greatness is, but I suspect the kind of wisdom at issue with CS is something along the lines of *knowing how to best live your intellectual life*. This know-how is partly negative, in that it means avoiding certain epistemically bad things, such as wishful thinking and false beliefs that are functioning as important guides in your intellectual life. But it also means positive things, such as adjusting one's confidence in certain ideas based on the overall evidence one is aware of, *even complicated or unflattering evidence*. For instance, I have learned that my judgment is poor when it comes to things like buying insurance, buying a home, planning a complicated remodel of a bathroom, following directions, managing office politics, and so on. Part of being wise involves not ignoring relevant evidence like that, even when it is unpleasant to acknowledge.

The relation of wisdom to knowledge is beyond the topics of this book. However, it is worthwhile to see how certain ideas about knowledge, if correct, suggest that being unwise when it comes to controversy might be consistent with having knowledge of controversial claims. Let me try to explain this odd idea.

In this book, we have not tried to defend a theory of the form "A person *S* knows a claim *C* just in case ____", in which we fill in the blank with something informative. Some philosophers used to think we could fill in the blank with "*S* has a justified true belief *C*", but we saw in the opening chapter that there are plausible reasons to think that's incorrect. So, what goes in the blank, really?

I have no good answer, but for the sake of argument, suppose that what goes in the blank, in order to generate a true theory of knowledge, is something that, roughly put, *heavily* emphasizes true belief. On this theory, having a true belief is about 95% of what is takes to have knowledge, if that makes sense. In response, some people are going to say, "Hang on. What about all the business about justification, ruling out alternatives, believing for the right reasons, and so on – the stuff we have been discussing in this book? Isn't it all super important, too?" Pfft. Just not that important, according to this truth-heavy theory of knowledge, as all that stuff makes up just 5% of what knowledge is.

We looked at such a theory earlier in the chapter: S knows C = S has a true belief in C and S arrived at and maintains that belief in a non-stupid way. According to this theory, there are three conditions on knowledge – belief, truth, and avoiding stupidity – and the fact that it's usually very easy for most of us to meet the third condition makes the theory truth-heavy.

Pretend for a moment that a theory along these lines is true. Pretend further that Fred thinks C, that second-trimester abortion is immoral; C is true; and Fred is aware that C is controversial in the sense described in my previous chapter.

(a) He knows that there is a large group of people, *each* of whom is generally very smart and has investigated C for a long time, quite thoroughly. (Of course, there are people who have opinions on C who aren't at all smart or who haven't put much thought into B. We aren't considering them here.)

(b) As far as he knows, these people have not collectively come to any significant agreement on C. He knows that a significant percentage think it's true, another significant percentage think it's false, and yet a third group of people hasn't made up their minds. But as far as he knows, it's not as though one group is three times as large as the other groups combined, for instance.

On a truth-heavy theory of knowledge, his awareness of the controversial nature of C might not be enough to ruin his belief's chance to amount to knowledge – *even though he is being unwise in having this belief*. Perhaps the fact that he retains C even when made aware of its controversial status is an epistemic blemish, so to speak, but it's not enough of an epistemic sin to make the belief no longer count as knowledge. Retaining C in the face of controversy is not epistemically wise, but it's not exactly *stupid*. If this truth-heavy idea is correct, then CS is true, but the ordinary person who is lucky enough to have true controversial beliefs actually *knows* they are true even though he or she is unwise in having them.

I don't know if knowledge is truth-heavy (and, of course, I haven't offered any good definition of it anyway). But I'm pretty sure that wisdom requires a great deal more than mere true belief arrived at and maintained in a non-stupid manner. I suspect that part of the reason why people find CS attractive is that they realize that being wise is not easy.

5 Controversy Skepticism and the Phenomenology of Confident Belief

I once had a girlfriend who insisted I was a degenerate criminal who was easily capable of – and maybe even planning – rape and murder. I disagreed. I would guess that her psychotherapists and psychiatrists would agree with me on this particular issue.

This section isn't about my love life. The germane thing about my (former, as you expected) girlfriend is that it seemed so *utterly clear* in her mind that she was right. Her conclusions about me were *inescapable*, according to her. The possibility that she was truly mistaken was merely academic as far as she was concerned. The reason I bring this up is that, surprisingly enough, something quite similar applies to most of the rest of us, even those of us who were not, like my *former* girlfriend, hospitalized multiple times for psychiatric evaluation and treatment.

Suppose you consider a particular issue that generates lots of controversy. View V, which is pertinent to this issue, strikes you as correct. In fact, it's much more than that. View V seems almost luminous in your mind. V just seems exactly right. It "fits" the issue so well! There is a real phenomenological, intellectual experience here when one considers a view, and it vividly strikes one as just completely right. I don't think I can put it into words, but perhaps I don't need to, since many readers have experienced it on occasion when it comes to issues in politics, morality, religion, and philosophy. It might take years for this experience to occur, but it could happen in a relatively short time as well.

The phenomenology doesn't stop there. You consider two or maybe three arguments for V. Again, they seem exactly right. The premises strike you – phenomenologically – as unquestionable for anyone who is thinking about it clearly, and any fool (within limits) can see that if the premises are true, then V is true, too. The arguments feel conclusive to your mind. It's not as though you think they are conclusive because all the authorities say so. It's not even that the weight of pro and con arguments is merely in your favor. It's more than that. You can just intellectually *see* that they prove their conclusion. Perhaps, although this is optional, the premises appear to capture, in some sense, the "real reasons" for V.

The third part of the phenomenology concerns your evaluation of the criticisms of V. As before, there is an intellectual experience here that I take it many of us have had. You look at the criticisms and can just *see* that they are weak. You can just see, in your mind's eye, the failure of these criticisms. This first criticism is *obviously* defeated by X; this other one doesn't even target V, for goodness sakes; a third is *clearly* question-begging. It's *so clear* in your mind.

In sum, there are the three pieces in the phenomenology of "seeing that V is true". The phenomenology isn't as extreme as "just seeing" that twice two is four or that you are currently awake. In these cases, you don't have arguments that you are relying on, both pro and con; but in the cases I am describing, your experiences of the arguments are crucial. After having all three parts of the phenomenology, it may strike you as almost ridiculous to think that V is actually false. It's just not in the cards, you think, given the strength of the intellectual experiences you have had. Indeed, it seems almost insulting to focus on the three experiences instead of the three alleged *objective facts* that V is true, its supporting arguments are sound, and the criticisms are fatally flawed. It's almost like my (former, remember) girlfriend with her judgment that I am on the brink of rape and murder.

And yet often enough, although not always, all this phenomenology occurs with just as much vivacity in other people, *ones who are experiencing it with respect to not-*V. That is, all that luminous intellectual experience in favor of V is had by others in favor of not-V (i.e., the view that V is false, not true). This is a *psychological* fact about the diversity of intellectual experience when it comes to controversial issues in politics, religion, morality, philosophy, and some other fields.

Two good examples are the beliefs "Second-trimester abortion is morally wrong" and "Second-trimester abortion is not morally wrong." Both beliefs are controversial even among people who have investigated them with real intellectual expertise and diligence. And for a great many people, one of these two beliefs is intellectually luminous in the three-part sense just described. Even the example I gave in my previous chapter, with my two physics professors disagreeing about the promise of "string theories", had the two participants having the three-part phenomenology – and in this case, the controversy came within science.

The people having that phenomenological experience with respect to not-V are often just as or even smarter or more experienced than you are and in the area(s) relevant to evaluating V. You can't deny that many of the people on the phenomenological not-V side are often not your intellectual inferiors but are your peers or even superiors, in the sense of being smarter or more relevantly experienced than you are when it comes to the issues involved in assessing V.

This symmetry of intellectual phenomenology – it occurs for both V and not-V – doesn't hold for *every* controversial view. Just because there are many people who disbelieve your view V, it might be the case that only a small percentage of them have the three-part phenomenology described earlier. But my experience in intellectual circles in physics and philosophy strongly suggests that it happens for a great many controversial views. I am certain that it happens in philosophy constantly, even among the best philosophers. The key, and intellectually troublesome, facts are these:

- It's highly probable that for a significant portion of your controversial beliefs that you have the three-part phenomenology for, there are many other people, just as or even smarter or relevantly experienced than you are, who have comparably vivid intellectual phenomenology for the negation of your view.
- There is little or no reason to think the numbers are on your side. For instance, it's not the case that 87% of people have the phenomenology for your view, only 3% have it for your view's negation, and 10% have neither phenomenology. Neither is it the case that the vast majority of the *super*-experts regarding the relevant issues agree with your belief, regardless of how one fills out "super-expert".

This is the situation of phenomenologically luminous controversial disagreement.

When personally confronted with the fact of phenomenologically luminous controversial disagreement among fully competent people, I think that many of us start out in *retreat*: the first thing we do is look back at our view V plus its supporting evidence, we experience the phenomenology again, at least in part, and think quietly to ourselves, "At the end of the day, V isn't wrong. They [my opponents] aren't seeing it right. They are making some mistake, or missing something. . . . Yeah, that's right."

But the inescapable fact is that *all that phenomenology is often happening for false views*, even among smart and experienced people. If I have the phenomenology for V and you have it for not-V, well, then this proves that that wonderful phenomenology is at least sometimes directed toward a false belief. Of course, on many occasions, one person says, "V is true", another one says "V is not true", and there is no conflict because of an equivocation of some subtle kind: we aren't really disagreeing at all. But there is little reason to think that that always or even mostly holds in cases of luminous phenomenological controversial disagreement.

Here is a vital question: how often does the luminous phenomenology latch onto a false view? 15% of the time? 50%? 85%? The mere fact that we know that *on occasion*, the phenomenology leads us to endorse a false belief should not make us stop relying on it. After all, even vision sometimes leads us astray, but it's not good advice to not rely on vision. So, if you think the luminous phenomenology gets things wrong only rarely, then you can keep relying on it, but if you think it gets things wrong often, then even though "often" is pretty vague, you shouldn't rely on it, at least to any significant degree.

For what it's worth, even though I have no data at hand, as I said earlier, my experience suggests that the luminous intellectual phenomenology gets things wrong often. I have lived for extended periods of time in five countries, and I have been emotionally and intellectually close to people from many countries, cultures, religions, economic classes, sexualities, and philosophical temperaments. In a great many cases, these people had the luminous phenomenology, at least approximately, and they had it for views that were straightforwardly inconsistent with one another. Again, this happens with respect to views in religion, politics, morality, philosophy, and even science. I think it often occurs for each of the topics in the list I gave earlier regarding areas in which there is significant controversy.

> Civil rights, censorship, free speech, abortion, capital punishment, affirmative action, the future impact of climate change, the future impact of the loss of biodiversity, the distribution of health care resources, the extent of racism, fascism, and misogyny, religious freedom, the proper extent of governmental

welfare, labor unions, the Electoral College in the USA, vaccine mandates, gun control, and foreign aid.

So . . . what are we supposed to *do* with this knowledge (or "knowledge") that luminous intellectual phenomenology gets things wrong many, many times? How should it make a difference in our lives?

For my own part, it has helped make me much less confident in my opinions. Even when I am strongly inclined to believe some clearly controversial claim, and this inclination is strong because I have the luminous intellectual phenomenology for it *after* I have assessed arguments pro and con, I am cautious in the sense that I do not accept controversial ideas with confidence. My degree of belief is typically quite low even when I have the luminous phenomenology. It can be difficult, when immersed in awareness of your own reasons for V, to vividly imagine that someone just as sharp and informed as you are has the phenomenology for not-V. But these people exist, and the experiences of the two of you guarantee that someone's phenomenology is profoundly misleading.

If you don't mind me saying so, I think that for most controversial claims that I am tempted to endorse, I'm a lot sharper than the vast majority of people who reject these claims. It's not that I think I was born a genius or have a super-high IQ or anything like that. Instead, it's because I have spent over 40 years studying mathematics, physics, philosophy, and logic – most of it fairly advanced. As you would expect, decades of intense study typically have fruitful intellectual consequences. But even armed with this significant advantage, I should not fool myself with flattering ideas such as "Well, even though lots of people disagree with me and even have the luminous intellectual phenomenology, I'm a lot more knowledgeable than they are when it comes to this issue." This idea is true, for me, but I also know full well that many of the people with belief inclinations the opposite of mine are comparably intelligent and informed and have the luminous phenomenology for the negation of my controversial views. Bluntly put, we should not focus on our disagreements with morons; we should instead focus on people who are our peers or superiors when it comes to the issues relevant to the disagreement.

When you are caught up in the phenomenological feeling that, for instance, second-trimester abortion is (im)moral, it can be difficult to remember that people just as smart and informed as you are have the luminous phenomenology for the negation of your view. It can seem outrageous: "There is NO WAY they could have that view and *really* appreciate the arguments against it!", one wants to say. Well, in a great many cases, they can, and they do. And when they don't? Well, why on earth would you think that you "really appreciate" the arguments against your view, when you just insisted that they failed to "really appreciate" the arguments for your view?

Summary

Every time I present an argument roughly along the lines of the argument for CS, people nod their heads but then explain why it doesn't apply to their controversial beliefs B1, B2, B3, or B4. That's convenient, isn't it? It's a bit like saying that *of course*, we should give money to the poor, or do something else noble, but you see, this requirement doesn't actually apply to me because of such and such. Uh huh, sure.

I remember years ago when I was married. I was having a disagreement with my wife about something practical, such as dealing with a bathroom remodel. I said X, she said not-X. We stated our reasons, as thoroughly and clearly as possible. She has graduate degrees in both philosophy and science, just like I do, so she can argue as clearly and thoroughly as I can. After exchanging arguments, it still seemed to me that I was right, and she was wrong. It seemed really clear to me.

But I remembered the brute fact that on issues like this, she is right much more often than I am. Her track record beats mine by a mile. It isn't even close.

So, I was faced with opposing thoughts: (i) I am definitely right that X is true yet (ii) she says not-X, and she is definitely better than I am at judging things like X. It would have been easy for me to defend my belief in X by saying something that starts with "Yes, but you see…". I didn't do it, and a couple weeks later, it turned out, again, that she was right, and I was wrong.

Similarly, even when it seems to you to be utterly clear that you're right and others are wrong, you need to set aside that "seeming" and consider things like track records.

Chapter 6

It Ends Here
Response to Frances' Reply

Michael Huemer

Contents

1 Debate and Consensus in Philosophy	178
2 Is "Know" Context-Sensitive?	180
3 A Moderate Conception of Knowledge	183
4 Understanding Strong Disagreements	184
4.1 The Need for Philosophical Education	184
4.2 Emotion and Ideology	186
4.3 Responding Rationally to Disagreement	190

I Debate and Consensus in Philosophy

I want to thank Bryan Frances for another stimulating discussion. I am also happy to announce that I have the answer to the titular question of his last chapter: The debate ends here, with this essay. Sadly, though, this won't be because we will have said all there is to say on the subject but rather because we will have reached our target length for this volume.

I did not entirely agree with Frances' portrayal of the history of philosophical debate (see Chapter 5, section 1). Frances is right to note the frequency of disagreement among philosophers throughout history. Where I think he erred was in suggesting that philosophers frequently give arguments that, at least at the time, seem compelling enough to generate a consensus on the issue they concern. Frances goes on to recount how this consensus is usually overturned and replaced with a new consensus in a subsequent generation, and another one after that, and so on. But as I read the history, philosophers rarely develop a consensus on an issue

DOI: 10.4324/9781003434931-9

in the first place,[1] and when they do, it has more to do with the prevailing zeitgeist than with any rational arguments.

I can name at least a few non-trivial philosophical views that attained a consensus in Western philosophy at one time or another. During the Middle Ages, philosophers agreed on the truth of Christianity. During the 19th century, if you can believe it, philosophers mostly agreed on idealism (as mentioned in Chapter 2, section 2.7). In the early to mid-20th century, there was a fair consensus on logical positivism. All of these views are now minority positions, indeed (with the possible exception of Christianity), *very small* minority positions. However, I think this is relatively rare – on most philosophical issues that we talk about, there was never a consensus. And even for the issues mentioned, I very much doubt that philosophers adopted these views primarily as the result of seemingly compelling arguments.

And yet, having said this, I am happy to report that, as it seems to me, there *has* been a pretty good consensus on the main topic of this book, external-world skepticism, over the course of the history of philosophy. Although there have been a few important skeptics here and there, the overwhelming majority of philosophers have always rejected skepticism. This has been a very lasting consensus; to this day, the great majority of epistemologists treat their task as one of explaining what is wrong with skepticism rather than one of figuring out whether skepticism is correct.

At least, that is how it appears to me. Admittedly, I do not have survey data on philosophers' views before very recent times. There is, however, a recent survey indicating that among contemporary philosophers, just 1.9% accept skepticism about the external world, with another 3.5% "leaning toward" it. This is a lot less than would be the case for the vast majority of philosophical views that one might see debated.[2] Even Bryan Frances doesn't seem particularly convinced of external-world skepticism, though he is among the most skeptic-friendly philosophers writing today. He seems more interested in the (much more plausible and less unpopular) doctrine of controversy skepticism. This reflects the sheer difficulty of finding someone to defend the "pro" side in a debate on external-world skepticism.

---

1. Or maybe it's just that we rarely *talk* about the issues on which we have consensus?
2. PhilPapers 2020.

I think this is pretty good second-order evidence that skepticism is false. Philosophers, after all, are the experts on this subject, if anyone is. Furthermore, they hardly come to agreements lightly – they are famous for disagreeing with each other and for exploring a wide variety of possible views. So if even philosophers, as cantankerous and intellectually neurotic as they are, mostly agree that skepticism is false, it is probably really false.

You might now be wondering why we created a book dedicated to debating skepticism and why it wasn't a waste of your time to read this far, if it is such a fringe view. I suppose the main reasons for creating the volume are that students are often tempted by skepticism and that going through arguments on this issue can teach you a lot about knowledge.

Summary

Philosophers rarely form a consensus on a philosophical issue, but surprisingly (*pace* Frances), there is a pretty good consensus on the denial of external-world skepticism. This is probably because skepticism is false.

2 Is "Know" Context-Sensitive?

Let's turn to an explanation for how ordinary people and philosophical skeptics could both be correct in their claims about "knowledge": maybe the meaning of "know" varies from one linguistic context to another, the skeptics are (correctly) using "know" in a very demanding sense, and ordinary people are (also correctly) using "know" in a much more permissive sense (see Chapter 5, section 3). This *contextualist* view might well be true; there are some pretty reasonable arguments for it. So perhaps, in certain philosophical discussions, to "know" P requires conclusively ruling out every logically possible alternative to P, yet in most ordinary life contexts, "knowing" P only requires having strong but fallible reasons (of the sort we often have) for P. (Or perhaps, per Frances' suggestion, "knowing" might require only having a non-stupid true belief.)

This, however, is generally *not* considered a skeptic-friendly diagnosis of the debate, and Frances acknowledges that most self-described skeptics would not be happy with it. As skepticism is usually understood, it holds that we lack knowledge of the external world in the sense of the word that correctly applies in normal contexts, not merely in some specially super-demanding sense of "know" that applies in philosophical contexts.

Be that as it may, I will now tell you my favorite argument against contextualism. Let's start with an analogy that helps to explain the contextualist view and its implications. Consider how we use the word "here": it typically refers to the place one is at the time one uses the word. Thus, as everyone knows, its reference shifts from one occasion of use to another.

So suppose we're outside in the summer, where it is 98°F, and I say, "Wow, it sure is hot here". Then we enter an air-conditioned building, where the temperature is 72°F, whereupon I exclaim, "Whew, I'm glad it's nice and cool *here*". You chide me for my "inconsistency": "Mike, first you said it was hot here; now you say it's cool here. Make up your mind! Is here hot or cool?" I reply:

> I stand by both of my assertions. It is cool here. This does not contradict my earlier statement, because when I said, "It sure is hot here", I of course did not mean that it was hot *here*.

Notice that all of this sounds perfectly fine, and any normal English speaker could understand my point. This makes sense given that "here" has shifted its reference: in my original statement, "It sure is hot here", "here" referred to the location outside the building, whereas the "here" at the end of my last sentence refers to the location inside the building. So I'm simply making the point that when I said it was hot [outside], I didn't mean that it was hot [inside the building].

Now suppose that the reference of "know" also sometimes shifts from one occasion of its use to another. Suppose, say, that mentioning the brain-in-a-vat (BIV) scenario has the effect of raising the standards for "knowing" such that one then has to rule out the BIV scenario in order to count as "knowing" anything about the external world. In this case, we should be able to imagine a dialogue analogous to the earlier dialogue involving the word "here" but using "know". Here's an attempt at this: imagine that we're in the supermarket, picking up some food for the upcoming philosophy department party, whereupon we have the following dialogue:

You: Hey Mike, do you know where the salsa is?
Me: Yes, I know where it is. It's in aisle 6.
You: How do you know you're not a BIV?
Me: You got me there. I guess I don't. So I *don't* know where the salsa is.
You: First you said you knew where the salsa was; now you say you don't know. Make up your mind! Do you know or not?
Me: I stand by both of my assertions. I don't know where the salsa is. This does not contradict my earlier statement because when I said, "I know where it is", I of course did not mean that I *knew* where it was.

Notice how the end of this dialogue perfectly parallels the earlier dialogue about "here". But this time, my last line sounds bizarre. This time, *I'm* the one who comes off as having some weird misunderstanding of English.

This suggests that the word "know" does not shift its meaning in the way hypothesized. You can also adjust the scenario to take account of other things that might be thought to change the standards for "knowing". The last line continues to come off as bizarre, whatever shift in conversational context you imagine.

I find the preceding argument half convincing. But despite the argument, it still seems as though "know" is used in stricter or looser senses in different conversations, as contextualists have pointed out. Perhaps what is going on in the earlier dialogue is that, by raising the BIV scenario, you signal that you meant "know" in a very strict sense to begin with, and you want the whole conversation (including the earlier part) to be interpreted using this strict sense. I, being cooperative, should normally accept this, whereupon I would have to concede that my earlier statement, "I know where it is", was false. Alternately, I might explicitly address the two senses, making the dialogue end as follows:

You: First you said you knew where the salsa was; now you say you don't know. Make up your mind! Do you know or not?
Me: I know in the ordinary sense, but I don't know in your sense of the word.

This sounds fine to me and is perhaps what we should say to skeptics in general.

I would add that what I here call the "ordinary sense" of the word strikes me as obviously more useful and interesting than the skeptic's sense of the word. The skeptic insists that "know" refers to something that never or almost never occurs. But why would we need a word for something that never happens? The dialogue about the salsa illustrates that what I call the ordinary sense of "knowing" is the sense most relevant in almost any context other than a philosophy seminar room. When someone asks if you know where something is, if you know what time it is, if you know someone's name, and so on, surely the relevant information to provide is almost always going to be whether you know in my sense, not whether you know in the skeptic's sense. Language exists to help us convey worthwhile information, so "know" should be interpreted in a way that enables it to do that.

Summary

If the meaning of "know" is inherently context-sensitive, then, after a context shift has occurred, you should be able to appropriately say that earlier uses of "know" did not refer to *knowing*. But this seems untrue.

Be that as it may, it often seems that skeptics are using "know" in a much stricter sense than people use it in ordinary life. The ordinary usage is much more relevant and useful, so I commend it to readers.

3 A Moderate Conception of Knowledge

Frances introduces the notion of a "truth-heavy" conception of knowledge, on which knowing is mostly about having correct beliefs. More is required for knowing than true belief (as all epistemologists agree), but perhaps that more is stuff that is very easy to do and hence not very important or interesting. That could help to explain how someone might *know*, say, that abortion is wrong, despite the existence of expert disagreement on the subject. Frances does not either affirm or deny that knowledge is truth-heavy in this sense, but since he raised the possibility, I will comment on it briefly.

I take a *moderately* demanding view of knowledge. It seems to me that no one knows whether abortion (say, in the second trimester, with no special circumstances) is ethically wrong. Some people have reasonable beliefs about this, but only dogmatic people would claim to *know*, given the persistent disagreement among ethical experts and the reasonable arguments that exist on both sides of the issue. It just doesn't sound right to me that I can know something to be true when there are multiple conflicting views that take into account the same evidence and are about equally reasonable. So I would deny that to know something, it's enough to be correct and non-stupid. One needs some pretty strong justification.

At the same time, it seems to me that many people know what continent Canada is on. There are *some* grounds for doubt about Canada's being in North America, but they are a lot wilder than the grounds for doubt about the morality of abortion. (They are things like "Maybe all of life is a dream, and the Earth doesn't exist" or "Maybe we are living in the Matrix".) So I deny that to know something, one must have some amazingly strong justification for it.

Dogmatists take an overly permissive view of knowledge, while skeptics take a ridiculously demanding view of it. The moderate view best matches our intuitions, the way the word is used, and the goal of communicating useful information with our "knowledge" discourse.

> **Summary**
>
> Knowledge is moderately demanding, not super-demanding nor super-easy to attain.

4 Understanding Strong Disagreements

4.1 The Need for Philosophical Education

Let us now turn to Frances' main topic of interest, the epistemology of disagreement. Frances discusses a particularly troubling type of disagreement, one wherein each party possesses a "luminous phenomenology" in which they seem to very clearly see that their view is correct, that the arguments for it are decisive, and that the arguments for the other side are terrible. Call this a "luminous disagreement". Frances wants us to consider how each party ought to react when such a disagreement occurs – presumably by greatly reducing their credence in their own initial view despite their luminous phenomenology. I think we should first wonder: how are such cases possible in the first place? Perhaps if we understood this, we would have a better handle on how to resolve such disagreements.

I think that *most* such cases occur when one or more parties to the dispute are inexperienced, ill-informed, or unintelligent. For instance, in my years of teaching, I have sometimes had students say that some famous philosopher's view that I tried to teach them about is obviously ridiculous. In most cases, if the student then explains why they say this, it will turn out that the student has completely misunderstood the issue and ascribed to the philosopher some simpleminded error that in fact no philosopher would be stupid enough to entertain for a second. In other cases, a person finds some philosophical view "absurd" without having listened to (and in some cases having pointedly refused to listen to) the arguments for it. This is often the case for such views as anarchism or ethical veganism, for example.[3] Claiming to have the "luminous" intellectual phenomenology with respect to a controversial philosophical issue is more common among people who lack philosophical training or are new to philosophy. This suggests that the remedy for most luminous disagreements is for the parties to more fully familiarize themselves with the arguments surrounding the issue and perhaps also to acquire several more years of philosophical training.

It is not impossible for a luminous disagreement to persist after these steps are taken. But I believe such cases are rare. I do not believe the abortion issue qualifies, for instance. To be sure, unsophisticated partisans often express very strong confidence in their opinions regarding the morality of abortion, and sometimes they express their utter confidence in one or more arguments for that view (which, by the way, typically turn out to be pretty lame arguments, much worse than those given by professional philosophers). But I don't believe I know any actual ethicists who talk this way. It appears to me that professional ethicists who have studied the abortion issue generally recognize that the issue is complex and that there are rational arguments on both sides. I would be very surprised, for instance, if I heard a professional philosopher say that either Don Marquis' argument against abortion or Judith Thompson's defense of abortion was obviously stupid. Maybe you could

---

3. On these, see my 2013 and 2019 books.

find *some* philosophers who would say such things, but I think we could plausibly view them as outliers with excessive levels of dogmatism or some other cognitive flaw.

4.2 Emotion and Ideology

As I've indicated, ignorance and inexperience are often the causes of overconfidence, and philosophical training tends to alleviate these problems, at least with respect to philosophical issues. Yet even experienced philosophers are sometimes highly overconfident about certain kinds of issues. One reason for this is that even highly trained scholars can be caught up in an *ideology*.[4] An ideology is a sort of secular substitute for religion – a belief system that gives people a sense of identity and meaning and a way of interpreting the world around them, especially the social world. Ideologies serve as tools of social bonding, such that our natural instincts for ingroup loyalty get attached to the group of people who share the ideology, and our natural suspicion of outgroups gets attached to those who question or deny the ideology. It is psychologically difficult for partisans to take criticisms of their ideology seriously because to do so feels disloyal.

In our present society, particularly in the academic world, the most common ideology is one that revolves around the (alleged) prevalence and awfulness of racism, sexism, and similar forms of prejudice and "oppression" in our society. Attachment to this ideology can lead people to embrace highly overconfident opinions on those subjects. To take one famous example, in 2005, economist Larry Summers, then president of Harvard University, made some controversial remarks on the subject of the underrepresentation of women in the sciences at leading research universities.[5] Summers noted that the distribution of intellectual ability differs between males and females, with the male distribution having a larger *variance* than the female distribution. (He did not claim that the male *average* was higher.) In other words, men are more likely to have either very high or very low ability, whereas women are more likely

---

4. Indeed, they may be *more* likely than ordinary people to be captured by an ideology. Drummond and Fischhoff (2017) find that education *increases* polarization for politically charged issues related to science but not for ideologically neutral issues.
5. For Summers' remarks, see PBS NewsHour 2005. For discussion, see Hemel 205; Cook 2013.

to be closer to the average. As a result, if a particular job requires people at the high end of the spectrum, there will tend to be more males than females who qualify. The higher the requirements (that is, the further from the mean one has to be to qualify for the job in question), the greater will be the disproportion between males and females who pass that bar. Summers advanced this as a possible partial explanation for the underrepresentation of women in the sciences at elite universities.

In case you're wondering, Summers' basic factual premise is well-documented in psychology; per most studies, IQ (along with a number of other traits) shows a higher variance among males than among females.[6] Summers' mathematical reasoning from this premise is also correct as a matter of statistical fact – that is, the higher male variance implies that the ratio of males to females who can be found at a given distance from the mean increases as this distance increases.

Summers was nevertheless met with howls of outrage at his blatant "sexism", leading to his resignation as president of Harvard. If questioned, no doubt some of his critics would claim to have the "luminous phenomenology" that Frances describes – they would report seeing very clearly that Summers' idea was sexist (and therefore wrong), that the arguments for this conclusion were decisive, and that the defenses of Summers were ridiculous. On the other hand, Summers had defenders who could clearly see that it was the critics who were wrong.

I assume that this is the sort of example Frances has in mind. But in this case, I don't think it is particularly mysterious what was going on. Summers' critics had fallen prey to the ideology I alluded to earlier, sometimes called "woke" or "social justice warrior" ideology. In this ideology, it is taken as dogma that all achievement gaps between demographic groups are due to racism, sexism, or other prejudice, and nothing else. So individuals who are emotionally attached to the ideology simply would not be able to listen to Summers' hypothesis dispassionately and evaluate it on its merits.

Ideologues are often to some degree aware of this dynamic in their own minds; hence, rather than criticizing the evidence on scientific grounds, they might simply say that they find it immoral or offensive to entertain the sort of idea that Summers advanced,

---

6. Hedges and Nowell 1995; Machin and Pekkarinen 2008.

which I take to be fairly close to an admission that their rejection of the idea stems from non-epistemic motives.

In other cases, ideologues will claim to be thinking scientifically; for example, they will say that Summers is doing bad science. And perhaps they will believe it. But I don't think this fact poses a particular intellectual problem for the rest of us; I think the rest of us can nevertheless reasonably suppose that the ideologues are basing their beliefs on their emotional commitment to their chosen political ideology and that their putatively scientific arguments function as rationalizations. This is the reasonable hypothesis given all we know about ideologies and their followers. What seems to happen when committed ideologues (or religious partisans) consider alternative views is that they feel an immediate, strong *aversion* to those views. It feels to them as though those views simply must be rejected. Most human beings, however, have imperfect and often self-serving introspection; thus, they fail to recognize that the source of their aversion is their emotional attachment to their ideology. They instead ascribe the aversion to the intrinsic, intellectual repulsiveness of the views being considered, whereupon they declare these views "ridiculous" or "obviously wrong".

When evaluating arguments, the ideologue's mind automatically, without the need for conscious effort or even awareness of the process, jumps to the most charitable interpretations of arguments for the ideology and the most uncharitable interpretations of opposing arguments. If there is more than one way of looking at anything (as there very often is), the way that is most friendly to one's own ideology will naturally thrust itself forward in one's mind.

As an example of this last phenomenon, consider the question of U.S. foreign policy vis-à-vis Russia. Since shortly after World War II, America and Russia have had an adversarial relationship, continuing even after the collapse of the Soviet Union. Now, one can easily see two perspectives on U.S.–Russia relations. One point of view is that the Russian government has been and is pursuing goals that are antithetical to American values and to the wellbeing of the world in general, and *therefore the U.S. government must stand up to the Russians*, demonstrate our strength, and clearly communicate the willingness to counter Russian aggression. Only then will the Russians back down.

The other point of view is that since Russia and the USA both possess thousands of nuclear warheads, it is of the utmost importance for the two nations to maintain peace, and *therefore the U.S. government must avoid antagonizing the Russians.*

These two points of view are approximately the opposite of one another. Notice, however, that both *make sense*. If you make an effort, you can probably *see* either point of view; when looked at in a certain way, each point of view seems obvious. But given the complexity of international affairs and the unpredictability of the future, there is no way of *proving* which approach is better. We can't prepare 1,000 Earths in the same initial state, try a hardline approach in 500 of them and a conciliatory approach in the other 500, and then observe the results. So the choice of approach remains a matter for speculative judgment.

All of which helps to explain the possibility of *shifting* one's take on the issue. For decades in the USA (I remember this from my childhood on), the Republicans were the party of anti-Russia hardliners, while the Democrats tended to support the more conciliatory view. All this began to shift when, in the 2016 U.S. Presidential campaign season, the Russian government supported the Republican nominee for President over the Democratic nominee, to the point of running deceptive social media campaigns designed to influence the election outcome.[7] Suddenly, Republicans (not least of all the Republican Presidential candidate) started to see the merits of developing friendly relations with Russia, while Democrats started to appreciate the importance of taking a strong stance against the Russians. This illustrates the point that when there is an issue that can rationally be seen in either of two (or more) ways, partisans will automatically view things in the way that most benefits their group. Sometimes their way of seeing things shifts on a dime, like the sort of gestalt shift one can have when viewing a Necker cube.

Now suppose there are a dozen different issues of that kind that each bear evidentially on your ideology. In each case, you adopt the view most favorable to your ideology. It will now appear that the cumulative case for your ideology is overwhelming, since consideration of *each* of the dozen different issues seems to you to point in the same direction. Opponents of your ideology must be extraordinarily blinkered to have gotten things wrong on all these different issues. What you don't notice (again, human introspection is often unreliable and self-serving) is that you perceive each of these issues

---

7. Walcott 2016. It remains unclear how much actual effect the Russian efforts had.

in the way you do *because* this way of perceiving them fits with your ideology.

4.3 Responding Rationally to Disagreement

All of this is meant as an explanation for how, with regard to ideologically charged issues, it can come about that intelligent and well-educated people form highly confident beliefs in contrary propositions. If what I have said is roughly correct, how ought we to react to the existence of such disagreements?

One answer, which I take to be roughly Bryan Frances' answer, is that we should withhold judgment about the issues on which such disagreement exists. And I certainly agree (as noted in Chapter 4, section 5) that many people ought to greatly reduce their confidence in their controversial political beliefs. However, this is painting with a pretty broad brush, and I believe we can give better, more finely tuned advice than this. Once we recognize the role that ideology plays in disagreements, we can take specific steps to counteract the ways in which ideology leads us astray.

For example, we can try to reduce our reliance on speculative and subjective judgments, knowing that these are more easily influenced by personal biases, and instead rely more on objective (e.g., statistical and other scientific) evidence. We can try to avoid anecdotal arguments, since these are more subject to bias in the form of cherry-picking. We can make a special effort to listen sympathetically to alternative viewpoints, to gather evidence from a variety of sources, and to avoid arguing for ideologically controversial points by appealing to other ideologically controversial points. Scrupulous efforts along these lines can result in our having much more justified beliefs.[8]

I would add – and perhaps here Frances might disagree with me – that we need not always significantly reduce our credence in a belief upon encountering controversy, even "luminous" disagreement. When there is a strong disagreement, both sides are not always equally biased; sometimes one side is much more ideologically biased than the other, and in some cases, as I believe, one can know pretty clearly which side that is. Take the Larry Summers controversy mentioned earlier. In that case, it is pretty clear which

---

8. For more on how to reason better, see my 2021, chapters 3–4; 2022, chapters 17–19.

side had an emotional horse in the race. Larry Summers had no particular emotional stake in his explanation; he would doubtless have been happy to find that the underrepresentation of women in the sciences was due to some other cause that could more easily be remedied. It was the woke ideologues who were deeply upset about Summers' hypothesis; it was they who felt their ideology being fundamentally challenged. The fact that they might deny that this was the case does not prevent the rest of us from perceiving it; hence, it does not force the rest of us, those who are not deeply emotionally invested in the issue, to give equal weight to the obviously emotionally charged opinions of the ideologues.

This case illustrates one important criterion for deciding whether you are subject to undue bias with regard to a given issue: if you feel emotionally upset by hearing others' opinions, and especially if you feel anger or a desire to hurt those others, that is a good sign that you may not be in a position to evaluate the issue objectively. Unfortunately, people who are very biased often have no interest in detecting their own bias, so they are unlikely to apply this criterion. Nevertheless, those who are *not* very biased can often apply the criterion. If you are *not* emotionally attached to any particular hypothesis on a given question, you can often know that this is the case, and you can often at the same time know that many other people *are* very emotionally attached to a specific hypothesis. You can then rationally attach less weight to the judgments of those who have very strong biases.

There is, of course, a temptation to use this reasoning solely to discount *other people's* biased opinions. I stress, therefore, that it is imperative to apply the lesson *to oneself* as well, to carefully observe one's own feelings in the effort to detect sources of bias. With respect to many issues, both sides are biased. For instance, concerning abortion, both pro-life and pro-choice partisans are often emotionally invested in their positions. If you introspect carefully, you will probably notice that either strong anti-abortion or strong pro-abortion positions are upsetting to you – which is understandable, given what is at stake; nevertheless, however understandable, your emotional reactions constitute a source of bias. Thus, it would be irrational to discount only one side's judgments as biased.

But to return to my point about the conditions under which one may rationally maintain one's belief in the face of controversy, let's consider another example. Frances relates an anecdote about a former girlfriend who was utterly convinced that he (Frances) was a degenerate criminal easily capable of rape and murder. Apparently, this was completely clear in her mind. Frances, not surprisingly, disagreed. Now, given the girlfriend's very strong opinion, was Frances rationally required to revise his belief about himself? Should he have said, "Well, she seems pretty convinced of it; maybe I *am* on the verge of homicide after all"?

Surely not. Frances (I assume!) knew himself to be a normal, non-criminal person. So when he learned of his girlfriend's opinion, he could conclude that something had gone very wrong in her thinking. Her complete confidence in a completely off-the-wall idea was presumably an indication that she was unreliable at judging this particular issue. Without detailed knowledge of the case, I of course can't guess what went wrong, but it is not exactly unheard of for people to have unreliable judgments about their romantic partners.

I suggest that we can take a more general lesson from cases like this: the mere fact that someone holds a belief with very high confidence does not obligate you to treat it as a serious possibility, particularly if you have no evidence that they are reliable on the subject. There are many ways in which human cognition can go drastically wrong; some of these ways are visible from the outside, and outsiders who can see this have no obligation to treat disordered cognitions as serious evidence regarding the facts that they concern. Most ideological beliefs are less extreme errors than the belief about Frances' potential homicidal tendencies, but it remains the case that outside observers can often see the signs of well-known types of epistemic malfunctions. This is why reasonable people can often retain relatively confident beliefs in the face of very strong disagreement from others.

Summary

Strong disagreements are common in such areas as philosophy, politics, and religion. Many of these disagreements can be moderated through the parties' learning more about the arguments and receiving general philosophical training.

Many strong disagreements are also caused by emotional commitment to an ideology, which leads to biased judgment. We can counteract this problem by making an effort to avoid speculative, subjective, and anecdotal arguments; by listening to contrary views; by gathering information from varying sources; and by avoiding reliance on arguments from ideologically controversial premises.

Although we should very often withhold judgment about controversial issues, we need not always do so. In some cases, when we can see that one side of a dispute is much more ideologically and emotionally invested in the issue, it is reasonable to give less weight to that side's judgment.

Further Readings

Following are some sources that readers may wish to consult for further discussion of skepticism in epistemology. We start with some skeptical writings.

Skeptical Views

Sextus Empiricus, *Outlines of Pyrrhonism* (2nd century AD)

> A collection of arguments from the ancient skeptics, gathered together by the 2nd-century Greek skeptic Sextus Empiricus. Sextus argues for suspending judgment on all things.

David Hume, *Treatise of Human Nature* (1739)

> Hume was among the most important figures in the past 300 years of philosophy. He presents skeptical arguments regarding the external world, morality, inductive reasoning, and even deductive reasoning. *Note:* if this book is too long for you, try his *Enquiry Concerning Human Understanding*, which presents many of the same ideas in shorter form.

Peter Unger, *Ignorance: A Case for Scepticism* (1975)

> Contemporary philosopher Peter Unger argues that no one can know anything, given that knowledge requires absolute certainty. He goes on to deny that anyone even believes anything or that anything is true.

Keith Lehrer, "Why Not Skepticism?" (1971)

> Contemporary philosopher Keith Lehrer defends the brain-in-a-vat (BIV) style of argument for external-world skepticism.

Bryan Frances, *Scepticism Comes Alive* (2005)

> Frances advances a form of skepticism based upon "skeptical hypotheses" that, unlike the BIV hypothesis, are advanced as true by some experts and taken seriously in their respective fields. This skepticism implies that, for example, you don't know that the sky is blue or that people have beliefs, although you *can* still know such abstruse things as that black holes exist.

Bryan Frances, *Disagreement* (2014)

> Frances defends controversy skepticism, as discussed in Chapter 1, section 4.

Robert Nozick, *Philosophical Explanations* (1981)

> Nozick advances the tracking account of knowledge, as discussed in Chapter 2, section 2.5.

Non-skeptical Views

René Descartes, *Meditations on First Philosophy* (1641)

> The classic, 17th-century source of some arguments for external-world skepticism, such as the dream argument and the deceiving God argument. Descartes tries to answer skepticism, but most people find his replies less persuasive than his initial presentation of the skeptic's arguments.

Thomas Reid, *Inquiry and Essays* (1983)

> Reid defends a direct realist view of perception and criticizes Hume, Descartes, and Berkeley for erroneously assuming that the direct objects of our awareness are ideas in our own minds. This book combines parts of Reid's

two most important books, *An Inquiry into the Human Mind* (1764) and *Essays on the Intellectual Powers of Man* (1785).

Bertrand Russell, *The Problems of Philosophy* (1912)

This is a good introduction to philosophy, mostly through epistemology. Russell discusses skeptical problems and explains his account of how we know about the external world via inference to the best explanation. Also covers a priori knowledge, universals, induction, and other topics.

G.E. Moore, "Proof of an External World" (1939)

Moore proves the existence of external objects by holding up his hands and discusses whether this really counts as a "proof of an external world".

G.E. Moore, "Hume's Theory Examined" (1953)

This article contains a good example of the G.E. Moore Shift, as discussed in Chapter 2, section 2.2.

Michael Huemer, *Skepticism and the Veil of Perception* (2001)

This book defends direct realism in the theory of perception, including Phenomenal Conservatism, and it rebuts four major skeptical arguments.

Michael Huemer, "Serious Theories and Skeptical Theories: Why You Are Probably Not a Brain in a Vat" (2016)

This article argues that the BIV theory is a bad theory, as discussed in Chapter 2, section 2.8.

Michael Huemer, "Debunking Skepticism" (2020)

Huemer argues that we should discount philosophical arguments for moral skepticism since philosophers are unreliable and have a general bias toward skeptical theses.

Hilary Putnam, "Brains in a Vat" in *Reason, Truth and History* (1981)

Putnam argues that the BIV theory is self-undermining because, if we were BIVs, then we could not entertain the hypothesis that we were BIVs, as discussed in Chapter 2, section 2.3.

Entertainment

Finally, here is some popular entertainment with skeptical themes:

The Matrix movie (1999)

> Neo discovers that he's living in a skeptical scenario – robots have taken over the world and placed humans in pods wherein their brains are artificially stimulated with a simulation of life in the late 20th century. This is a classic movie with many sequels.

Star Trek: The Next Generation, S6:E21, "Frame of Mind" (1993)

> Commander Riker gets trapped in another skeptical scenario. Is he dreaming? Is he insane?

Star Trek: Voyager, S4:E4, "Nemesis" (1999)

> Chakotay helps an alien race fight a war. But maybe he doesn't fully understand what's going on.

Glossary

Bayes' theorem The theorem of probability that says $P(h|e) = P(h) \times P(e|h)/P(e)$ (read: the probability of h given e equals the probability of h times the probability of e given h, divided by the probability of e). Also sometimes given as $P(h|e) = P(h) \times P(e|h) / [P(h) \times P(e|h) + P(\sim h) \times P(e|\sim h)]$.

Bayesian reasoning Probabilistic reasoning in accordance with Bayes' theorem, especially reasoning that a theory is likely to be true because some known evidence would be more likely to occur if that theory were true than if it were false.

Begging the question The fallacy of giving an argument in which one or more premises *is* the conclusion, or presupposes the conclusion, or depends for its justification on the conclusion; circular reasoning.

BIV Acronym for "brain in a vat"; a brain that is being kept alive in a vat and artificially stimulated to produce a simulation of living in the real world.

Certainty skepticism The view that we know (at most) very little because almost none of our beliefs are absolutely certain.

Closure Principle for Justification The view that if one has justification for believing P and P entails Q, then one has justification for believing Q (or something like that).

Closure Principle for Knowledge The view that if one knows P and knows that P entails Q, then one can know Q (or something like that).

Contextualism *See* Partial Contextualism; Full Contextualism; Debate Contextualism.

Contingent Said of a proposition that could have been true and could have been false, that is, it is neither necessary nor impossible.

Controversy skepticism The view that, when one knows that many equally or more qualified people disagree with one's belief, it is unwise to retain one's belief.
Debate Contextualism The view that, due to the truth of Full Contextualism, assertions of skepticism are true in contexts in which BIV and similar scenarios are under discussion and being taken seriously, while assertions of realism are true in normal contexts in which BIV and similar scenarios are not under discussion and being taken seriously.
Direct knowledge Knowledge that is not based on any other knowledge.
Direct realism The view that perception gives us direct knowledge of the external world.
Epistemic Having to do with knowledge.
Epistemology The branch of philosophy that studies knowledge, the justification for beliefs, and related matters.
External world The world independent of one's mind.
External-world skepticism The view that no one knows any contingent truths about the external world due to the fact that our external world beliefs almost always have inadequate justification.
Externalism The view that the degree of justification that a belief has depends partly on factors outside the believer's mind. Hence, there could be two people with the same internal mental states but one of them might be justified in believing *P* while the other was not, due to some difference in their environment.
Foundational Said of a belief that is justified in a way that does not depend on its being supported by other justified beliefs.
Foundationalism The view that (a) some beliefs are justified in a way that does not depend on any other justified beliefs, and (b) all other justified beliefs depend upon the beliefs mentioned in (a).
Full Contextualism The view that Partial Contextualism is true *because* the standards for a belief to count as "knowledge" vary depending on the conversational context, that is, sometimes there are higher standards than at other times.
Idealism The view that there are no contingent external objects; there are only minds and "ideas" (mental states), and "physical objects" exist only as ideas in our minds.
Indirect knowledge Knowledge that is based on some other knowledge.

Indirect realism The view that perception gives us direct knowledge only of something in our own minds, which enables us to acquire *indirect* knowledge of the external world.

Intentionality The property of representing something, being "of" or "about" something.

Internalism The view that the degree of justification that a belief has depends solely on factors internal to the believer's mind; the denial of externalism.

Justification skepticism The view that we know (at most) very little because almost none of our beliefs are justified.

Justified Said of a belief that is sufficiently likely to be true that it is rational to hold.

Necessary Said of a proposition that could not have been false, that is, its negation is impossible.

Partial Contextualism The view that "S knows P" could be true when said by one person in one context but false when said by someone else in another context, even though they are referring to the same S and P and the same time. (Requires the meaning of "know" to vary with context.)

Phenomenal Conservatism The view that if it seems to you that P, and you have no grounds for doubting this seeming, then you have some justification for believing P.

Realism The view that there is a world outside our minds and that we know many things about it.

Regress Argument (a) The Regress Argument for Foundationalism: An argument that says that foundationalism must be true since this is the only way to explain how we have justified beliefs without relying on either circular reasoning or an infinite regress. (b) The Regress Argument for Skepticism: An argument that says that no beliefs are justified, since we cannot have foundational beliefs, we cannot have beliefs justified by circular reasoning, and we cannot have an infinite regress of justified beliefs.

Relevant Alternatives Theory The view that knowing P only requires ruling out *some* of the alternatives to P (the "relevant" ones), often understood as the alternatives that were objectively possible given the circumstances.

Reliabilism The view that knowledge = true belief formed by a method that is *reliable* in the sense that it tends to produce true beliefs a great majority of the time.

Self-Defeat Argument for Phenomenal Conservatism An argument that says that alternatives to phenomenal conservatism are self-defeating since they are based on how things seem to the person giving the alternative view.

Skepticism The view that we know nothing or almost nothing.

Sound Said of an argument that is valid and has all true premises.

Subtle skepticism The view that all or almost all our beliefs are epistemically impoverished.

Tracking account of knowledge The view that knowledge is true belief formed by a method that would not have produced the belief that P if P were not true.

Traditional skepticism *See* skepticism.

Valid Said of an argument whose premises entail its conclusion, that is, it would be impossible for the premises to be true and the conclusion false.

Bibliography

Audi, Robert. 1988. *Belief, Justification, and Knowledge*. Belmont, CA: Wadsworth.

Beckwith, Christopher. 2015. *Greek Buddha: Pyrrho's Encounter with Early Buddhism in Central Asia*. Princeton, NJ: Princeton University Press.

BonJour, Laurence. 1985. *The Structure of Empirical Knowledge*. Cambridge, MA: Harvard University Press.

Brons, Robin. 2018. "Life without Belief", *Philosophy East and West* 68: 329–51.

Christensen, David. 2009. "Disagreement as Evidence: The Epistemology of Controversy", *Philosophy Compass* 4: 756–67.

Conway, James L., dir. 1993, May 1. *Star Trek: The Next Generation*. Season 6, episode 21, "Frame of Mind". United States: Paramount.

Cook, Katharine. 2013, August 2. "Is Larry Summers Really Sexist?", *American Enterprise Institute*, www.aei.org/society-and-culture/is-larry-summers-really-sexist/, accessed October 17, 2022.

Davidson, Donald. 1986. "A Coherence Theory of Truth and Knowledge", pp. 307–19 in Ernest LePore (ed.), *Truth and Interpretation: Perspectives on the Philosophy of Donald Davidson*. Cambridge: Blackwell.

DeRose, Keith. 2009. *The Case for Contextualism: Knowledge, Skepticism, and Context*, vol. 1. Oxford: Oxford University Press.

Descartes, René. 1984. *Meditations on First Philosophy* in *The Philosophical Writings of Descartes*, edited by John Cottingham, Robert Stoothoff, and Dugald Murdoch. Cambridge: Cambridge University Press.

Dretske, Fred. 1970. "Epistemic Operators", *Journal of Philosophy* 67: 1007–23.

———. 1981. "The Pragmatic Dimension of Knowledge", *Philosophical Studies* 40: 363–78.

Drummond, Caitlin and Baruch Fischhoff. 2017. "Individuals with Greater Science Literacy and Education Have More Polarized Beliefs on Controversial Science Topics", *Proceedings of the National Academy of Sciences* 114: 9587–92.

Feldman, Richard. 2006. "Reasonable Religious Disagreements", in L. Antony (ed.), *Philosophers Without Gods: Meditations on Atheism and the Secular Life*. New York: Oxford University Press.
Frances, Bryan. 2005. *Scepticism Comes Alive*. Oxford: Clarendon Press.
———. 2010. "Disagreement", pp. 68–74 in Duncan Pritchard and Sven Bernecker (eds.), *The Routledge Companion to Epistemology*. New York: Routledge.
———. 2013. "Philosophical Renegades", pp. 121–66 in Jennifer Lackey and David Christensen (eds.), *The Epistemology of Disagreement: New Essays*. Oxford: Oxford University Press.
———. 2014. *Disagreement*. Cambridge: Polity Press.
———. 2018a. "The Epistemology of Real-World Religious Disagreement Without Peers", *Philosophia Christi* 20: 291–9.
———. 2018b. "Scepticism and Disagreement", in Diego Machuca and Baron Reed (eds.), *Skepticism: From Antiquity to the Present*. New York: Bloomsbury.
———. 2021. "Religious Disagreement", in Stewart Goetz and Charles Taliaferro (eds.), *Encyclopedia of Philosophy of Religion*. Hoboken, NJ: Wiley-Blackwell.
———. 2022. *The Epistemic Consequences of Paradox*. Cambridge: Cambridge University Press.
Fumerton, Richard. 2010. "You Can't Trust a Philosopher", in Richard Feldman and Ted Warfield (eds.), *Disagreement*. New York: Oxford University Press.
Goldberg, Sanford. 2009. "Reliabilism in Philosophy", *Philosophical Studies* 124: 105–17.
Goldman, Alvin. 1979. "What Is Justified Belief?", pp. 1–23 in George Pappas (ed.), *Justification and Knowledge*. Dordrecht: D. Reidel.
Hedges, Larry and Amy Nowell. 1995. "Sex Differences in Mental Test Scores, Variability, and Numbers of High-Scoring Individuals", *Science* 269: 41–5.
Hemel, Daniel J. 2005, January 14. "Summers' Comments on Women and Science Draw Ire", *The Harvard Crimson*, www.thecrimson.com/article/2005/1/14/summers-comments-on-women-and-science/, accessed October 17, 2022.
Huemer, Michael. 2000. "Direct Realism and the Brain-in-a-Vat Argument", *Philosophy and Phenomenological Research* 61: 397–413.
———. 2001. *Skepticism and the Veil of Perception*. Lanham, MD: Rowman & Littlefield.
———. 2003. "Non-Egalitarianism", *Philosophical Studies* 114: 147–71.
———. 2005. "Is Critical Thinking Epistemically Responsible?", *Metaphilosophy* 36: 522–31.
———. 2006. "Phenomenal Conservatism and the Internalist Intuition", *American Philosophical Quarterly* 43: 147–58.

———. 2007. "Compassionate Phenomenal Conservatism", *Philosophy and Phenomenological Research* 74: 30–55.

———. 2013. *The Problem of Political Authority*. New York: Palgrave Macmillan.

———. 2015. "Why People Are Irrational About Politics", pp. 456–67 in Jonathan Anomaly, Geoffrey Brennan, Michael Munger, and Geoffrey Sayre-McCord (eds.), *Philosophy, Politics, and Economics*. Oxford: Oxford University Press.

———. 2016. "Serious Theories and Skeptical Theories: Why You Are Probably Not a Brain in a Vat", *Philosophical Studies* 173: 1031–52.

———. 2019. *Dialogues on Ethical Vegetarianism*. New York: Routledge.

———. 2020. "Debunking Skepticism", pp. 155–76 in Michael Klenk (ed.), *Higher-Order Evidence and Moral Epistemology*. London: Routledge.

———. 2021. *Knowledge, Reality, and Value*. Kindle Direct Publishing.

———. 2022. *Understanding Knowledge*. Kindle Direct Publishing.

Hume, David. [1739] 1992. *A Treatise of Human Nature*. Buffalo, NY: Prometheus.

———. [1748] 1975. *Enquiry Concerning Human Understanding*, in *Enquiries Concerning Human Understanding and Concerning the Principles of Morals*, edited by L.A. Selby-Bigge. Oxford: Clarendon, https://en.wikisource.org/wiki/An_Enquiry_Concerning_Human_Understanding.

Klein, Peter. 1995. "Skepticism and Closure: Why the Evil Genius Argument Fails", *Philosophical Topics* 23: 213–36.

Klein, Peter. 2007. "Human Knowledge and the Infinite Progress of Reasoning", *Philosophical Studies* 134: 1–17.

Kornblith, Hilary. 2010. "Belief in the Face of Controversy", in Richard Feldman and Ted Warfield (eds.), *Disagreement*. New York: Oxford University Press.

Kraft, James. 2012. *The Epistemology of Religious Disagreement: A Better Understanding*. New York: Palgrave Macmillan.

Kuzminski, Adrian. 2008. *Pyrrhonism: How the Ancient Greeks Reinvented Buddhism*. Lanham, MD: Lexington Books.

Lehrer, Keith. 1971. "Why Not Scepticism?", *Philosophical Forum* 2: 283–98.

Machin, Stephen and Tuomas Pekkarinen. 2008. "Global Sex Differences in Test Score Variability", *Science* 322: 1331–2.

Moore, George Edward. 1939. "Proof of an External World", *Proceedings of the British Academy* 25: 273–300.

———. 1953. "Hume's Theory Examined", pp. 108–26 in *Some Main Problems of Philosophy*. London: Allen & Unwin.

Nozick, Robert. 1981. *Philosophical Explanations*. Cambridge: Cambridge University Press.

Oppy, Graham. 2010. "Disagreement", *International Journal for Philosophy of Religion* 68: 183–99.

PBS NewsHour. 2005, February 22. "Harvard President Summers' Remarks About Women in Science, Engineering", www.pbs.org/newshour/science/science-jan-june05-summersremarks_2-22, accessed October 17, 2022.

PhilPapers. 2020. "2020 PhilPapers Survey: Main Survey Results", https://survey2020.philpeople.org/survey/results/all, accessed October 19, 2022.

Pritchard, Duncan H. 2015. *Epistemic Angst: Radical Skepticism and the Groundlessness of Our Believing*. Princeton, NJ: Princeton University Press.

———. 2019. *Scepticism: A Very Short Introduction*. Oxford: Oxford University Press.

Putnam, Hilary. 1981. *Reason, Truth, and History*. Cambridge: Cambridge University Press.

Quine, Willard van Orman. 1951. "Two Dogmas of Empiricism", *Philosophical Review* 60: 20–43.

Reid, Thomas. [1764, 1785] 1983. *Inquiry and Essays*, edited by Ronald Beanblossom and Keith Lehrer. Indianapolis: Hackett.

Russell, Bertrand. [1912] 1997. *The Problems of Philosophy*. New York: Oxford University Press.

Sextus Empiricus. [2nd Century A.D.] 1994. *Sextus Empiricus: Outlines of Scepticism*, translated by Julia Annas and Jonathan Barnes. Cambridge: Cambridge University Press.

Singer, Alexander, dir. 1999, September 24. *Star Trek: Voyager*. Season 4, episode 4, "Nemesis". United States: Paramount.

Smythies, John and Robert French, eds. 2018. *Direct Versus Indirect Realism: A Neurophilosophical Debate on Consciousness*. London: Elsevier.

Thune, Michael. 2011. "Religious Belief and the Epistemology of Disagreement", *Philosophy Compass* 6: 712–24.

Unger, Peter. 1975. *Ignorance: A Case for Scepticism*. Oxford: Oxford University Press.

Wachowski, Lana and Lilly Wachowski, dirs. 1999. *The Matrix*. United States: Warner Bros.

Walcott, John. 2016, December 9. "Russia Intervened to Help Trump Win Election: Intelligence Officials", *Reuters*, www.reuters.com/article/us-usa-election-cyber-russia-idUSKBN13Z05B, accessed October 18, 2022.

Index

absolute certainty 56–7, 59
appearances 60, 89–94, 95, 100, 141, 150, 151
arguments 112–16

background knowledge 114
Bayesian reasoning 85
Bayes' theorem 85
begging the question 29, 77–9, 128, 145–6
belief 6, 8–11, 14, 41–2, 44, 47–52, 72, 89, 97–8, 109, 110, 130, 143–5, 152–3
Berkeley, George 80, 101
brains in vat (BIV) scenario: direct realist response 79–82; factual lack 123–5; incomplete meanings 31–2; indirect realist response 82–5; K-justified belief 122–3; notion of 13; premises for not being 15–26, 35, 36, 59–60, 61, 109, 111, 120–5, 127, 137–43; relevant alternatives theory 74; responses to argument 61–86; ruling out 20–1, 23, 25, 26–7, 39, 59, 65–70, 73–4, 79–80, 115, 138, 139–43, 149; unknown truth 26–30
brains in vat hypothesis (BIVH) 26–9, 32, 35, 60, 69, 82–5, 123–4, 128, 139, 141, 149, 150

certainty skepticism 56–9, 82
cheating 115–16

circularity 86–7, 152
claim 9, 35
closure principle: counter-example 76; justification 77, 86; knowledge 72–3, 75; notion of 72n3
closure principle for justification 77, 86
closure principle for knowledge 72–3
common sense 9, 20, 102, 108, 155
consensus 178–80
contextualism *see* debate contextualism; full contextualism; partial contextualism
contextualists 166, 180–1
contingent 55–8, 60, 61–2, 109
controversial beliefs 47–52, 95, 100, 104, 171, 174, 177
controversial opinions 104, 156, 157
controversy skepticism (CS): argument for 50, 104, 156–7, 169, 177; defense of opinion 100–3; excuses 132–6; irrationality 96–8; notion of 41–2; objections to arguments for 50–2; obviousness of 95–6; peers 99–100; phenomenology of confident belief 172–7; role of disagreement for 42–50
counterintuitive truths 146, 150
crazy truths 146–8

debate contextualism 167–9
Dennett, Daniel 101
Descartes, René xi
direct knowledge 80, 81
direct realism 79–82, 86, 87
disagreement: argument for existence of God 112–14; controversies 135–6; controversy skepticism 102–3, 104; knowledge and 42–50; philosophical debate 161–4, 178–80; responding rationally to 190–2; suspension of judgment 4–7; understanding 184–92

Earth diameter 62
emotion 186–90
epistemic achievement 118
epistemic credit 119
epistemic crucial thing 108
epistemic standards 110
epistemic superiors 5
epistemology 25, 40, 126, 132, 145, 184
error theory 99
evidence 6, 21, 23–4, 35, 95, 134–5
evidential support 124
excuses 132–6
experts 5–6
external conditions 141–3
externalism 126–7
external world 55–8, 60, 61, 65, 71, 75, 79–80, 86, 87, 101, 109, 117, 140, 142–3, 149–51, 180, 181
external world claim 29
external world skepticism 55, 56, 59, 60, 61, 65, 94, 96, 138, 153–4, 156, 179
extrasensory perception (ESP) 93

fallible justification 138, 140–1, 147
falsehoods 146
foundational 86–8, 94
foundationalism 86–8, 94
frostbite 22, 24, 26–30, 109, 115, 125
full contextualism 166–7, 169

"G.E. Moore shift" 63–5, 91
God 80, 112–14
group disagreements 4–5

historical variability. 6–7
Hume, David 65, 101

idealism 80, 179
ideology 186–90
incomplete meanings 31–2
indirect knowledge 80, 81
indirect realism 80, 81–2, 86
infallible justification 138–40, 147, 153
infinite regress 87, 94
intentionality 66–7, 69–70
internal conditions 141–3
internalism 24, 55, 138, 142–3
intuitions 92–4, 147
irrationality 96–8

judgment 4–7, 135
justification skepticism 57–8, 60, 71, 82
justified 14, 38, 47, 49–52, 57–60, 63, 65, 71–2, 75–80, 100, 102, 109–11, 116, 122–3, 130–1, 138–42, 144, 147–8, 150–2, 156, 170
justified belief 50, 76, 80–2, 86–8, 90–4, 110, 117, 119, 122–3, 126, 130–1, 151, 155, 156, 190

Kant, Immanuel 101
K-justified 115, 118–20, 122–3, 128–9, 151–2
knowledge: as achievement on part of knower 117–22; belief and 8–11; closure principle 72–3, 75; closure principle for knowledge 72–3; consistency with 37–40; context-sensitive 180–3; disagreement and 42–50; fallible justification 140–1; internal conditions 141–3; moderate conception of 183–4; notion of 25, 163, 168; opinions and 9; plausible claims 148; practicality of 30–1; relevant alternatives

theory 74; requirements 14; tracking account of 73–4; truth-heavy theory 171–2, 183–4; without justification 70–2

Lewis, David 101
linguistic ambiguity 164
linguistic complexity 164–9
logic 63

Mackie, John 101
Madhyamaka Buddhism xn1
McTaggart, J. M. E. 101
Meditations on First Philosophy (Descartes) xii
misinterpretation 127
misunderstandings 148–50
Moore, G. E. 63
motion 62–3

necessary 55, 87, 94, 101, 102, 149

opinions 4, 5–6, 8–9, 13, 30, 41, 44, 48, 54, 95, 96–8, 100–3, 104, 117, 132, 156, 157, 171, 176, 185, 186, 191–2
ordinary knowledge 23

partial arguments 112–13
partial contextualism: notion of 166, 168–9; self-defeat argument 91–2; as theory of justification 90–1
peers 99–100
perceptual experiences 66–7
phenomenal conservatism (PC): criticisms of skepticism 128–32; vs. external-world skepticism 94; notion of xii, 88–94; pre-theoretical beliefs 143–5, 150; principle of 89–90; self-defeat argument 91–2, 95; as theory of justification 90–4
philosophical beliefs 91, 101, 102–3, 104
philosophical debate 161–4, 178–80
philosophical education 184–6

philosophical method: begging the question 145–6; crazy truths 146–8; misunderstandings 150; pre-theoretical beliefs 143–5
Plato 101
Popper, Karl 101
pre-theoretical beliefs 143–5
Pyrrhonism x–xi, xn1
Pyrrho of Elis xn1

Quine, W. V. 101

radical skepticism ix–xii
rational belief 110
realism 14–15, 37, 125–7, 164
real world hypothesis (RWH) 82–5, 86, 128, 141
reasonable belief 110
regress argument 87
relevant alternatives theory 74
reliabilism 71
reliable belief-forming mechanisms 32–4, 92–4
ruling out 20–1, 23, 25, 26–7, 29–30, 33, 39, 59, 65–70, 73–4, 79–80, 115, 125, 138, 139–43, 145, 148, 171, 180
Russell, Bertrand 65
Ryle, Gilbert 101

self-defeat argument 91–2, 95
self-refutation 61–2, 65–6, 69
sensory experiences 13, 22, 26–8, 65–8, 70, 81, 123–4
silly beliefs 152–3, 155
S-justification 151–3, 155
skepticism: argument for 15–26; begging the question 29, 77–9, 145–6; certainty skepticism 56–9, 82; challenging argument 26–34, 107–11; continuing debate 161–4; controversy skepticism (CS) 41–52, 95–103; direct realist response 79–82; forms 54–5; indirect realist response 82–5; living life as skeptic 12, 34–6; notion of 7–36, 54; as philosophical puzzle xi; realist criticisms 128–32;

self-refutation 61–2, 65–6, 69; as stance xi; subtle skepticism 37–40, 41, 42
socio-epistemic justification 110, 151–2, 155; *see also* S-justification
straightforward linguistic ambiguity 164
subtle linguistic complexity 164–9
subtle skepticism 37–40, 42, 51
Summers, Larry 186

tracking account of knowledge, 73–4
traditional skepticism *see* skepticism

traffic accident 107–9
truth 28–30, 36, 55–6, 125, 146–8, 171–2

uncontroversial beliefs 104
unicorns 96
unknown truth 30, 125

visual experience 66, 68, 87, 93

wisdom 170
wise beliefs 152–3, 155

zebras 75–7
Zeno 62

For Product Safety Concerns and Information please contact our EU representative GPSR@taylorandfrancis.com
Taylor & Francis Verlag GmbH, Kaufingerstraße 24, 80331 München, Germany

www.ingramcontent.com/pod-product-compliance
Lightning Source LLC
Chambersburg PA
CBHW071409300426
44114CB00016B/2237